THE GOLDEN
SOVEREIGN

Books by RICHARD CHURCH

Over the Bridge
The Golden Sovereign
An Autobiography

THE GOLDEN SOVEREIGN

A conclusion to *Over the Bridge*

BY

RICHARD CHURCH

E. P. DUTTON & CO., INC.

New York

1957

Copyright ©, 1957, by Richard Church
All rights reserved. Printed in the U. S. A.

FIRST EDITION

¶ No part of this book may be reproduced
in any form without permission in writing
from the publisher, except by a reviewer
who wishes to quote brief passages in connection with a review written for inclusion in
a magazine, newspaper or broadcast.

Lithographed by The Murray Printing Co.

LIBRARY OF CONGRESS CATALOG CARD NUMBER: 57-9003

Contents

THE DIFFICULTY is not only in the gaps and illusions of memory—though that is bad enough—nor does it lie in the way the lit-up theatre of childhood puts the later years into a half-light, so that we seem to have lived the rest of our lives as a mere bemused audience of our own past. The real trouble is that we find no ground under our feet when we start to write; the subject that looked familiar and ready-made turns out to be no less than the total wilderness and mystery.

— V. S. PRITCHETT

THE GOLDEN
SOVEREIGN

CHAPTER ONE

The Golden Sovereign

IT WAS THE 23rd May, 1911, an inconspicuous date, but I found it heavily emphasised because it was pay day, and I was going home to my rooms with my first full month's salary as a permanent Civil Servant in my pocket: three golden sovereigns.

I was aware of a sense of security, an odd state of mind in a boy of eighteen. But I welcomed it, and recalled that I had recognised it earlier in the year on the day that I received the letter from the Civil Service Commission (signed by one J. L. le B. Hammond, a name at that time strange yet attractive to me, but later to be more familiar).

My brother Jack, a qualified school-teacher earning £100 a year, took me for a walk that day, and as we tramped over Champion Hill, past Mr. Bessemer's observatory, I was given some advice about not being content with that first step on the ladder of an official career, and the wisdom of taking further examinations, toward a higher rating in the Service.

I half agreed with him, as I was to agree with so many other well-wishers who subsequently offered the same good counsel: but it was the passive half of me that agreed. The active half had been in command since before my mother's death a year ago. That active half was a conflagration which has been raging ever since, still to throw out fitful flames today, over my elderly years, and to light up my veteran mind as though it were an ivy-mantled tower in a monochrome by Victor Hugo.

That active half was the obsessed and opinionated self dedicated to poetry, convinced of a vocation that would place him among the immortals by some magical and timeless process yet to be worked out in detail and method.

I had taken the first step in the making of that schedule of the work which was to occupy my life. I was now assured of bread and butter by means of a job that would rob me only of seven hours a day and from which I should retire at the age of sixty on a pension. My brother failed to convince me, though his argument lasted from Champion Hill, through Dulwich Village, and half-way up College Road past the tollgate, that to be content to remain as an Abstractor Clerk, on a salary beginning at £45 a year and rising by annual increments of £5 to a maximum of £150, was really rather supine, even though I might contrive to disguise that fact by sitting with Shakespeare and Milton in the pantheon of English Literature.

My confidence, however, was to be shaken within the next week or two, because I failed the medical examination. Once more that ass, Brother Body, had dug in his pretty little hooves. I was given the option of appealing against the report of the local doctor, who had accused me of defective kidneys. For another week I was plunged back into the nervous fears and uncertainties which had beset me since I left school in 1908, at the age of fifteen, three years before. I wanted no reminder of the events, and the states of mind, of these three years. For two of them I had nursed my mother during the last stages of her mortal sickness. She had died in my arms. My universe had been shattered and, to my shame, I had found a new and even more enticing universe rising from the ruins of the old: to my shame, because I was horrified at what could only be lack of loyalty to the mother in, and for, whom I had lived with such passion and service.

I hastened, therefore, to clamber out of this new uncertainty. Within a week I presented myself at a consulting-room in Harley Street, where I was interviewed by a frowsty old man who began his scientific and specialised enquiry by asking, in a grumpy tone, "Did they tell you what the fee would be?"

"No," I quavered.

"Oh! I see. What's your father?"

"A sorter in the Post Office."

"Hum! Poor devil. Mother living?"

I could not reply. Something had gripped my throat. The

old man glanced at me, then looked down at the dossier quickly.

"Humph! I see. Bronchial asthma? Nonsense! Nobody dies of asthma. And what's the matter with you, eh? Kidneys? Fiddlesticks! Go home and drink a glass of water once an hour. You'll grow out of it. Must have had measles some time or other. Ever remember having measles, my boy, eh? Or chicken-pox, or scarlet fever?"

I had them all, in the course of my febrile years, but I thought it wise not to confess. I could see that the old curmudgeon didn't care a damn, and was openly on the side of the weak battalions. He expected no reply, and went on to the real business. "My fee's three guineas; but a guinea will do."

That was fortunate, because my father had foreseen that a guinea would cover the fee, and I had left home with twenty-five shillings, to include the bus fare, and a steak pudding at an eating-house after the ordeal.

I left Harley Street, once again secure in the certainty of my future, protected from the wholly unknown jungle of the competitive wage-earning world. I was so relieved that I sank into a featherbed complacency, which blinded me to the possibility that I might also be groping my way back to the nursery, and to apron strings which Death had torn from my hands a year ago.

On the 8th of April, within a day of the first anniversary of the loss of my mother, and after two years as a temporary Boy Clerk in the Civil Service, I became established and pensionable. It may be a sign of my poor physical vitality that instantly I began to look forward to the pension, as to an era of release when I should be able to give myself with even fuller abandonment to the activity for which I believed myself to be destined. Or it may be that I was born out of my time, and had entered the world with a sense of privilege, and the right of patronage, more appropriate to the eighteenth century than the early twentieth.

Treasury pay day, in 1911, was on the 23rd of the month, and that is why my first full month's pay, in three golden sovereigns, was in my trouser-pocket when I got off the tram at Camberwell Green, on a glorious afternoon in May.

My sight was dimmed, and my arm numbed, because I had been strap-hanging during the journey from the Elephant and Castle to Camberwell Green. I had found that by walking from Billingsgate, over London Bridge, past Chaucer's 'Tabard Inn' in The Borough to the Elephant, I could get to the Green on a penny fare. On the journey to and fro each day, for six days a week, this economy saved a penny a day. Sixpence a week meant a new volume of Everyman's Library, or a World's Classic, every fortnight. And several other such devices might permit me to add a Nelson's Sevenpenny Classic as well.

Not only that, but I enjoyed the walk, especially in the morning, for it gave me pause, to fortify myself against the stomach-probing ordeal of entering the grimed and forbidding portal of the Custom House, climbing those eighty-odd stone stairs, and being absorbed unwillingly into the routine and discipline of the Government Laboratory. So too, on the homeward journey, that walk to the Elephant and Castle gave me opportunity to shake off the manacles, to free my mental limbs, and to reassure myself that, like the young Coleridge careering with waving arms down the Strand, I was free "to swim the Hellespont".

My sight was dimmed, that bright day of spring, for during the strap-hanging inside the L.C.C. tram I had been studying Archbishop Whateley's *Logic*, bought some days previously from the twopenny box outside a second-hand bookshop.

I made slow progress amongst the syllogisms, although I had also waded through Jevons's book on the same subject, having been driven to this dusty task by the urgings of unease. From the time I left school three years earlier, I had been assailed, between the spasms of self-glory, by misgivings about intellectual equipment. This must have been partly due to my brother's monitorship. He disapproved of my head-in-the-air attitude, and my tendency to claim a principality in the realm of letters. He was one for correct spelling, uncleaved infinitives, and logical sequence in presentation of ideas.

This insistence on academic correctitude was odd in a person of temperament so emphatically emotional, even disastrous and never to be fathomed. He had the ravaged look of a Savonarola, and emanated a similar power. But in action he was spinsterly and precise. He abhorred extravagance, unjustifiable claims, and even the minor symptoms of an untidy mind.

Thus, if a visitor should light a cigarette, and drop the extinguished match on the carpet, Jack's melancholy face would wince, his lips tighten in a nervous twitch, he would rise slowly from his chair, extend a hand (the Holbein drawing in flesh and blood, but not too much blood), pick up the match between finger and thumb, *convey* it to the fireplace and *deposit* it among the flames. Those are the correct verbs to describe the small ritual of disapproval. At the same time, his lustrous brown eyes gleamed with humorous recognition of his own irritability.

It is small wonder that, after a childhood spent under such tonic vigilation, I should be subject to qualms of conscience because of my wayward attack on every task, whether of my own choosing or of necessity. I have never lost that sense of guilt, and when in the nineteen-twenties I read or heard my contemporary T. S. Eliot inveighing against the use of the word 'inspiration' in connection with poetry, I knew what he was driving at, though I believed he was driving too hard.

So, to compensate for my deficiencies in academic training, I was putting myself through this course of study in the elements of logic as an auxiliary to the more enjoyable and self-indulgent study of the dictionary, and books on words, such as those by Richard Chevenix Trench and Professor Weekley of Nottingham University (the man to whom D. H. Lawrence owed so much).

I was encouraged in the dreary discipline by the discovery that much philosophic pleasure is based on the knowledge of language and the part played by the words themselves in the processes of thought. I realised already that the accuracy involved would act as a drop-keel to my temperament, which tended to carry too much sail.

My daily return to Camberwell Green was always over-stimulating. For me, this complex junction of main roads was the gateway to the South. Now the South figures largely and permanently in my life. I had not been living in Dulwich for more than a few weeks, at the age of twelve, before I was enriched by this faculty for recognising the South. It came from the marriage of the Sun and the enormous elm trees which dominate that village. I saw, for the first time in my life, how the sun moved round them, with a burning approach, a withdrawn embrace, casting their shadow as a moving reminder of his power. The relationship stirred my imagination, heated my blood. I smouldered over the discovery, became an eavesdropper of this universal attraction and acceptance.

On my way to school, I learned to touch the tree-trunks on the sunny side and on the shady, my palms comparing the difference in sensation, to convey it to my half-conscious mind in the form of a panic drama, or love-making, that stirred me to incoherent and anguished longings.

The sun; I knew my way to the sun! I must always look southward, arranging my life to that direction, or I must shrink and die. Merely to turn round on my own axis, to face north, evoked a sinking sensation in my body, and a foreboding in my mind, a vague worry, a shadow of despair. The idea of travelling north increased these emotions to the point of inhibition, and half a century was to pass before I could bring myself to visit the Scottish Highlands, though both intellectually and æsthetically I knew that such a visit would be an experience worth the violation of my own address.

Camberwell Green summed up that attraction. It lies due south of London, and is a gateway to the South. It is dramatically placed, though strangers probably pass it without a second glance, hardly realising that it is anything more than one of those traffic-knots with which the inner suburbs of London are punctuated; points that are made, as it were, by a reverse process from that of the forming of pearls. For these points of aggravation were once the centres of small, picturesque villages within a morning's trudge, or an hour on horseback, of the City or Westminster. But as the Wen grew more tumid, it overran these quiet high streets and cross-roads, fixing their geographical shapes into a grotesque and inconvenient exaggeration. Clapham, Tooting, Islington, Highgate, Lewisham, Shepherd's Bush; there are dozens of such centres into which the traffic of the twentieth century piles, and is blocked, to make a fuming and poisonous over-lay upon the original scenes, blinding these pearls one after one.

To the casual observer, Camberwell Green must be such a typical junction, even today, after the removal of the trams and the rails on which they ran. A generation of citizens is already growing up which will not know the London dominated by the equalitarian tyranny of the L.C.C. trams, those dull-brown, top-heavy canisters on bogie-carriages with massive iron fenders at each end, which in their thousands carried the workers in their millions day by day, hour by hour, into and out of the centre of London, from home to work, from work to home, winter and summer, the year round, in a ceaseless shuttle of clangour and grind, the deep and despairing din reverberating along the rails and the subterranean live-wire, so penetrating to the very soul, and violating every privacy of the cockney universe.

For almost exactly half a century the L.C.C. trams were the dominant feature of mobile London, and especially South London. Every main road was laid with the steel rails. In the poorer suburbs, whose local authorities could not afford to maintain the road surface, the rails gradually emerged some inch or more above the broken setts, wood-blocks, macadam, their edges sharpened and polished like sword-blades by the friction and grind of the wheels, which at every curve resisted the confinement of the permanent-way, thrusting with heated flanges, metal against metal, and raising an outcry of shrieks, scratchings, groans, and dull sound-blocks as of a community of machines suddenly animated with hatred.

At the big road-junctions this metallic hell made night and day hideous and terrifying. The constant movement of the brown monsters, giants with neither head nor tail, eyes nor limbs, nothing but bellies of steel and glass; the inter-weaving yet blind movement of these trams, impervious to the contest of free traffic that rushed, dodged, avoided and cut in around them, mounted during rush hours to a nightmare fantasy. The roar of it, the clangour of the gongs, the sudden formations in a halted procession, a dozen or more of these expressionless land-arks, the surge forward, the partings, with shrieks of vehicular agony at rail-points; and the vision of the half-mortals packed on the lower deck, the upper deck, swaying together in one soporific inertia, drugged with tobacco smoke, the night's over-hang, the day's labour, and the subconscious certainty of this enduring slavery; the menace of the road surface, with its oiled and tyre-polished setts, its armoury of razor-edged rails; all these things, a piling up of threats and horrors, came to a sinister perfection at Camberwell Green.

I know it from A to Z. I saw it grow. I have seen it suddenly disappear, melted away like a slug sprinkled with salt. It hung over London between 1904 and the early 'fifties like a dragon over a fairytale city. And now it is gone. Yet it was thought to be a blessing, the healthy child of democracy. But then, democracy has some very strange offspring.

This Caliban, the L.C.C. tram, served a good purpose, and was a dutiful slave in spite of its hideous shape and raucous conduct. It carried me, and millions like me, at a minimum cost, enabling us to save a ha'penny or a penny a day, which could be accumulated to buy a book. It was thus a patron of culture, of the arts. It took part in the maintenance of the university of self-education where I, and so many fellow aspirants, learned to walk the invisible cloisters with as much ease and seclusion as the undergraduates in the college gardens of Oxford and Cambridge—or almost as much.

My cloister stretched from Camberwell Green to the Elephant and Castle. Between those hell-gates of steel rail, I stood twice a day in the belly of the tram, and sometimes sat, book in hand. My anxiety was that I should be driven by the crush of passengers to ride on the upper deck. There the sway-ing of the top-heavy monster induced an equivalent of sea-sick-ness, aggravated by the dense clouds of treacly-sweet smoke from pipe-tobacco. But even so, I read, acclimatising my stomach to the dip and fall, the swing and lurch, as well as to the fumes of shag, the cough, hoick and spitting of my fellow passengers.

I was more comfortable, more serenely academic, inside the tram. I might even find a place to rest my buttocks, and balance my bag of books, wedged into a few inches between two warm human bodies on the seats that ran along each side of the lower deck from one end to the other. I cannot say from back to front, for this tram, this servitor to my scholarship, had neither back nor front. It was shaped, like the blindworm, to a primeval ignominy.

It was a good friend to me. It carried me in all weathers, all seasons, to work, and brought me back again to my privacy, another aspect of my secret university. For these years were of intensive study. The routine began when I was eighteen, and was maintained for four years. Thus it was the equivalent of a normal number of terms at a substantial university, with a year for post-graduate work.

The only drawback to my *alma mater* was that it did not provide me with a tutor to supervise my reading and to guide me in the maze of conflicting intellectual enticements. I found a substitute for fellow students in the daily company of my colleagues in the Government Laboratory. This lack of a steersman is a deprivation which affects all self-educated people. Though I have since found that there is no other form of education than self-education, I know that the person who has started along the road of scholarship alone, guided only by instinct, is in danger of protecting himself, or herself, within an armour of solemnity. There is often no pedant like the pedant who has had to find out for himself, and at great pains which he cannot forget—or pardon.

We instantly recognise, too, the learned fellow who in his youth had to emerge, by an obstinate and distasteful struggle, from a family environment of illiteracy and insensitive manners. He carries the scar where the chip has rested on his shoulders. Sometimes, even, the chip is still there, weighing him down under its imaginary ponderousness, a vast tonnage, spoiling his stance, his gesture, in a more polite and sophisticated society. He is to be pitied, the dear fool, because his tale of courage, endurance, solitary hope and gradual achievement is concealed and goes for nothing. He is shunned as a bore, a dogmatic crank, the victim of self-arrested development.

In the early part of this century, when the struggle of such people to emerge was so violent, and that emergence so rare as to single them out and make them self-conscious and lonely within their later environment, this social disease was not uncommon. It survives today in some of the veterans. Scholars in the new dispensation of the Welfare State have no such complex. Their problems are of a different pathology, and are largely based on the fact that there are now too many students thrust up from the main body of the ever-increasing population, to storm the universities and the realm of scholarship. It is equivalent to an army bursting into an ancient city, with tumult, crude and special appetites, and an ignorance of comparative as well as absolute values. The looting is still going on as much in the mansions of learning as in the ancient monuments.

The journey, on that afternoon in May, had been tiring. because the tram was full, and I had stood, strap-hanging, with my bag of books between my feet, and Whateley's *Logic* open in my free hand. A premature burst of warmth had hit the town like a slap on the back. I was wearing an overcoat, whose weight sagged round my neck, almost pulling me over backwards. Sweat trickled into my eyes, and as both hands were permanently engaged I could only endure the salt irritation, blinking hurriedly at each invasion, then resuming my study of the syllogism.

Thus, with one thing and another, I was in a shaky condition when I reached Camberwell Green. Blinking, trembling, my mind still chasing along the unfrequented path of pure logic, I tottered across the steely death-trap at the junction, making my way by instinct to the southern side and the approach to the road that led uphill, past Coldharbour Lane and the Camberwell Music-hall, to my own country, Denmark Hill.

In that lay the magic of this gate to the South. Approaching the Green along that abject slum, the Walworth Road (once the fair-ground where the child Robert Browning marvelled under the lamp-hung trees), I could see in the distance, rising beyond the Green, a church spire, and a tree-clad hillside set still with Victorian mansions where hardly more than half a century earlier rich merchants, German bankers, steel magnates (Bessemer, the pioneer) had lived, within brougham-distance of the City.

Even in winter that prospect, with its recollections of something other than industrialism and lower middle-class monotony, inflamed my mind. I knew that Mendelssohn had stayed in one of these great villas, and had composed his 'Spring Song', now a hackneyed piece for the pianoforte, in the grounds overlooking the cross-roads at Camberwell and the Walworth levels. Richard Wagner also had stayed on Denmark Hill, guest of the German banker—and an exacting guest he must have been, with his craving for silks, his overweening egoism, and his menagerie of Nordic deities.

There too, among those lush gardens, chestnut groves and bowers of syringa, Ruskin spent his childhood, and returned later, mother-ridden, to write his billowy prose, to dream of a non-predatory society of man, and to give his books such absurdly florid titles as *Sesame and Lilies* and *The Crown of Wild Olive*.

The distant church spire stood up that day against a gentle blue sky. I saw it afresh as my eyes cleared themselves of sweat-drops and regained a normal focus after being dilated by logic. I heard a thrush singing in the ornamental trees of the Green, protected by railings from the surge of omnibuses, trams, lorries, and the still-surviving horse-traffic. I felt the hot sun caressing my face, and saw the clamour of light he made in the south-western sky beyond the Music-hall, filling Coldharbour Lane with fire.

My eighteen-year-old heart responded instantly. I accepted this largesse as a personal tribute, offered by a Presence who had seen through the incognito under which I travelled, morning and evening, happily assured of my princedom in the realm of poetry. With superb confidence I crossed the road, picking my way over the protruding rails that flashed in the sun. A tram gonged angrily, but I skipped forward and reached the pavement, Archbishop Whateley's *Logic* still in one hand, the bag of books in the other. I had not yet sufficiently collected

myself after the minor crucifixion in the tram to be able to put
the book back into the bag, along with volume two of Hughes's
edition of Spenser's *Faerie Queene*, a correspondence college
course on précis-writing, a primer on inorganic chemistry,
another on double-entry book-keeping and a manuscript-book
already dog-eared with my own poems.

I had come to Spenser at the suggestion of my most intimate
friend and mentor, John Keats. At that time I did not possess
the whole of *The Faerie Queene*. I had picked up three volumes
in a little shop in The Great Turnstile, the alley leading from
Lincoln's Inn Fields to High Holborn, the year before, while I
was a Boy Clerk in the Land Registry. These volumes—four,
five and six—had cost me a penny each: published in 1750
and bound in calf. Some years later, when reading Boswell, I
found that Dr. Johnson had referred to Hughes's edition of
Spenser. This gave me a pleasant sensation of being in the
literary family; for in spite of my large assumptions, so naïve
and innocent, hardly even self-conscious, in the matter of poetic
ambition, I was watchful for the smallest objective acceptance
of my claim, as it were a nod from the gods.

Some months after this purchase, I was walking through
Richmond High Street, on my way to the Park, and I found
volumes one and two of the same edition. I accepted that co-
incidence as something more significant, more personally
indicative than chance. A person to whom this could happen
must surely be dedicated from birth. I was almost reverent
toward myself as I walked up Richmond Hill, past Sir Joshua
Reynolds's square house overlooking the view immortalised by
Turner. I studied my reflection in shop windows, and was
prepared to bow to it, as to a mystery half-revealed. I had that
day received another assurance, though the price had gone up
to threepence a volume.

So complete was this day-dream that by the time I entered
the park, to be lost in scenes not dissimilar from some of those
pictured in the two books flapping against my legs, one in each
pocket of my mackintosh, I had conjured the belief that I
should have only to find volume three of the set of six, to
ensure universal recognition of my undisguised self as one of the

immortals, to be with Keats and Shelley and this wonderful Spenser whose "verse prolongs Eliza's reign".

Forty-five years have passed since that illuminated afternoon on Richmond Hill, and I am still looking for volume three of Hughes's edition of 1750. Had I more fully mastered Archbishop Whateley's *Logic*, I should now be in a desperate mood, acknowledging defeat, as a corollary to that adolescent premiss. But during this long and still pursued apprenticeship to the arts, I have learned that logic has its undertones (as Nietzsche also discovered), which reward us unfairly, while defeating the textbooks. The divine cheat by which the creative artist pronounces his authority is still something that has not yet been explained. The secret, after all, may lie in that dangerous word 'inspiration', the refuge of the fraud as well as the fortunate.

Safely across the road, I realised at last that I had to do something about my supper, my usual practice at this stage of the homeward journey. The fish-shop was but two doors up the road, and there I stopped, to examine the display on the marble slabs, and the little aquarium of goldfish that crowned it, the living over the dead. My choice was always limited, because I could not afford more than a few coppers. Even the sense of wealth, of being amply cushioned against the possibility of starvation and the hazards of the gutter, which I felt on this, my first full pay day, could not tempt me to extravagance, or even attract my attention to fillets of salmon, halibut and turbot.

I was schooled by experience, and by long family tradition, to frugality and thrift. The Victorian economic matrix had shaped my bones. The idea of over-spending, of falling into debt, was quite unrecognisable. It hardly entered my consciousness, except as a vague fear, an abhorrence. I believed that money come by in any way except that of hard work was come by dishonestly. Thus betting, or any other chance (which oddly enough included inheritance), was outside the pale. Perhaps my prejudices were fed by contact with my father's inarticulate but obstinate socialism. For some years before our home broke up I had read his copy of Robert Blatchford's weekly newspaper *The Clarion*, and had accepted something of its utopian simplicity, its *News from Nowhere* message, passed on from William Morris, who had translated pre-Raphaelitism into terms of parochial politics.

My theory was as simple as that. My deeper conviction was a class instinct: that of the slow-growing, patient, dutiful lower middle class which had emerged out of the Civil War nearly three centuries earlier, applying its puritanism to its purse. This principle was in my bones and blood, and had not yet been challenged by other and more mysterious inheritances from quite other sources, to which I have referred when describing my father's origins and his birth in the neighbourhood of Woburn Abbey.

Unaware of these hereditary directions and contradictions, I decided to buy a bloater, and, the occasion being somewhat special, I picked out a large one, from the slab marked '2d.'. Still somewhat confused, physically and mentally, I asked the fishmonger to ensure that my choice had a soft roe, and while he was investigating with thumb and finger I freed my left hand of its burden, plunged it into my trouser pocket, and drew out the little envelope containing the three golden sovereigns.

But my hand shook. It was still under the influence of logic, as well as being restricted by the book under that arm. The three noble coins, too much wealth to be thus concentrated, too heavy and too precious, rolled out into my palm. One stayed there. The other two slipped through my fingers. I stood frozen, watching them, my mouth and jaw fixed half open in a kind of tetanus of dismay.

Several eternal seconds passed while the fishmonger and I—he arrested with the bloater in his raised hand—watched the two sovereigns, on their milled edges, the one following the other tandem-fashion, roll swiftly across the pavement to the gutter. The first one faltered, wobbled, turned aside, and collapsed on the kerb. The second ignored this, rolled on past its fellow, leaped off the kerb, and disappeared between the bars of a drain.

"Gawd! Some people can afford to chuck it about!" said the fishmonger. And he grinned. I looked back and forth

between the open drain and the grinning mouth. Slowly the
ancient comedy, the age-old indifference and kindly cruelty,
dawned upon my mind. I left the shop, retrieved the one poor
coin, and leaned over the drain, as though agony could draw
the golden sovereign up again.

But this high drama could not be sustained. The bloater had
been slapped into a sheet of newspaper, wrapped up, patted
with a scaly palm, and was now being held out to me, with the
expectation of payment.

"Tuppence!" said the fishmonger, the spectator, the spokes-
man of the rest of the universe.

I offered him the prodigal sovereign. He looked at it, then
at me, and frowned.

"Ain't yer got nothing smaller?" he demanded.

I shook my head, dumb and bewildered. I had touched
bottom. Finally I murmured "Pay-day"; returning the third
sovereign to the envelope, and the envelope to my pocket.

My audience melted. An instant recognition warmed the
eyes in that beefy face. He saw the whole tragi-comedy.

"Blimey!" he said. "Look 'ere, son; you want to 'old on to
it, see?" He produced the 19/10d. change, leaned forward and
examined my empty hand. "Better 'ave it all in silver, eh?
Now 'old it tight this time!"

Half indignant at this patronage, consumed by fear and
despair over the consequences of this disaster, I left the shop
carrying the bloater in one hand, *Logic* still under that arm,
the bag of books in the other hand. I walked slowly up the hill,
looking neither to right nor left, nor at the blaze of Maytime
sunshine, the hawthorn, chestnut and laburnum blossom
shining and fragrant in the old gardens and the sacred triangle
by Champion Hill, once a plague-pit during the mass-burials
of 1665.

I was cold. All that I was conscious of was that I had
£1 19s. 10d. to last until the 23rd of June. I could not turn
to my brother because he was desperately in love, had been
so since he met his fate at the Goldsmiths' Training College in
the autumn of 1908. He was putting away every penny that
he could save, in order to get married to the austere and half-

reluctant lady. Nor could I approach my father, for reasons which will appear in another chapter.

I was alone. Gradually, while I dragged my tired body up Denmark Hill, turning off by the plague-pit, along the front of the lofty Georgian houses that stood behind lush, over-crowded gardens now glorious with flowering trees, gradually I began to feel warmth returning to my limbs and paralysed stomach. The sense of nausea died down, to be replaced by heat and an impulse to diarrhœa.

I was no longer convulsed, frozen. The recent experience had become a confirmation of that major evidence offered me a year ago, after my mother's death. The grim but bracing lesson was beginning to take a firmer hold, that "in the end is the beginning".

I breathed the perfumed air, drawing it deliberately into my lungs, sending it by an effort of will and imagination, like a wine, into my belly and legs, round my shoulders and up the back of my head into my brain, feeding it with a draught of renewed courage. Once more the familiar sensation of growing lighter than air filled me, and I rose an inch or two from the ground, contenting myself with that elevation so that passers-by should not notice anything untoward or critical in my passage.

My mind began to work again, telling me that I was specially protected, and that these downfalls, these pains and humiliations were part of a testing process, incidents in the life of a knight-errant of poetry, which I must accept. I began to laugh inwardly at myself, and my recent helplessness. I even recalled a line from the opening stanzas of *The Faerie Queene*:

> "But forth unto the darksome hole he went
> And looked in . . ."

and the joke rumbled round my warm body like the sound of drums and trumpets, heralding me home to my rooms, where I arrived, eager as ever, and bloater in hand.

CHAPTER TWO

First Glimpse of the Phœnix

I SPEAK OF 'my rooms' as though I were a hermit living in solitude. It is a slight exaggeration, for my brother Jack and I were still together, and he bore the major part of our domestic expenses, though he was seldom in the rooms. The fellow student whose reserved manner and girlish aquiline beauty had captured his fastidious attention was an only child who lived with her parents in an end house, in a quiet cul-de-sac on a Camberwell hill-top, ten minutes' walk from our rooms. Jack was absorbed into that *ménage* from his own choice, since this arrangement enabled him, the ardent moth, to hover closer round the cool candle-flame.

There was also some distaff influence to draw him there, the household being one quite unused to the intrusion of strangers; even of a fourth personality. He had to be examined, graduated, moulded, preparatory to becoming a permanent member. Thus he would compensate in some degree for his revolutionary proposal to convert this exclusive and intensely private trio into a quartette.

The father was a Yorkshireman, of some small property. As a youth, he had come down to London to work as a pupil-teacher in a school in Chelsea, and he had the distinction of being examined by Matthew Arnold. That must have been Greek meeting Greek, for this young man from the West Riding, cautious, conservative, monosyllabic, with a nose ridged like that of the Duke of Wellington, was equally as un-bending as the distinguished and by that time silent poet.

The mother was a daughter of London. Her father and his family before him built racing skiffs in a boathouse by Putney Bridge. She was as loquacious as her husband was silent; an ample woman, smartly dressed, vigorous and benevolently dominating. She knew what people needed to do them good. She was quite fearless and was only once defeated in her resolution to run those near and dear to her. She never succeeded with my brother Jack, and to the end of their long domestic association (for they lived under the same roof after his marriage to her daughter) she was puzzled by him, afraid of him. Of the two young males, I believe she preferred me, because I was naïve, innocent and, like herself, outspoken and candid.

She had a recipe for my good. My skeleton frame, my burning temperament, worried her vastly. She described me as "that poor boy", and whenever I went to the house I was fed with a boiled duck's egg; or if I were particularly dilapidated, with two duck's eggs. I could never persuade her that even chicken's eggs gave me violent nausea, or that the glasses of rum-and-milk with which she almost forcibly fed me were too painfully reminiscent (by their odour) of the drink which I had been used to preparing for my mother every night after I had got her, so laboriously, into bed, during the last two years of her life.

My brother had no sooner shewn the orientation which was to direct the rest of his life than, of course, the two mothers had to meet. It is a time-honoured situation, worn threadbare by playwrights and novelists. I found it nerve-racking from every point of view.

Two women could not have been more dissimilar. The future mother-in-law abounded in health. She had a massive confidence in herself as ruler of her small world. She was comfortably off, well-dressed, tolerant but unmovable. My mother too was a queen in her own small country; but she was a dying queen, subject to illusions, haunted by fears and anxieties. She had always been imaginative, passionate, vaguely hostile to a world which at some time or other in the past had cheated her, making her distrust her fellow women though they adored her and longed to serve her. It was an original, elusive personality, enriched by charm and physical beauty, qualities with which she had endowed her elder son.

I knew that the visit would disturb her. I could see for days beforehand the obstinacy and suspicion gathering in those brown eyes, sunken with suffering. The effect on her breathing was instant, and she had to take to her bed, though she insisted on getting up to receive this intruder, this other woman who, she insisted, would be hostile. "What does she think?" I was asked. "Isn't my son good enough for them?"

It would have been bad politics to suggest that the other party probably had the same prejudice. I was, fortunately, adept at coaxing her. I had to be, for I could not have ministered to her racked body if I had not perfected a technique for persuading the spirit still burning, with almost the rage of genius, within it.

No situation could have been more repugnant to Jack. There was much of his father in him too, notably a distrust for emotional and moral crises. He winced before any exuberance and excess. Loud noise of any kind affected him physically. He shrank. His eyes retreated to the back of their caverns, crouching like those of a wounded leopard. His huge beaky nose went white, and one Düreresque hand, half-transparent, rose to his lips, as though to prevent him from groaning.

It was not that he was unemotional. On the contrary, he lived in a secret world of spiritual tempest, an antarctic continent of the soul where all moods and feelings were stark, archetypal, infinitely dangerous. That may be why he submitted himself, and would submit me and the rest of civil humanity, to a repressive discipline, by which thought, reason, formality should hold down the cosmic storms within.

He saw the least argument as a breach in the defences; thus the everyday debate which most of us enjoy would make him irritable with apprehension. His distress would be so apparent that even a parlour conflict of opinion would falter and die out in his presence. It was a constant paradox, that this queer, reclusive personality, an apostle of quietness, remained so dominant in company, attracting first attention, then sympathy, and finally devotion.

To me, he was a universe, a system of law, outside which I moved, ever observant, a young and awe-stricken astronomer.

How acute, therefore, was my anxiety that day when the two mothers met. I worried about mother. I worried about Jack. Father was not present. The day being a Saturday, and he being off duty from the Post Office at two o'clock in the afternoon, he was over the hills and far away, cycling to Margate with a couple of his colleagues, intending to ride back through the night. "Take care of our mother, my boy," was his parting remark as he wheeled out his Osmond racer (a beautiful lightweight machine) at seven o'clock that morning, on his way to work. "A pity you can't all come with me. Ah! my boy, how I miss you. Remember those days, when Mother was well, and you lads on your tandem . . . ?" He sighed, brushed my cheek with his moustache, mounted, and shot off down the empty road of our sleeping suburb, one of the Sons of Morning.

I spent hours after breakfast getting the house ready. It would not do for the visitor to find anything to criticise. I dusted and swept in the drawing-room (including the leaves of Mother's forest of aspidistras), lighted the huge, pagoda-like gas fire, burned a small tray of asthma-powder in the room, and by mid-day had got Mother installed there, propped up with cushions in an armchair, with the oxygen apparatus at hand, to augment her breathing just before the visitor was due to arrive.

Jack too had gone. He disapproved the whole situation. From my terrestrial observations, I had detected faint signs of hostility between him and his future mother-in-law. After I had met her, I was not surprised at this opposition of temperaments.

She was utterly forthright, factual, and certain. Her sympathy and consternation over my mother's health were too clearly shewn. Mother resented it. I had to deal with that afterwards. During the interview Mother said nothing provocative. She was not capable of action, though the recent dose of oxygen had brought a lovely flush to her cheeks, and a light to her eyes. She looked very frail in comparison with her visitor; the blood could be seen coursing through the veins in her temples and neck, and over the backs of her sculptured hands.

Mother listened to the monologue, the tale of the daughter's virtues, needs, the childhood and the desired future. She agreed about that, for she had already approved of Jack's choice. She bowed her head, to shield a mood that might have been angry pride, when Jack was accepted, with certain reservations about his vitality, his 'shyness', his health. I listened to this too, and I had the illusion of Jack glowering from the depths of his cave. I heard him growl, and shrink further back against the rock of his stubborn personality. I was also quickly aware that the kindly visitor did not share this imaginative picture of my brother; and never would.

All went well, however, though afterwards, while I was administering another dose of oxygen, Mother said, cryptically and with great effort between one artificial inhalation and another: "She'll never understand people like us!"

Mother was right, but nevertheless I was to find a good friend in that healthy, matter-of-fact woman. Her normality was a relief to me, and during the years to come I liked to sit in her semi-basement morning-room, amongst a litter of family treasures, sideboards, cutlery, biscuit barrels, framed photographs, an armoury of fire-irons, while I listened to her cockney philosophisings and her occasional malapropisms that stood out like gargoyles on her Gothic conversation.

Very shortly after that first meeting, she offered to take me to the theatre. Off we went together to the West End, a rare occurrence. Jack stayed at home that afternoon, to look after Mother, who had suddenly rallied, as though determined to show any possible rival that she too could give the appearance of being hale and hearty.

The play was *The Three Musketeers*, with Lewis Waller as d'Artagnan. I recollect some wonderful swordplay. I remember also that my companion was 'taken bad' as she called it, and had to leave the gallery, after managing to command me to 'stay where you are'. But I could not. My interest in the picturesque gangsters was destroyed by concern for this kind half-stranger. After a while, I crept out (our seats fortunately being on the end of the row) to the stone staircase, where I found the lady collapsed into a mountainous heap. With expert, experienced hands, I was about to offer first aid, when she roused herself furiously, and barked out: "You go back and enjoy it. You're wasting my money!"

Her complete unself-consciousness was always a source of joy to me. It was different from my father's, which had an element of evasive cunning in it, so that sometimes one doubted his spontaneity, and if one were prejudiced (as I had been of late), his gay good-humour and boyishness savoured of the bluffness of Iago. But my new, elderly friend could not possibly harbour a double motive.

Her complete candour, however, had to be compensated, or it might have led to trouble in that triangular *ménage*. She had a habit, disconcerting to visitors, of uttering loud asides about the characters, habits and motives of her husband and daughter! The only way of recognising these interpolations into her direct monologue was by seeing her hand go up to her half-turned mouth, stage-fashion. Father and daughter obviously had a compact to regard these asides as wholly *sotto voce*, unheard by them. What amused me was that when my brother became a permanent member of the *ménage*, he too was included in this convention, and accepted it just as placidly as did the other two, his wife and father-in-law.

This last had his conversational habits too. Every evening, about to go out to his local Conservative Club, he would come into the morning-room, look round (the light flashing on his Wellington nose and in his blank blue eyes) and say: "Min! Seen my pipe?"

Min's response was equally automatic. Up went her hand, as she leaned heavily and conspiratorially to my new sister and to me (Jack more usually being upstairs in his music-room). "Old fool's lost his pipe!" Whereupon she would produce it from behind a photograph on the mantelpiece, where he always left it.

This tiny comedy would be followed regularly by another, with similar dialogue, relating to his hat. It took place in the hall upstairs, so it meant a slight heightening of tone in the wifely aside and response to his helpless request.

All this took place in another house, which I shall presently describe. In speaking of it now, I am revealing that I was not firmly balanced after the break-up of my concise little world, after Mother's death. Recalling that period today, I still fall into uncertainty and confusion; still hear the axes laid to those singing aspen trees that were an integral part and surety of the circumscription of our home on the outskirts of Dulwich Village. The impressions made by events when we are seventeen years *young* appear to be made for ever, and to reverberate through our lives.

I am able to realise, however, that it was not so much the events as the lack of events which most deeply and permanently affected me during the rest of 1910 and through 1911—those endless deserts of time beyond the frontier of childhood.

Up to then, and especially during the final months of my mother's illness, I had found small opportunity for introspection. Fear loomed large, but my world was still intact. I still had Mother at the centre of it, tangible, passionate. I refused to allow myself to believe that this state of affairs could come to an end. I have already described how I prayed that it should not, imploring my newly discovered God, an actual, personal Christ within whose Church I had been confirmed a year earlier in 1909; imploring with such fervour every night that the sweat poured down my face and neck, and I got into bed shivering, exhausted, but reassured sufficiently to carry my body, and my eager mind, through the night and to a hopeful morning.

After the funeral at Highgate Cemetery, father and sons returned to the silent house. Something was over. Something was finished. I did not know what it was. I am not sure that I know today, nearly fifty years later. These fundamental experiences are outside the definition of language and the images of art.

The immediate effect was to make all three of us shy of each other. Father seemed even reluctant to enter the house. He hesitated at the front door, key in hand. Nobody awaited us. Mother's two sisters had gone to their brother's house in North London, a foreign country to us.

Father put his hat down on the hall-stand, turned, and

looked forlornly at us. I shut the door and, as usual, it stuck before closing, causing the familiar little jolt that made the knocker outside give a ghostly rat-tat.

Then, in silence, Father wept. Jack turned away, his face darker, more Spanish-looking than ever, his mouth moving as though he were memorising words that threatened to escape. I looked from Father to Jack, seeing two strangers; for my brain had stopped working, had come to an end. I could feel nothing, realise nothing. I was not even cold. I had gloves on; and I remember taking them off and putting them down gently beside Father's hat. Everything was slowed down; the whole process of time. There was no purpose, no future. Something had been betrayed. The prayer and sweat, the imploring confidence had been useless.

We still stood in the hall. Ages had passed. Jack had put a hand on the knob of the dining-room door. My mind had raced round the house, looking for something, and finding nothing, not even in the bedroom which Mother had left only a few hours ago, and left for ever. I did not disbelieve that, for I did not even consider it. A more dreadful apprehension was gathering within me, over the frozen emptiness. Numbed, uncomprehending, I stared inward across the vastness. But realisation was not yet. It had to come later. All I could sense now was that this was not the worst. The exploration of death was not complete, because I had not found the strength and courage to look into my own self.

All I could do now was to stand, watching my father, longing to say something to comfort him as he wept, half-turned from us, bewildered and helpless. But I was dumb; and Jack shrank back, a retreating shadow.

Someone knocked at the door, behind which we stood. The knock was repeated.

Father shook his head, and made a gesture with his hand.

"See who it is!" he muttered, and fled to the kitchen. Jack's hand turned the knob of the dining-room door, and he too disappeared. I opened the front door.

The visitor was the friend of Mother who lived with a brother at the 'Bricklayer's Arms' at Penge, the quiet and modest lady who loved music and had a pianola. She was devoted to Mother and had been coming habitually to see her every few weeks, to sit with her, not saying much. She was one of those rare people who do not need to speak, being sufficiently articulate and sympathetic in their physical person.

I looked at her now, and at the sheaf of springtime daffodils on her arm. I saw her quiet glance, her timid smile. I heard her say: "And how is Mother?"

"She's dead," I said, with a distant voice. "We're just back." I did not say from what.

Mother's friend stood silent. She could not believe me, perhaps. I saw her eyes go blank. She looked up, without moving her head, then to right and left, as though making some further enquiry, in another place of some invisible agent.

At last she spoke, her voice flat, impersonal. "Then she won't want these," she said, and savagely flung the sheaf of daffodils down under the privet hedge. She turned and walked away. I have never seen her since.

But I have often thought about her, because I valued her devotion to Mother, and I know that this gesture of hers, so final, so complete in its despair, summed up the gathering power of events and revelations to which my life was being submitted. And this sudden concentration of reality woke me up.

It was a strange awakening. My conscience, my passionate loyalty to Mother, cried for an equally demonstrative outburst of grief. I expected, and demanded of myself, that everything should now come to an end, in a final cataclysm of heart-break.

Nothing happened. The hours began to move on. The day of the funeral closed. We had eaten a supper, real food, and Father had become Father again, no longer quite so pitiable. Jack still was silent; but that was only in character, especially in times of crisis.

To my horror, I went to bed and slept. I slept with unbroken oblivion until the morning, and woke to hear a blackbird shouting in one of the ancient elm trees that stood down the middle of the pavement along Half Moon Lane. I looked out of the small square window of my room, over the felled trunks of the aspens, and the plats of ash where the twigs and buds had been burned. I saw the elms shining in the Easter sunlight, dewy and coralline with flower-tufts and tiny leaf.

I wanted to feel guilty, but I could not. I stared angrily at this evidence of spring: the blue sky; the cloud-billows sailing over Herne Hill station; the massive elms. I smelled the dampness from the forsaken farm meadow, and the tart whiff of the wood-ash. The builder's men would soon be busy there, and all would be changed, nothing left as Mother had seen it, known it. I tried to fan the rebellion in my heart, aghast at the treachery there. But the song of the blackbird distracted me from this hopeless purpose. Nor would my other senses be coerced. I saw the grand riot of misty golden light rolling over the world. I watched the little stirrings of wood-ash flickering beyond the fence that bounded Ruskin Walk, like the phœnix about to rise from its own sacrifice.

CHAPTER THREE

Tuning Up Again

Two days after the funeral, Jack had the piano-tuner in, the bluff rustic-looking man who wore leather leggings and a tweed hat, which gave him the appearance of a gamekeeper. It was he whose devotion to my brother was like that of a sheep-dog to its master. He had negotiated the exchange of our infamous Broadwood-White pianoforte for the little eighteenth-century five-stop pipe-organ from Park Walk Chapel, Chelsea.

Jack had remained silent, irritable, pallid through the past tumultuous days. He complained that the premature spring weather had made the Klingmann pianoforte fall out of tune, and that the Open Diapason stop of his organ was ciphering. This must have been the reason why the tuner appeared, unexpected by me, for I had resumed work at the Land Registry in Lincoln's Inn Fields, befriended there by sympathetic but discreet colleagues, particularly my friend Arthur Sullivan, and my chief, a barrister named John Stewart-Wallace, who made it his business to put through the probate on my mother's will, and to encourage me by examining and discussing with me a set of six volumes of Macaulay's works, in Everyman, which I had bought during that first official lunch-hour under the new dispensation—my empty world.

I entered the house that evening, carrying my books loose, to hear music. Jack looked round as I opened the drawing-room door (he would never sit in a room with the door open), nodded severely, and continued with the Mozart sonata which was sparkling out from the refreshed strings of the German instrument. There was nothing defiant, enquiring, or challenging in his nod. It was absolute. "This is reality, the continuum" it said. So I read it, and I knew I was right because I knew my brother, changeling though he may have been, unlike his parents except in minor traits, unlike any other mortal.

I held up my books, knowing better than to interrupt the flood of formal gaiety with its under-current of melancholy, an element which Jack always contrived to pronounce wherever it was latent in music. A gleam of sardonic amusement lit his eye, and he nodded again. I felt a glow of warmth, the pleasure of being understood. It was the first time I had felt really warm since time stopped, the Saturday before. And now Thursday was nearly gone, another warm spring day. Had I been asleep, drugged, during the week, moving in a trance between home and office, yet responding with an almost exaggerated consciousness to overtures of kindliness from people with whom I had to make contact?

The music was delicious again. It perfumed our death-tainted home. But it also emphasised the emptiness. I put down the books, retreated to the kitchen, and began to prepare tea, methodically filling the kettle, lighting the gas-stove, laying two cups and saucers, noticing the hollow tick of the Swiss clock on the mantelpiece over the heavy cooking-range. The music followed me, cool yet impetuous, refusing to be excluded from my sorrow. The clock ticked out the increasing distance from the shore of my childhood and its premature burden.

I stood listening both ways, my hearing doubly acute. The blood once again pounded in my body, demanding something that I dared not understand. The conflict was so violent that I cried out involuntarily: "Oh, no!" and was instantly astounded. I had been standing with the tea-caddy open in my hand, I don't know for how long. But the kettle was boiling away and had filled the scullery with steam. The music had stopped, and Jack stood at the kitchen door.

"Did you call?" he asked.

"No," I stammered. "No."

"Father's left this note," he said. "He's got a week's leave and has gone on his bike to Wakefield."

I took the note and read it. Father also said that this was his *last* ride. Jack and I discussed that, but could come to no conclusion. It was impossible to imagine Father doing anything desperate or tragic. He enjoyed life too much, and also disliked decisions.

"He's working it off," said Jack, who understood him better than I did, and was closer to him.

I agreed, and we sat down to tea together in the motherless house.

"The tuner's put the organ right, too," said Jack. His irritability had disappeared, and a spot of colour kindled in his sallow cheeks. "Will you be all right if I go over the hill this evening? She can't very well come here—now!"

I reassured him. I knew what he meant by 'going over the hill'. I could see that he was torn. I could also foresee that this was how life would shape itself in future. I must not be a burden on him. He was the last person to saddle with such a responsibility. The first winds of solitude sighed around me.

After he had gone out, I sat down at the kitchen table, not daring to go upstairs to my room, or to wander about the house. I knew that I must resume my interrupted cramming at the detested subjects for the Civil Service examination, which, once passed, would make me a permanent clerk, assured of that pension and a bread-and-butter security. I tried to convince myself that I saw my way clearly; that Father's objection to my accepting the Art Scholarship was after all for the best, since this setback had shewn me my true vocation: the dedication of my life to poetry, following the example of John Keats, now my most intimate friend and consoler.

CHAPTER FOUR

The King is Dead! Long Live the King!

OUR CONJECTURE about Father's statement in his note proved to be right. There was no sinister or morbid intention in his reference to a *last* ride. He was preparing us for his next move forward into a fuller life. And he made that move the day after King Edward VII died, exactly a month after Mother.

I went to work as usual that day, but was held up at the Temple Bar, to hear the Herald proclaim the accession of King George V; yet another change to increase the distance between Mother's continent and this shapeless world where I was still walking backward, desperately trying to discern the details of the familiar sureties now diminishing. But behind me the counter-attractions grew more insistent. I must soon turn and face them. But how to do it, without a sense of treachery toward the past, and that dear person enshrined at the centre of it? Enshrined! I had already begun to accept the fact that she was now motionless, deified, no longer warm, no longer sharing life with me, no longer sick and demanding my service and vitality.

I got back to the house to find Father out under the glass verandah, crouched on his heels, examining the new arrival—a Humber motor-bicycle.

I had come in by the garden-door at the end of the verandah, and thus had a side-view of Father. He turned his head quickly, and I saw his grey eyes moisten. It was a recognised gleam. I had seen it whenever Mother rebelled against his boyish acts and moods. He knew, and he knew that I knew too, that she would have rebelled now. His desire to be up-to-date as a knight of the road had always kept him alert to what was going on in the world of cycling and, latterly, that of motoring. But the cost and the danger had frightened Mother. Her veto had been emphatic, absolute, and Father had submitted.

But he had not forgotten. That was why I now saw a woeful little smile playing under that handsome moustache, and the equivocal gleam in his eye. A kit of tools was unrolled before him like a praying-mat.

"Ah! There you are, my boy!" he cried, just a little too heartily. "A surprise for you!"

It was indeed a surprise, though for the past two weeks I had noticed a certain secretiveness in his comings and goings. Jack also had remarked this, but we had accepted it as part of the structure of his grief. He had depended so utterly on Mother that he was now bewildered; a ship without a rudder. That was how we interpreted his conduct, his slight avoidance of us. We saw him as an old man, his zest for life shattered, his enthusiasms widowed. We deluded ourselves that he looked physically older. He seemed to stoop, to be springless. To our young eyes, his age, forty-three years, was sufficiently autumnal, and this, with the burden of sorrow, would explain his tendency to creep away from us, memorials of his past happiness.

These reflections flashed ironically through my mind during that instant while he looked up at me and I at him. I said nothing. Foreboding, heavy with dread, made me silent.

That hesitation widened the rift which both he and I had suspected to lie between us since the incident of the Art Scholarship.

"I had to do something, my boy," he said. "Couldn't go on like that. I'd lost heart for the old velocipede. It reminds me too much of the days when Mother—you boys——" but words failed. His head drooped, and a dewdrop gathered on the tip of his aristocratic nose. I could not resist such desolation. I had to shew sympathy, enthusiasm, though I was deeply embarrassed, and indeed suspicious. I told myself that I was being unfair (a fact that Jack had already brought to my notice at one of our councils of action during the past month). Father was still Father; and I was clinging desperately to all that survived of the home, the world, which Mother had made so stable. I knew that she would have stood by Father. I must do the same.

I sat down on my heels beside him, and drove myself to ask questions about the mechanism that shone brand-new before us. The effort was not difficult, for I shared his passion for efficient machines. Unless a bicycle or a car is tuned up to concert pitch and is kept spotlessly clean, I fuss and fidget and lose my sleep. If I wake in the night, and hear a clock strike the hour, I have to check it against the luminous dial of my wrist-watch, and if it is a fraction of a minute fast or slow, a minor mood of doom and disaster takes me. Next morning the necessary regulation has to be made before I can settle to my work.

This passion for accuracy in mechanical matters I have inherited from Father. He also trained me to it, as the one form of discipline which he could fully understand. For him, a watch or clock had to be right to the second, a pocket-knife razor-sharp, a cycle chain oiled in every link. He had a natural gift for this kind of military mastery.

I remember once that he and I were cycling alone on a Saturday afternoon, bound for Leighton Buzzard. Somewhere in Hertfordshire we saw an inn with the sign 'The Load of Hay'. This took Father's fancy. "Ah! My boy!" he cried, "We'll have a cup of *tay* at 'The Load of Hay'." Delighted with his rhyme, he lodged the tandem against a bench, and led the way to the garden beside the inn. It opened on to a meadow, with woodland beyond. Three men, one of them the landlord in his shirt-sleeves, were occupied in examining and discussing a Service revolver in his possession. Then one of the men threw up a clay pigeon, at which the landlord fired—and missed.

Father, who was irresistible to strangers, walked up to the landlord.

"Gun practice!" he said. "Bravo! Years since I handled a Webley. Mind if I have a shot, before we start tea?"

Nobody resented the intrusion. Father took the pistol in one hand, plunged the other into his trouser pocket, withdrew a penny and flung it spinning high into the air. As it reached its zenith and was about to drop, Father fired. The penny disappeared.

"Well 'done! You've kept it in fine fettle," said Father magnificently, as he handed the revolver back. The three men stared at him.

"Now for some tea," he said. "Any fresh eggs, landlord?"

That was a part of his character which always emerged in moments of physical crisis: an utter fearlessness, directed by a lightning dexterity. He was a soldier, whose regiment happened, by mischance of birth, to be the Post Office Service.

This character took command now, at a time when he was in danger of being wholly demoralised by grief. His grey eyes brightened, his hands came to life and moved about among the tools, while he explained to me the principles by which the internal combustion engine worked. I was spellbound. Here at least was something concrete, demanding all my attention. It offered an excuse for escaping from the burden of that larger, anterior process of thought, the slow, ceaseless articulation of conscience and imagination, which for me was "that two-handed engine at the door" of my waking life, and whose pounding I often heard in my sleep, the ground-bass of accusing dreams.

That hour, spent sitting on my heels beside Father, was perhaps the first occasion when I became conscious that to be 'busy', to be up and doing some immediate job, was always a good excuse for putting off the *real* exercise of the mind, that agonising, racking athleticism of creative thought, which exhausts us body and soul, and usually gives such intangible results.

Jack was less exercised than I over Father's perfidy toward Mother's wishes. His emotional life was sufficiently tied up elsewhere, and he could look with a detached coolness at the changes, broken allegiances, reckless innovations, that were gathering momentum in our home, breaking it open, like a horde of *sans-culottes* invading the boudoirs and sanctuaries of a Parisian house during the Revolution.

Further, he had, and in a more intellectually developed degree, Father's delight in machines. It gave him the power of concentration on the substance of things, on the way they worked. That could be a satisfactory interest, while for me, plagued with the ungraspable and profitless question about origins and ultimate value, the problem was only an added poison, lulling me to an indifference toward immediate assets.

Jack had tested the motor-bicycle several times, before my turn came. On that occasion, I went out only as passenger, in a second-hand side-car which appeared within a day or two of the advent of the Humber.

The two were joined together in Holy Mobility on the day of King Edward's funeral, 20th May, memorable also because it was a premature summer day of great heat, with the sun blazing down from dawn to dusk. The day was a public holiday, so both Father and I were free.

"Let us fare forth!" said Father. "We'll take the road!" But Jack had already disappeared, so Father and I assembled the Humber and the side-car in the street, outside the garden door. This had to be done every time we went out; with the concomitant dissembling on our return.

The great open day, humming and vibrating with life, signalled by continuous song of blackbird and thrush in the chestnut trees, whose buds swelled hourly, glistening with gum; the flinging open of the gates of summer, took us along too, breaking away the cords that bound us to our recent loss. Like two conspirators against our own selves, Father and I worked with spanners and bolts, thrusting tubes into sockets, tightening up the connections, and finally surveying the assembled combination.

It would look old-fashioned today. The motor-bicycle had long and groping handlebars, rather like a pair of boat tillers set at an angle, so that the rider should sit bolt upright. The machine was of the latest design, and thus had a three-speed gear in the back hub, in which the changes were made by thrusting a steel pencil through the drumful of cog-wheels. We were to become better acquainted with that during the course of our first outing.

A person today, seeing that side-car, would believe that Father and I were taking part in a historical pageant. The body was made of wicker-work, and it was shaped somewhat between a conch-shell and a cornucopia. It threw out scrolls in all directions—round the top and back, and at the sides to provide arm-rests. The interior was lined with livid oilcloth, decorated with foliage that might have been peonies, or pickling-cabbage.

It swung over a framework of curved tubes, and was so delicately balanced that it shivered at a touch. Father, anxious for my comfort, went indoors and reappeared with a small cushion. It was one of three formerly used to make Mother comfortable when sitting up between the paroxysms of asthma. I said nothing, and sat down deliberately, to test the new purpose, and to justify it.

We locked up the house. Father wheeled the combination out to Half Moon Lane, waited for the hourly horse-bus to trot past, and then mounted the saddle. He had bought himself a new cap, and wore it perched forward to shade his eyes. At the back it stood up vertically, where it had been folded in store.

There was no difficulty in starting, for Father had already mastered the new technique. He twirled the handle, and the machine coughed apologetically. He tapped the plunger of the carburettor, and a tiny fountain of petrol spurted out. He twirled the handle again, commanding me to hold the throttle-lever open. There was a roar that startled the neighbourhood, unaccustomed to such sounds, and a moment later we moved off.

It was a strange, intoxicating sensation, to glide away without exerting a muscle. I knew that it made me feel drunkenly helpless, yet eager to accept this invisible force outside myself which had picked me up and was carrying me along the road, faster and faster. I gripped the sides of the demented bath-chair in which I sat, and pressed my feet against the up-curve of the floor, trying to counteract the dropping of my stomach, and the giddiness that made me close my eyes and throw back my head to avoid the surface of the road, racing toward me and seemingly disappearing into my intestines.

"Steady on!" said Father. I recovered sufficiently to open

an eye and glance at him. He sat calmly, leaning forward, his new cap vibrating, his hands shaking but in control of the several levers on the far ends of the handlebars. He was on the road again, and his *real* self. Through his teeth, he began to whistle 'I'll Sing Thee Songs of Araby', breaking off for interjections of encouragement, or to instruct me to lean to right or left, appropriately, as we turned corners, the basket-work squeaking its resistance.

So, with Father's song "charming me to a sigh", we roared through a diminished Dulwich, up College Road to the Crystal Palace, down Sydenham Hill into the traffic of Penge and Anerley (Father wholly unperturbed and persuading his mount as though he had trained it from birth), out through Beckenham, over Hayes Common, to Keston, where we stopped.

We stopped suddenly, after Father had shot the steel pencil through the barrel of cog-wheels in the rear hub, to change gear at the top of the Common. A rending sound, as of teeth being torn out of an obstinate jaw, warned Father that some-thing was wrong, as also did the racing of the engine.

A thoughtful mask fell over his face, and silenced his song, which at that moment was 'The Deathless Army'. Calmly he drew off the road and we came to a standstill, in solitude, on the turf. The rest of the community must have been drained from the Home Counties, to attend the royal funeral. We had Keston Common to ourselves.

The quiet, after the roar of our pioneer internal combustion engine, the creaking of the side-car, the rush of air past my tingling ears, was more than positive. It was a comment, a criticism. The sun blazed in the blue dome, where a choir of larks trilled and lingered, rose and dropped. The heat shim-mered on the gorse-bushes and short croziers of bracken, carrying up a general perfume of sap and greenness.

I got out, chilled and stiff, to feel the warmth of May surging round my body. Father sat in the saddle, thinking things out, humming contentedly.

"What is it?" I ventured.

"Oh, nothing! Nothing at all. Get it right in a jiffy," he replied.

Out came the mechanic's praying-mat, the roll of tools, and as by instinct Father located the trouble after tinkering about for only a few minutes. He found that the steel pencil, instead of shooting through into top gear, had stopped, like the Laodicean, between two determinations, thus setting up an internal conflict of cog-wheels. It was this revolt which had reached our ears, and brought us to a standstill.

Having found the fault, Father could not so easily correct it. Nothing would induce that steel pencil to shoot backward and forward through the right positions. Father, in his boyish enthusiasm, had entered the motoring world too soon. It was still at the experimental, pioneer stage, as he might have learned from the unreliable motor-buses which were beginning to replace the horse-buses in the streets of London. His object, however, was not to arrive, but to be on the road.

Fortunately, I had one of my new Everyman volumes of Macaulay's works in my pocket, and I sat by the roadside reading the opening chapters of the *History of England*, while Father tinkered happily with the defective transmission of the Humber, squatting on his heels near to me, alternating bouts of balladry, conversations with himself, and sometimes calling upon me to "Hold this!" or "Lend a hand, son," to which I responded affectionately, though with some absence of mind, owing to my being half-suffocated under Macaulay's voluminous prose.

My heart was warmed by Father's restoration to his former self. He was, indeed, on the road again, utterly content, for the moment, to be waylaid in the open air, with the dusty macadam at his feet, and the invitation of the highway that mounted the hill. The sun had already recognised and embraced him, and his cheeks were ruddy, his nose gleamed, his black moustache shone. I watched his hands at work, shapely hands and leisurely. I could see by the tentative efforts, however, that this new medium, the motor engine, was beyond his comprehension. He was really only fiddling at it, by a childish process of trial and error. But I was content, for the day was warm, and the odours of earth and new green life made music to my senses, restoring me as well as Father to a healthy share in the life of the world, after so much dreadful travel elsewhere.

The hours passed, and the sun moved over Keston Common. Our solitude remained unbroken. Father was still unsuccessful with the gearbox, and consented reluctantly to wipe his hands on a tuft of grass and a duster from the tool-kit, so that he could share the bread and cheese and bananas which I had brought from home in a paper bag supplied by a multiple store called David Greig Ltd. I patronised this shop because of a self-indulgent fancy that this David Greig might be an emigrant relative of the Norwegian composer Edward Grieg, whose work enchanted me by its longing to escape from the North. This nostalgic urge toward the South, the sun, and the Latin way of life seems to be common to artists born above a certain degree of latitude. There must be a fundamental rightness in the symbol of Apollo, the sun-god, as the father of the arts.

He shone down benignly upon Father and me that afternoon. The obsequies of King Edward VII were over long before we left Keston Common. Somehow or other Father contrived at last to persuade that steel pencil to function. We started up again, but our return journey was spasmodic, and consisted mostly of coasting downhill, and hand-pushing the combination uphill. This ignominious progress was helped by occasional bursts of co-operation from that experimental gearbox in the back hub.

We reached home long after dark, to find Jack, self-consumed with damped-down passion, bent over the dining-room table in the desolate house, designing a gramophone which he proposed to build from this new kind of wood called three-ply. He listened to Father's tale of our adventures, then dismissed it while he explained how he intended this new gramophone to show no external horn. It would stand four feet high, be lacquered black, with Watteauesque paintings on the sides and within the lid. The sound would be amplified by a trumpet-like scroll occupying the major part of the square cabinet. "Fine, my boy. Fine!" exclaimed Father. "You should have been with us today, though. The road! The trees bursting! That's the life. You want the fresh air, Jack, you're looking pale. Too much brooding! All work and no play makes Jack a dull boy. How long is it since you've been out on your bike? We must persuade Grace's parents to buy her one. Then you can go off together, healthy and strong, just as your mother and I did, when you were little fellows. Remember those tandems, eh?"

This recollection plunged him into a mood almost as sombre as the gloom which had re-settled over Jack as he realised his father's utter imperviousness to the revolutionary scheme for a gramophone without a visible horn. I knew, however, that the project would not be quenched, but I was too tired to say anything encouraging that night.

The wrongness of the house settled over us again, and we went to bed in silence, each to his separate cell.

CHAPTER FIVE

The Sap Continues to Rise

SUMMER CAME EARLY and took swift hold. I went to the Land Registry every week-end, resuming my lunch-hour explorations with the Titian-haired Arthur Sullivan, either standing to read at the bookshelves of Denny's in the Strand, or Glaisher's in High Holborn (the managers seeming to vie with each other in their hospitality toward our hungry intellects), or sitting in the gallery of St. Clement Danes Church, or St. Anne's, Soho, bemused by Bach's mathematical forms, or the lighter confections of Rheinberger and César Franck, while the steak and kidney puddings, previously consumed in a cabmen's eating-house, rumbled round our digestive systems, and in the process temporarily drained our immature brains of blood.

It was a period of weltering purposes, bewilderments, delusions. It was also empty. Although I was swotting (a different activity from studying) for the Civil Service examination, and reading with the utmost recklessness such authors as Spenser, Oscar Wilde, Ella Wheeler Wilcox, Milton, Stevenson, Keats, Shelley and Bret Harte, putting in a seven-hour day at the Land Registry, and continuing to carry my usual share of the household chores at home, yet my life was empty. I had the sensation of groping my way along a vacant corridor.

Nothing appeared to happen. I was waiting. At the same time, I was being hurled along. I could grasp at passing impressions, but they dissolved at my touch. The home that was no longer a home stood in the flood of this strange, quiet nightmare, but it was a castle of sand, slowly crumbling. The furniture, formerly the anatomy of my accepted universe, became unfamiliar. I found myself sitting alone in the drawing-room, or in my own room, looking around me in surprise, as though I had used the wrong door-key, and were a trespasser there.

I observed a change, too, in myself. I read books in a different way. I was more self-conscious, and no longer lost myself absolutely in the scene, the situation. I looked coolly at the words. Some faculty of alertness, of utter identification, had died. I asked myself, was this what death meant? Was this how death came home to the living survivors, laying its cemetery in their minds, their hearts? Grief, then, must be a negative; loyalty to the memory of the dead little more than a cauterisation. I grieved the more, despairing in the very elusiveness of grief.

With all this, my physical health improved. I was constantly hungry. I was no longer responsible, or proxy, for Mother's suffering. Wherever she was, she did not need me now. My nerves were not drawn to that necessity. In this respect, I was idle. Even prayer, that misplaced and abused exercise, was dropped, as an agent in the puzzle, the cheat.

Everything else, indeed, that might rouse my emotions, re-awakening forces best left alone, was dropped. I could hear the fall, the world-wide subsidence of all sensation, all meaning, as the cosmos I had built around my mother's person collapsed, card by card.

Strangest of all the new sensations was this uprising of physical vitality. It was like the tumult of a mob approaching along a deserted street. It affected my mind, making me feel that revolution was in the air. I was half frightened. Could these be my own limbs, that craved for violent movement? Was this warmth racing through my veins, bracing my back and stomach (normally such inert areas), quite acceptable, and to be trusted?

But I did not consciously ask myself these questions. I was only half aware of the changes, as a fisherman idling by the seashore between deep-sea voyages will see, without seeing, that the tide has turned and is flooding in.

The effect of this enlargement was to drive me out, cycling or walking, obedient to a muscular craving aided by my reluctance to be left alone in the house; a mood obviously shared by Father and Jack, who each went his separate way. We were blown apart, litter from an explosion, part of the wreckage of our home.

Father made an effort, however, to keep things together. He found a woman willing to come in during the mornings to clean up the house, and gave her a door-key so that she could let herself in after we had gone to our day's work. I encountered her one morning, because she had come earlier, to spring-clean the parental bedroom—the all too familiar bedroom. I stared at her powerful arms and heavy bust, as at something abnormal. The blood surged up, over my face and neck. I knew too much of this business: the structure, the ways of womanhood. It still claimed me, this precocious knowledge; but I wanted to escape.

She responded to my equivocal glance, mistaking it for friendliness, and I was quickly made a confidant about her aches and pains, her ailing husband and her five children. I might have been the family doctor, or a parish priest. I murmured something consolatory and fled from the burden.

Father's next step was to seek out old friends. Fatuously pursued, it was to lead him to years of trouble, and also to affect my freedom and development. Its first effect, however, was happy. He and I went one Sunday afternoon—Jack having already gone 'over the hill'—to North Side, Clapham Common, to call on one of his Post Office cronies.

This was a musician named Harry Bridge; semi-professional, because in his off-duty hours he played the viola in the local Shakespeare Theatre orchestra on Lavender Hill, and also conducted an amateur orchestra which, at some national festival, had been warmly praised by Hans Richter, who had shaken this modest English postal worker by the hand and told him that he was an artist.

So he was; and a saint as well. He was a modest little figure, worn out by overwork, and distrait through sheer simplicity of spirit. He seemed to be wholly ignorant of the ways of the world, and might have been a character conceived by Hans Andersen, put to music by Humperdinck. His true love was

Haydn, though this quiet, reverential passion did not detract from his devotion to his wife Annie. She was even simpler, a gentle soul with a voice like a distant flute heard through woodlands and hardly distinguishable from the accompanying complaint of doves. She ministered to her Harry and to their two sons, whom Jack and I had met once or twice during our infancy, they being just two years, respectively, older than us.

Now Father, perhaps with a view to doing something toward our musical interests, sought out this other-world family. We were instantly welcomed, but with no hearty display. The little house in a turning off Clapham Common received us as it were into the eighteenth century. We might have entered Doctor Burney's music-room at Deptford. The air was filled with resin-dust, from the rubbing of bows; violin, viola, 'cello and bass, all the stringed instruments being played in that household.

Nothing was said about our recent loss. Annie Bridge took me by the hand, and made a little murmuring sound, as of a bee approaching an isolated flower. I could distinguish no word, but instantly I was comforted.

We discovered that the two boys were already professionals, both having won scholarships in the Royal Academy of Music, the elder for the 'cello, and the younger, Bertie, for the double bass. Bertie, two years senior to me, was a male version of his mother Annie; gentle, simple-hearted, almost overwrought with sympathy for all living things—and quietly, deeply religious. He was already playing third bass in Covent Garden Opera House, and was remarked in the profession as a master of his instrument.

The elder brother, the 'cellist, was a handsome fellow, touched by a gentle frown of perplexity, as though living in dread of being parted from his violoncello and bow, a fatality that would have made him wholly inarticulate and helpless. Gentleness emanated from him, too, as from the rest of this extraordinary family, but only to form a kind of mist, through which he could be but dimly perceived as a personality, while he must have seen the world through it as no more than a vague series of irrelevant masses, remotely connected with his music.

Father and I stayed to tea, that June afternoon, and Bertie and I talked together, recalling how in our distant infancy we had played with his toy trains. Then music engulfed us, and for the first time in my life I listened to the earlier of the two trios by Schubert.

While the meal was in progress, Harry Senior sitting not at the head of the table but beside Annie, with only a tea-cosy between them, over which from time to time she reached to place a buttered crumpet on his plate, the while glancing at him with reproachful affection on account of his absent-minded toying with his food; Harry Junior exactly emulating his father, sitting half-turned from the table, one elbow on it, his hand buried in his long brown hair, meditation weighing on his eye-lids like sleep—in the midst of all this, and to the interruption of my Father's monologue upon the intricacies of the route between Stow-on-the-Wold and the Wye Valley, there entered an addition to the party.

He was Old Harry's brother, Uncle Charlie. No two close relatives could have been more unlike Whereas Old Harry was small, narrow-chested, with lined features set in the cast of gentle abstraction and tinged with pallor over brow and cheek, Charlie was stout, rubicund, bald. He was also a little irascible.

I instantly sensed that something was amiss. The harmony of this musical family did not extend outside the home to its further members. Annie fluttered in nervous apprehension, and I strongly suspected her of saying, almost aloud, "Oh, dear!" as she gathered herself together in order to fetch a boiling kettle from the kitchen, to re-fill the tea-pot and lay another cup and saucer. As she passed her husband, beside whom I sat, I heard her whisper, "Now, Harry, you're not to say anything! Don't start it!"

But it was Young Harry who seemed most perturbed. He looked up at his Uncle Charlie, and his already lined young forehead crinkled like a concertina. The sleepiness left his eyes, and I could see that he was prepared for battle.

All this mystified me. I was uncomfortable, for like my brother I hated controversy and argument, loud quarrels or bickering.

No hostility broke out, however. The truce lasted through tea, and Uncle Charlie and my Father engaged in a hearty dialogue about other colleagues. It appeared that Charlie also was a Post Office man, and had formerly worked with Father and old Harry in Hobart Place, Victoria, until the family feud caused him to apply for a transfer to another district office, out of daily contact with his brother.

Later in the evening there entered a third brother, very like old Harry in appearance, but deaf and dumb. This disability had prevented him from entering the Post Office as a sorter, but he made a safe living as a wood-carver. A panel of his work, fruit and foliage in the manner of Grinling Gibbons, hung over the door of the sitting-room where we were all gathered at tea (a double-room with folding doors removed).

The meal finished under some restraint, and Uncle Charlie wiped his head with his handkerchief, wheezed irritably, and suggested 'a little music'. I saw Annie tremble. This was the moment. Then the genius of compromise shone from the younger son Bertie, the bass player. He suggested the Schubert trio, and there was immediate assent. We left Annie to clear away the tea things, and withdrew to the front half of the sitting-room, where stood a boudoir grand by Broadwood (*not* the spurious Broadwood-White) and a small copse of music stands. What with the bulk of the piano, the splay legs of the stands, the bass lying on its side and the 'cello (with extended peg) lolling over an armchair, little room was left either for performers or audience. I sat on the curb of the fireplace, and Bertie joined me, for he seemed eager to further our acquaintance.

Our conversation was enthusiastic, for we were discovering, moment by moment, mutualities of interest in music, and country matters, and religious adventure. I quickly found that he did not read much, and that my self-dedication to poetry was something of a novelty to him, which he found endearing but incomprehensible. But he respected it, and said so. I needed no more encouragement. A proud gratitude welled up and almost overwhelmed me. I must have shewn it, for he smiled and nodded at me, exactly as his mother had done over our bereavement. The evening sunlight flickered through the lace curtains and hovered like butterflies around his handsome head. I could hardly see him, because my eyes were suffused. I had to take off my spectacles and wipe them, thus changing the scene to a mass of glowing shapes, the sunlit Broadwood, the gilt music-stands, the vague figures of the performers, or rather those about to perform.

For the music of Schubert had not yet begun to flow. The score was being handed out, examined, commented on, hummed at, while discussion went on as to who should play which instrument. It was finally decided that as Bertie was in deep conversation with me, he should not be called upon. Young Harry sat down at the pianoforte, perplexity still written on his brow. He wiped his hands with his handkerchief, tucked it up his cuff, and leaned forward to examine the score, frowning still more as he did so, as though to suggest that what with the mysteries of music on the one hand, and the distractions of having to contend with everyday life on the other, he was likely at any moment to resign the contract made so shyly at his birth, by dear Annie and Old Harry.

This last was to play the violin part, and for that purpose he now had to make up his mind which of two ready instruments he should use. Three were examined, but one was out of court as being quite distasteful to him. How it had got into the house, he explained somewhat querulously, no one knew, but he suspected his brother Charlie of having bought it at an auction. Charlie accepted the accusation meekly, or absent-mindedly, for he was busy fitting a string to an out-of-commission 'cello, a garishly red instrument for which he plainly had little respect. But Young Harry allowed nobody to touch his own violoncello, and there it lolled, a spoilt darling, ready for utterance, still in the main armchair.

With a grimace that drew the muscles of his mouth sharply, as from toothache, Young Harry touched a key to give the tuning note. He played a few chords—and rapture flooded over me as though a caress had surprised me, touching the hair at the back of my head. The velvety tone of the Broadwood was softer, more woody, than that of our Klingmann; but it compensated by coming from an open grand—with that instant contact which is always just lacking in an upright piano.

I paused in my excited flow of conversation with Bertie, and he looked at me, half enquiring, but wholly patient, for I believe that he was letting the content of my speech flow over him. Our friendliness, our mutual warmth, were enough, though most of my references to things and persons literary and philosophic were unintelligible to him.

This sudden pause in our conversation resulted in one of those social silences which are said to occur either at twenty minutes past or twenty minutes to the hour. A marble clock, with figures of a blacksmith and a husbandman supporting it, affirmed the superstition. The time was twenty to seven, and the sun at that same moment withdrew from the room, leaving us to contract our range of consciousness, and to concentrate upon the universe of the ear, privy from the distractions of that of the eye. Dusk was falling.

The effect of the silence was galvanic upon Young Harry. He suddenly returned to the current world, a spasm shook him, and he leaned across the keyboard of the piano, his brown eyes alight with a touch of malice, and said to his Uncle Charlie: "And are you coming to hear *Tannhäuser* on Thursday?"

Annie was out in the kitchen, and thus no feminine influence was present in the darkening music-room to prevent the explosion that followed. Uncle Charlie struggled to his feet, bow in one hand, the other hand grasping the reddish 'cello as though it were a turkey which he had just strangled. His face grew purple, his eyes stared glassily.

"You're young," he gasped, "Harry, you don't know yet. You haven't lived long enough. But people like him come between father and son; they are blasphemers. They crucify all that is good and sacred in music. We've had this out before. It's upset our family. I've been kept away from you all—and now, the first time I come to see what can be done, you say this to me! I tell you, young Harry, and you're my own nephew; I tell you once and for all, that I'll have nothing to do with this wicked charlatan, or his damnable works. Let them bring him to Covent Garden, with his Ring of the Nibble-*lung*ens, and his

Tan-houzers! It doesn't make him a musician; it doesn't change my belief that you and Bertie are being ruined as instrumentalists by playing his horrible works, with their wicked tricks and fraudulent discords. It's enough to make me weep!"

And he did weep, to our intense embarrassment. The tears gathered in those bulging, glassy eyes, like blood out of stone, and Old Harry, with his fiddle under his arm, trembling and quavering, muttered over and over again.

"Oh, come now, Charlie. There's no call for all this. The boys are young. You can't expect . . . old heads on young shoulders . . ."

What might have happened if Annie had not returned to the party, I dared not think. Indeed, I was incapable of thinking, for the storm appeared to be blowing all round me. Bertie had put his hand on my knee, in concern over my distress.

"They don't understand," he pleaded with me. "You can't expect them to. It's all so big—everything different—but they can't see that it had to come. Verdi has said all that could be said in the old forms. But Wagner is another world. The more I play his work, the more I learn. He's more like a god than a man. But what's the use of arguing about him—quarrelling about him?"

"Now, now," quavered Annie, "what is all this? Why haven't you begun your music? Who began it *this* time?"

She looked reprovingly, but with infinite timidity, from one to another of her menfolk, the four musicians (two of them also Post Office sorters), and I could have sworn that she shook a finger, as in a kindergarten of naughty children. "Now come along, Harry dear," she said to her husband. "Just you get along with it."

But Young Harry, who had caused the disturbance, was too upset to settle down at the keyboard. He flung back his hair, looked at his uncle accusingly, and stood up.

"No!" he cried, "I can't take the piano part after that. You'd better. I'll play the 'cello."

And he picked up his own instrument, bent over it, his hair almost sweeping the strings, and began to tune it, screwing the keys, and his own features, simultaneously, as in a kind of nervous agony.

"Uncle Charlie's old-fashioned," whispered Bertie to me, leaning across the fireplace. "Father doesn't really understand Wagner either, but he's more tolerant. That's due to Haydn, whom he worships. Haydn was an experimenter too. Father is kind of—of *prepared* for the change, you see."

His further words were drowned under an expostulation of tuning up, this time with a still angry and lachrymose Uncle Charlie at the piano, giving the note. Old Harry was trembling at one knee, and from moment to moment his head nodded violently in the aftermath of the storm. I gathered, however, from Bertie's innocent stage-whisper that Uncle Charlie had not been near the house for six months, and that when his brother had refused to take sides in the previous quarrel— though his tastes were known—Charlie had put in a request to be moved from the South-west District Post Office in Hobart Place in order to withdraw himself from even this remote contagion from Wagner.

Schubert bowed himself into the room through an atmosphere of constraint. His boyish gaiety and bubbling outburst of good-humour were quite incongruous with the expression of set obstinacy on the face of the pianist, the worried anxiety of the fiddler, and the anger of the 'cellist.

But that made no difference to the movement of the music; music that came running up the shore round me, sunlit, foaming out of the deep, as playful yet strong as a flooding tide, sun-drenched, and pungent out of the mid-ocean of genius.

I leaned forward, half-losing my nervous distress, and, clasping my hands between my knees, stared at the whitening knuckles, unaware that my fingers were aching, conscious only that I was moving into another and larger chamber in the house of music. And I was conscious, too, that I was here without Jack, and that this was an intrusion I could not help since he had gone off on another pursuit that demanded all, perhaps more than, he could give.

CHAPTER SIX

And Buds Burst

THE EXCITEMENT of this new friendship that suddenly had come to flower out of a seed set long ago in childhood made me insistent to share it with Jack. I could see there was so much to enchant him, lighten his melancholy temperament, and even to dilute the intensity of his love-passion, in this family circle where music was the daily bread.

One Sunday, when it was inconvenient for him to go 'over the hill', and Father was absent again—somewhat mysteriously —with his Humber motor-cycle, plus the sociable side-car (which I had helped to assemble), I persuaded Jack to come with me to Clapham Common. The occasion made us both shy, because we realised that this was the first time we had been out together since Mother left us.

The afternoon, of a sunny day in July, was hot, and the streets of suburban London were deserted. A placid smell of dust and privet hedges charged the air with laziness and sleep. We had been busy during the morning, cleaning up the house while Father roasted the joint. Now he had departed, blurted down Half Moon Lane, temporarily ruffling the silence of the afternoon. But it closed again after him, like pond water settling over a flung stone.

Hardly a sound disturbed the neighbourhood when Jack and I set out at a little before three o'clock. The elms in Half Moon Lane stood in the dark mantle of their own shadows. From one of them floated the lifting murmur of a pigeon's voice, and the abrupt stop. The suburb was digesting its Sunday dinner, with the *News of the World* over its head as a shield from the light. Even the light itself was subdued.

Jack and I walked toward Clapham, breaking our reserve

by shy, generalised remarks as though we were strangers. Indeed, we were so, for we had come together again for the first time since Love, and then Death, had entered our home, and shewn it to be so fragile.

I watched my brother while we walked. The intensity of his emotions, concentrated now upon the timid and inexperienced person of the girl whose cool beauty and reserve had thrown him into a perpetual state of enthralled frustration which even her gentle loyalty could not assuage, had fined down the sufficiently sparse flesh. He was more than ever like Savonarola. I almost had the illusion of seeing his great beak of a nose protruding from under a cowl, his eyes invisible.

He stooped as he walked, and a little hunched, guarding something.

"Don't you dare to fall in love," he said suddenly, as we approached Brixton.

"Why?" I asked, equally guarded.

"It's torture!"

With that we went on in silence again, but sensibly drawn closer to each other. After a while I ventured upon some consolation.

"It'll be all right when you're married."

His head drooped a little more forward. "But when—when?" he demanded. "We come out of College this term, and start teaching in September. I shall just be turned twenty-one, and she's only twenty. Her people won't hear of it. You can't blame them."

Then he stopped, turned, and stared at me, deeply, consumingly. I stopped too. It was impossible to pass this barrier of fire.

"And what about *you*? Mother's been gone three months and what is Father doing? Where does he go lately?"

The passionate query meant less to me than to Jack. Father had always been somewhat of an absentee in my life; his enthusiasms remote, his enormous physical vigour unintelligible. I saw now that Jack, who had been his companion, though a slightly reserved one, all through the cycling years, was frightened. Perhaps he was trying to shift the burden.

After all, he had been the first to break, in 1908, the enclosure of our unique family life, with its involved emotions and interest.

He must have read my thoughts, for he went on, as we resumed our way toward the haven of the Bridges' home: "And there's you. I can't leave you alone: not yet."

I had not contemplated these possibilities. I lived removed from the immediate drama of events and actualities, and thus had little political sense. I had not learned to put two and two together. I was otherwise occupied with the excitements of the dictionary and the drug of verse. The only reality that I could appreciate was the prospect of a room to myself, somewhere close to the assurance of food and warmth, where I could fulfil my verbal dreams without interruption.

Even now I did not fully grasp what Jack meant. So I said nothing. The idea of being left utterly alone in the world was one I could not entertain, except under the conditions of my monomania. I could desert the world, in order to pursue my purpose: but the world must not desert me.

This self-concern made me respond with some ardour to Jack's words. He was seldom given to demonstration; signs of affection or expressions of praise from him loomed up like hillocks on a plain. So though I accepted this surprising gesture in silence, I was inwardly eloquent. I seized him by the arm, and walked along with him for at least a dozen paces. Then I realised that his artesian emotions had sunk back to their normal depth, escaping from my exuberance. The spiritual contact survived, however, and we walked on in silence or intermittent conversation, very happy together, he in his responsibility for me, I in my faith in him.

The Bridge family made Jack as welcome as they had made Father and me a week or two earlier. Again the Sunday tea-table was spread in the back-room, with Annie fluttering like a moth behind the tea-cosy, and Old Harry at her side, dependent upon her even for the conveyance of bread and butter, with bloater paste, to his plate. He accepted visitors as he accepted the rest of his life's furniture, with an impersonal sweetness. But his character managed to give an assurance, in spite of its *distrait* habit, that he knew the true value of things and people, and that he would recoil with obstinacy from a fake Stradivarius, as well as from a pretentious friend or musician. I had already noticed how affectionately, though somewhat dismissively, he had received my father. I now saw him accept Jack with a more continuous interest. Throughout tea-time he studied Jack's hands. They appeared to fascinate him.

Meanwhile, my brother warmed up. He sat opposite Old Harry, listening and responding to a technical cross-talk about counterpoint, a subject the two Bridge boys were struggling with in their studies at the Royal Academy. Jack emerged from his cavern and sat there in the full glare of debate, while I amused myself as a listener, trying to count the threads of the argument, and to see them as a living demonstration of the art of counterpoint, the fact being that each enunciation by Jack, after provoking a babel of voices, was repeated by Young Harry lower down the scale of the tea-table.

I realised, too, that throughout my life I had never before seen Jack in other than our own domestic setting. He must have felt the same about me; but I had nothing to demonstrate. I was in a state of foreboding. Jack's remarks during our walk to Clapham had come home to me with belated effect. I watched this still united family of four, and it brought back to my mind the disaster which had crept upon our home, with gradual stealth, and then suddenly struck: only now was I beginning to realise with what shattering force.

After tea, I retreated into a corner, beneath one of those novel phonographs which Young Harry had introduced to the house. It stood on a pedestal above me, its horn sticking out above my head. Young Harry demonstrated it, playing a cylindrical record of Caruso singing an aria from *Il Trovatore*. It sounded like a tiny, far-off voice from fairyland. Harry then showed me Caruso's autograph in his album, embellished by a self-caricature drawn by that warm-hearted master.

All this, however, was but a preamble to the business of the evening, the usual Sunday night quartette-playing. Uncle Charlie had not appeared. He was still sulking in his tent, after the last altercation about Wagner. Old Harry accordingly had a suggestion to make, as though it were something utterly unprecedented, an inspiration belatedly showing itself in his autumnal years—that the evening's music should start with one of Haydn's thirty trios for strings.

"There, Harry, and very nice," said Annie, who might not have heard this suggestion every Sunday night for the past twenty-five years.

With his dear wife's encouragement, Old Harry began to explore one of the piles of sheet-music which stood about the room, in the corners, on the chairs and sofa, in and on cabinets, under and on the grand pianoforte. Jack volunteered to help him, and immediately the two were withdrawn from the rest of us into a world of 'unheard music', that magic still merely in notation, dumb within the confinement of the staves.

I recognised in Jack's absorbed activity the power that had so often caught me up in those distant days of childhood, æons ago; sweeping me on out of my station of day-dreams, only to leave me higher up the slopes of that dangerous range of fantasy.

But more was happening. Jack had stopped sorting over the piles. He was immersed in something particular. I knew by the poise of his whole body that he was concentrating upon one of his enthusiasms. It was much the same physical stance as that of a kestrel when it halts upon air, its wings spread and still, yet at the same time vibrant in a lifting intensity, a throb of directed purpose, before the plunge. "Mr. Bridge!" he said; or rather, he commanded.

Conversation died away, and Young Harry nervously lifted the ruby needle from the revolving wax cylinder on the phonograph, thus snatching the voice of Nellie Melba into oblivion.

Jack rose from the floor, still looking at the opened sheets in his hands.

"We ought to play this," he said. He spoke quietly, finally. There could be no denial, no opposition. "I've never heard it, but I've had the score out of the library. It's one of the greatest things I've ever heard."

"You mean *not* heard," said Young Harry, wryly, smiling his whimsical, half-distracted smile.

"This is Brahms at his best," Jack went on, soliloquising rather than addressing himself to us. "It's the Piano Trio in C major."

"Dear me, that's very difficult," said Old Harry indulgently, shaking his head to indicate that Brahms was not to blame.

"But it's astounding!" cried Jack. "It's so—so *tense*, with the hesitation of strength in the first movement. I long to hear the effect of that when it's played. It's not easy to follow on the page. But all that comes after: the gaiety of the second movement, and this remote Hungarian music of the *andante*, with the solid peasant dance of the last movement, festive yet tragic. Oh, it suits me, it suits me!"

I stared at him. Never before had I seen him emerge so far. Not even on the occasion when, as a boy of thirteen, he built a steam locomotive that made a record run and then blew up, nearly braining him in the explosion, had Jack shewn himself so triumphant.

Nobody could withstand that force. Within a few minutes, Jack was at the piano, Old Harry at the violin, and Young Harry at the 'cello. One or two differences of view about tempo, a false start, owing to a defective tuning of the fiddle, and then the music launched out into the open, Jack playing from sight, his great nose white, his lips indrawn, the muscles of his cheeks twitching, his silky hair lying lank over the neat skull. I could *feel* the knowledge, instantly translating itself from theory to living music, as it flowed from his hands. They appeared to cling to the keyboard like hungry birds alighting there, for he had devised a muscular stance (after reading an exposition of Tobias Matthay's method) in keeping with his own character, so that much was done with a minimum of effort, the full significance and authority finding expression mostly in what he did *not* do or say.

It was almost a devastating experience for me. I saw, for the first time, my enigmatic brother's personality stripped naked, and I was both awed and charmed. Apart from my wonder at the bravura of playing such a work at sight, I recognised that this particular trio by Brahms, which I have never heard performed since that Sunday in July of 1910, might have been composed as a prophetic portrait of my brother. He, too, had the passionate reserve, the latent force of lyrical joy and humour, the basis of robust sanity, the sudden soaring up into self-immolation under the prompting of agonised emotional sacrifice.

Bertie and I sat together again during this performance, and I had the illusion that we were kneeling side by side at a sacrament. The wry humour of the last movement (*allegro giocoso*) must have touched Jack at the very core of his nature, for he played it as though he were possessed, and actually broke into a sardonic chuckle, in time with the heavy beat of the dance rhythm. The sweat glistened on Old Harry's time-tonsure; and Young Harry at the 'cello, at each emphasis of the detached string quavers, gave a rapid bob over his instrument, causing his mane of hair to fly over his face and almost to flick the strings, adding an unwanted *pizzicato*.

Annie, sitting with her sewing in the back room, spoke up when the triumph ended.

"That last piece was very loud, Harry dear," she said.

But Old Harry paid no attention to this gentle criticism. He was trying to say something to Jack. Words failed him, however, and, after an effort that shook his whole frame, nothing came but tears. They flowed down his withered cheeks, tears of joy, and he groped for his handkerchief to assuage them. But what with this effort, and the attempt to pat my brother on the shoulder and the burden of the violin and bow still in his hands, he finally gave way, and stood in helpless confusion, vaguely murmuring: "Good boy! Good boy!"

Young Harry meanwhile resumed the manner of the tired professional, the mask of perplexity over his features, the wrinkles in his forehead, while he tossed back his hair, and worked at a bit of silent stopping up and down the 'cello strings. He was waiting for more.

"Come along, Bertie," he said. "It's time you took a turn. Give us a bass solo."

Bertie eased himself up from the fender, where he and I had been sitting like two dumb tailors. The great double bass

was turned round from its dunce-posture, face to the wall in
the corner by the doors into the back room, and Bertie (his
fingers and thumbs already slightly splayed at the tips, an
occupational distortion) began to tune up. It was like a shire-
horse rousing from sleep.

Accompanied by Young Harry, who sat at the piano as
professionally as he sat at the 'cello, Bertie gave us a bravura
little lyric by Giovanni Bottesini; a touch of love-laughter
among the giants. We all made merry over it, and on this note
of comedy over the pathetic emotions of the instruments that,
like Atlas, carry the sphere of music—the double bass, the
bombardon, the bassoon, the big drum—Jack and I left, with
the assurance that the home was always open to us, Old Harry
seeing us to the door and still trying in vain to say something
to Jack about his miraculous bit of sight-reading. He patted
Jack again on the shoulder, before closing the door.

"Nice old boy," said Jack, walking glumly beside me.

CHAPTER SEVEN

Or but a Wandering Voice

THIS NEW AND EAGER FRIENDSHIP with Bertie Bridge brought me back to sensation again. The result was painful, like the return of blood to a numbed limb. I was afraid of further attachments, after the treachery of events which I had so recently known. But this young musician, partly through our association in that intact world before my mother died, partly because of his exquisitely sensitive gift of sympathy, came into my life as a proxy for the trust I had lost. He filled —or at least obscured—the gap left by Mother and Jack.

For I knew that Jack could never resume quite the old relationship which had made my infant years so secure and my boyhood so sensibly monitored. He had neither the time nor the vitality for it. Something was beginning to tell upon that vitality. More than ever, he looked older than his age; his sombre sagacity still more marked. Most of his free time was spent 'over the hill' in that *ménage* where he was ultimately to be settled, or domiciled; for the idea of settlement was as incongruous for this strange, pulsing character as for one of our latter-day radio-active elements.

What he did there, hour by hour, night after night, he never disclosed to me. But he came back after each session moody and self-consuming. Perhaps our recent loss had crippled him as deeply and unchangeably as it had crippled me. But it took different forms, as I was soon to discover. For the time being, however, I was bemused by grief, and believed that I was never again to be capable of strong feeling; nothing that was not guarded by art, as in my purpose to become a writer, or by gentle good-humour, as in this new friendship with Bertie Bridge.

The summer opened out, and during my lonely week-ends, when Jack was 'over the hill' and Father away on his motor-bicycle—always with the side-car, I wandered about Dulwich Village, haunting the picture gallery and the old garden behind it. I had given up drawing, turning from it with perverseness that surprised me. I knew the cause of this irrational mood, but I could not cure it. Indeed, it festered and settled into a poisonous centre that threatened to ruin my relationship with Father, whose limited imagination had been the cause of my disappointment over the relinquishing of the scholarship at the time of the award by the Camberwell Art School, two years earlier.

At present, however, any kind of open antagonism was inconceivable. I still saw Father as being permanently injured, like myself, by our loss, and my immediate compassion for the lonely widower overcame any other feeling. Perhaps his frequent absences enlarged this compassion. I imagined him wandering over the English countryside, seeking those places where he had always longed to take us on the two tandems. He had been sadly frustrated, but, even so, there were many rendezvous to which he could return, there to live over again happy and carefree hours spent with his united family. I knew his propensity for harping on the past, and also his dread of solitude.

I took it for granted that he and I should go for a summer holiday together. Jack and his fiancée had both left Training College, and would begin their careers as school-teachers next term. Neither Jack nor I had any conception of the possibility of free adventure in the world. The idea of a need for a regular income was paramount. We had been born into a home where that idea had never been questioned. I know that sometimes I looked, apprehensively, over the wall of that sense of security, and wondered with dread how people dared to live otherwise; to marry, beget families, subject to the caprice of an individual employer, or the vagaries of the market.

It never occurred to me that a man might have confidence in his ability, or his trained skill in a craft, or even in his brute muscles, by which to ensure his livelihood. Perhaps I had an instinctive knowledge that the vocation I had chosen, or which had chosen me, was quite outside the general run of workaday activities, and that I must be prepared to sacrifice self-confidence in practical affairs, in order to exaggerate it in the world of letters.

I was really wading out of my depth, and a guide at that stage would have been useful, though I might not have appreciated him, for I was beginning to swim wildly out to sea, on this ocean of day-dreams, concerned only with the novel discovery that I *could* swim. University tutors must know all about such gestures, the prancings of the colt when he first feels the collar.

Father could do nothing, for he was unconscious of the problem. Jack from time to time showed his old authority, but more and more intermittently. This was due partly to his own struggles and the complications of a new loyalty, partly to his reluctance to intrude on my demands for freedom. I could see his shyness, and the affection behind it. I told myself that behind his severity was a brotherly belief in my determination to become a poet, though I was starting with but a meagre capital of grey matter, physical vitality, or the elements of a sound scholarship. My only assets were an insatiable curiosity into the goings-on of nature and mankind, and a great capacity for happiness, a power which objectified even my sorrows.

This sounds complicated, but at the time it was simple enough, and I lived with but few hesitations. Having dismissed worldly ambition, and the healthy spirit of competitiveness, as part of the satanic side of life, I believed my future ascendancy, and public recognition of it, to be assured. And all this certainly was arrived at within a few weeks of passionate emotional quiescence (a paradox, a living contradiction in terms) after Mother's death.

Thus firmly settled on my cloud, I went away with Father almost happily. Before us lay a fortnight of freedom, at high summer.

Jack had already gone with the other little family, to the West Country. Father and I shut up the house, heartily glad to escape from its silences and whisperings. After assembling the motor-cycle and side-car (I was by now expert in slotting one tube into another and tightening the nuts), we slammed the back gate, and tied our baggage on the carrier. Taking my place in the side-car, I noticed that the little cushion was sadly flattened, and that the new open-air life was bleaching out the all too familiar pattern of its cretonne cover.

We were bound for Folkestone and a comparatively sedentary holiday. Father was secretly unhappy about that unreliable gear-change mechanism. As we plugged our way through Dulwich Village, stopping to pay the due at the toll-gate in College Road, he talked airily about the gear having 'let us down' on several occasions. But seeing my puzzled glance of enquiry, he changed from the plural to the singular, recalling that never, since that first trip on the day of King Edward VII's funeral, had I been out with him when the gear misbehaved.

"Have to do something about it, my boy," he said, anxiety making a grim set round his jaws, as he slotted into bottom gear up the hill at the approach to the Crystal Palace.

"What, a whole new gear?" I enquired, still puzzling over his previous remark.

"No; it may mean a part exchange. I've been thinking about a Triumph machine. Fine work there, son. English at its best!"

We were now rapidly leaving the diminishing world of that dear critic who had vetoed motor-bicycles altogether, as being dangerous in themselves and financially disastrous to our nicely balanced domestic economy. The open country of Kent lay before us, lush, and a wanton invitation to adventure. The glorious summer day blazed, and the chalk downs glittered under their thin quilts of green. We took the road to Maidstone. "The Broad Highway!" cried Father, "Onwards! To the Sun, my boy!" And he lifted a hand from the long tiller-like bars, snatched his tweed cap from his head and held it aloft in salute to that very visible deity on whose face we dared not look, though his caress was reddening our skin, and causing the pegamoid cover over my legs to give off a smell as of burning rubber.

Father had taken lodgings at the back of the town, under the shadow of the high viaduct carrying the railway to Folkestone Harbour. The little streets of working-class houses were dwarfed by this Romanesque grandeur.

I got out of the side-car, overcome with shyness and stiffness of limb, to stare at the arches. Their slender height instantly caught up my imagination, and I felt a momentary spasm of excitement, of rapture; but no word can define that mood, by now recognisable, with which I responded to things, people, events, and ideas possessed of *quality*. I had already begun to sort out these experiences, and to hoard them instinctively, as material toward the rebuilding of my shattered universe.

I was so much under the spell of this magnificent gesture in brickwork that I did not turn my head when the front door of the tiny villa opened. Thus only out of the corner of my eye did I see a girl standing there, smiling. Father was more appreciative.

"Are you the lassie of the house, my dear?" he cried, with a familiarity that made me feel I was all feet and hands, and altogether too much in evidence.

The young woman, who must have been about fifteen or sixteen, tossed a heavy plait of brown hair, and wrinkled a small, freckled nose. She obviously thought Father was a card, but she was also somewhat guarded, as she bade us good afternoon.

Father would not take this.

"Very well!" he cried. "Come and give us a hand with the luggage! This is my baby!" He patted me on the shoulder, again to my dismay.

She now definitely thought him to be eccentric, and a half-nervous snicker touched her features, screwing up that little nose even tighter, and drawing my attention to the mischievously protruding eyes.

But she was obliging, and came out to the pavement, to give me a quick but searching glance of enquiry. It was friendly, and I became interested. I had no means of shewing my interest, however, for I had no knowledge of how to deal with a young

female of my own age. I was also still acutely embarrassed by
being introduced as Father's 'baby', especially as he emphasised this ridiculous sentimentality by pronouncing the word
as 'babby'. It gave the girl an unfair start.

She took advantage of it by accepting the suitcases from
Father, and immediately passing them to me. I was saved
from further humiliation by the girl's mother, a pretty little
grey-haired woman, who came out, apologising for having
been at the back of the house.

"Maudie!" she said, reproachfully, to her daughter, and
seized the bags from me with such determination that she
almost carried me indoors too, as though I were merely a label
attached to them. Maudie again tossed her pigtail quite
prettily, but submitted to the reproof, and followed us into the
tiny passage and front sitting-room.

I saw a piano, and at once felt at home. Here was something
I knew all about. I opened the lid, nodded my head, and
muttered: "Challen!"

The daughter looked at the mother, as though to accuse her
of introducing *two* oddities into the home. But her mother was
intent on making us feel that, for the time being, this was *our*
home. I had no standard of comparison in the character of
landladies, but I was alert enough to realise that Father and I
were in luck, and that we were being welcomed to no com-
mercially run seaside lodging.

My intuition was confirmed when Father appeared, smiling
and handsome, to be told that he must pardon any mistakes, as
she had only just begun to take summer lodgers, owing to the
illness of her husband, a printer on the local newspaper.

This last bit of information affected me as the viaduct had
done. Anything connected with writing was enough to set me
off on my monomania, in headlong and famous career. I was
at once an Editor. Fate was pointing the way again. What
else could this mean; that we should have been led to lodge in
the house of a printer?

This fact, and my rise in temperature at the sight of that
lofty viaduct, with the welcome given by the eager little woman,
and the challenge by that sunburned replica, her daughter,

made me assured that the holiday was likely to be a success, and I settled into that tiny house like a complacent cat before a bright fire, upon the thickest of hearth-rugs.

Such comfort, after a long period of austerity, must have made me spiritually drowsy. I recognised the cosy family atmosphere, the closed little world of small importances and local dramas; but the over-warm, half-secretive feminine conspiracy created by the mere physical presence of a mother and two daughters, diluted by the convalescent personality of a modest father, was narcotic to me.

For there was also an elder daughter; tall, gaunt, protective of the younger. She was going to be a school-teacher, and I smiled to myself, amused by the coincidences and similarities which cropped up so frequently in my life. She too was a kind and friendly person, blunt and matter-of-fact, with none of the elusive playfulness of her younger sister, the flirtatious accompaniments of good looks, and another gift which I was soon to be shewn, and to appreciate only too well.

Before the first evening was over, I had taken note of those pretty features, the trim figure so lovingly adorned by the mother's patient needle-work, and also of the somewhat kittenish tricks and gestures, revealing an innocence which the girl pretended not to possess.

I studied her from the near distance, fascinated by the novelty of being drawn into a household where the talk was of clothes, cookery, chapel friends, while my dulled senses began to revive, heavy with a tragic sense of recognition, at seeing feminine garments lying about—a hat on a sofa, gloves on the piano, some underclothes being ironed in the kitchen.

For I had been invited into the kitchen before the evening was out. I must have given the impression of being a lonely boy. Father had gone round to the stable near the gasworks, where he had found a shelter for the Humber. He wanted to overhaul it after the journey, just as a good cavalryman would tend his horse.

The kitchen was hot, for the mother was at the ironing-board, and this task demanded a fire in the range, to heat the two flat-irons. Sitting at the table was the father of this delightfully unself-conscious family: a small, grizzled man, temporarily enfeebled by convalescence after a long illness. He had little to say, but amid the chatter of his womenfolk he maintained a mild dignity that shewed itself in the deliberation with which he concentrated on the task in hand.

Before him on the kitchen table was spread a copy of the newspaper in the setting up of which he made his living and maintained his family in this intimate warmth. But he was not reading it now. His two dry hands were fluffing up and mixing three piles of tobacco. To this blending process he brought a dexterity both serious and experienced. I had the feeling that something of major importance was in process.

I at once began to question him about his work in the printing office, and we were soon in close discussion about the compositor's technique, and the routine that led to the appearance of a daily newspaper. So vivid was the craftsman's description of his work that I had the illusion of being in the printing room. The better to study the machines, I raised myself (unconsciously) a few inches from the floor. Only as the conversation subsided did I realise that not since Mother's death had I used this dubious device, accidentally learned years ago during my convalescence at the Yarrow Home in Broadstairs, on a memorable winter morning at sunrise.

Half ashamed of myself, I dropped instantly to earth, broke off the conversation, and found the mother looking at me quizzically, with a smile that was both indulgent and surprised.

As Father did not return, I was given high tea alone in the front room, temporarily our sitting-room. I felt somewhat sick and giddy after the long ride of eighty miles, followed by the din of the printing machines, though the latter experience had been only through my perfervid imagination. It was no less real, and fatiguing; for I have always been susceptible to noise. Ten minutes in a motor-bus reduces me to incoherence and semi-coma.

I sat there, embarrassed at being waited on by the hostess and the elder daughter, both contesting in kindness, the one serving a haddock cooked in milk and butter, the other offering to pour the tea.

"I've never known Father talk so much," said the mother. "Goodness me, how you *did* draw him out!" "It's done him good," added the daughter, whom I had heard addressed as 'Elsie'. "None of us shows any interest in his work. He just comes and goes every day. That's what has pulled him down. I think."

"Oh, go along, girl!" said the mother, pausing to close the lid of the piano, which had been left open since I raised it to see the name of the maker. I saw her readjust a strip of green felt, embroidered with daisies and leaves, along the ivories.

"What is that for?" I enquired.

"To keep them white," she said.

I thought this a charming device, and my attention began to concentrate again. I had misgivings about the instrument. Its case was too much like that of the Broadwood-White which had played such a sullen part in our Battersea home.

"Is it an under-damper action?"

I did not address her by name, because I had not yet memorised it. My first acquaintance with people has always been a sufficiently nerve-shaking experience to paralyse my wits. Was the name Denham? Was it Parmoor? But I had totally lost it, and one part of my mind was casting madly into the stream of good manners, trying to draw up the right name so that I should neither offend nor hurt this motherly little woman who was shewing more and more kindness to me, and proffering it with such respect that the daughter was both puzzled and amused, as I instantly detected. I looked at her, and I believed the laughter in her eyes conveyed a slight criticism, which she put into words.

"I should have thought it was you, and not your Father, who would be tinkering with that new motor-bicycle," she said.

"He's never happy indoors," I replied, hoping to defend him from a stranger's disapproval.

"Well, really, you *are* an old-fashioned boy," she cried.

Her mother was shocked.

"Elsie, you mustn't be forward!" She spoke as though her daughter had been pert to an elderly gentleman.

After that, I was left alone to proceed with my abundant meal: the haddock, a plate of watercress, white and brown bread and butter, a pot of honey, and a cherry cake, all served upon napery lavishly edged with crochet work, which I knew to be home-made, having noticed it with an experienced eye immediately I sat down at the table. Crochet, tatting, Goss china, model locomotives and railways, pianos and organs, harmoniums and American organs, phonographs, home-made cameras, bicycles, and now motor-bicycles; I was knowledge-able about all of them, as ingredients of my family life; know-ledgeable, but only as an onlooker. My practical skill as a cyclist and an oarsman was dexterous enough, for I had been expertly drilled, but owing to the mysterious pains and fevers of my childhood I lacked the muscle to put this skill to good use. Nobody knew better than I how to drop the ankle when pedalling uphill, or at what angle to lean against a head wind. And I knew to an inch how just *not* to feather with the flat scull in rowing, so that on the off-stroke the boat should not be slowed by the touch of the blade on the surface of the water.

Father appeared while I was still at the table. "Ah! Good!" he cried, loudly enough to attract attention from the kitchen. The other half of the haddock appeared, and the landlady stood in consternation, staring at Father's hands. They were covered in black grease.

"Bless you!" he said. "You're looking at my hands. No ceremony, now! I'll go into the scullery and wash them with Monkey Brand!"

I heard him. He was now jockeying up the master of the house, hail-fellow-well-met. The lack of response crept through the walls to my apprehensive nerves. Out in the scullery, Father was singing to the accompaniment of running water. "I am waiting for thee, Asthore," he carolled, in his light baritone. I heard laughter and badinage. Then he returned.

"Nice girls!" he confided to me. "Good homely wenches. We'll take them out after tea. Do us good to stretch our legs, my boy."

And when the landlady looked in to see how we were getting on, he congratulated her upon "your two handsome daughters.

Makes me long to be young again. I'd be courting them both!"

By this time I began to feel exhausted, and thought wistfully of Jack, longing for his support in the effort to swim against the stream of Father's rapidly reviving flood of youthful bonhomie.

He had his way about the walk, and we spent the evening strolling along the Leas, he with the elder girl, and I with the younger. The crowd moved ant-like around the bandstand; the music waxed and waned upon the shifting breeze; the westering sunlight struck down from the sky and up from the solid sea.

I saw my pretty companion curiously distorted by these contradictory lights. Her brown eyes glittered, her cheeks looked puffed, her throat artificial. A thin chain round it ran as though it were liquid, and a tiny cross flashed as she breathed. I *felt* her breathing; a firm, healthy animal respiration. The magnet began to draw me; the novelty of a perfect young body, fair to look at, so assured, so proud.

"Is it you who plays that Challen piano?" I asked, half whispering, so awe-stricken was I at the touch of my hand as it drew to her arm, and rested on the sleeve of the coat made by that industrious little mother. "You don't lose time," she said.

I was puzzled.

"Lose time? Good heavens, no! There's none to spare. Why, Shelley was dead at thirty, and Keats when he was twenty-five!"

I spoke so emphatically that she withdrew her arm from my hand, before replying, in a *demi-voce* that instantly captured my attention by its beauty of tone, so that I ignored what she was saying, and was enraptured by the voice that said it.

"What *are* you talking about?"

"You haven't told me about the piano," I urged. "And what else do you practise? That throat! It's like a thrush's breast!"

She was almost offended.

"You shouldn't say things like that!" she said: and now her voice was full, metallic and hard. "It's not nice." But a moment later she relented. "Perhaps you didn't mean anything."

We threaded our way among the holiday-makers, all

strolling out of time with the 'Valse Triste' of Sibelius, from the band. I recognised it, and one strand of my consciousness was vibrating gloomily in response, while the rest of me hovered about the tantalising person by my side. This was something new in my life, calling upon me to wake, to come back to the flood-tide of the world, to break the funereal spell of the whispering aspens whose last lament, before they were felled, had come too appropriately with our family disaster.

I had no means of understanding why this young girl had been startled, and taken offence, when I compared her throat to a thrush's breast. I could think of nothing more complimentary. I heard that glorious song in the elm-tops as I spoke. She drew her filmy scarf protectively over her bosom, and pretended to pout.

"You ought to sing," I explained. "I mean you ought to sing. It's in your voice; when you speak softly I can hear it!"

She changed instantly. She almost snuggled up to me.

"Really, you are a strange boy! How did you know?"

I chuckled, and took her arm again. "I don't know how I know. But there are certain things—but I can't explain. I am——"

She interrupted, looking at me as though I were on stilts.

"There you go again! What is it about you? Suddenly you get taller. I saw it when I looked into the kitchen. You were talking to my father while he was mixing his week's tobacco, and your head nearly touched the ceiling."

She laughed merrily, and again I caught that revealing throat music, more bird-song than human. I closed my eyes for a moment, lost in sensuous rapture.

But now she was suddenly serious. Her moods came and went like those of a kitten playing with thistledown.

"You frighten me," she whispered. Her large brown eyes, slightly protuberant, flashed with tearfulness, reflecting the fairy lamps along the parade. "That's what it's all about."

I waited for her to explain. I knew the confidence was coming. All my sympathy opened to her, to all women. My over-stretched emotions, stunned since April, began to revive, to take on where they had left off, deeply and superbly pro-

tective of all womanhood, its weaknesses, its vulnerable body.
I pressed the young stranger's arm. It was like that of a statue,
hard, permanent. I noticed the difference and was almost
shocked; but my mind was concentrated on what she now
began to tell me.

"It's Daddy," she said, almost in tears now. "And Mother
always sides with him in a matter like this."

She was struggling with her conscience. The idea of taking
her troubles to someone outside the family was frightening her.
I felt myself to blame, as though I had hypnotised her, stolen
her will-power. But by now I wanted to help. She was
appealing; and that I could not resist.

"You see. I *do* sing! I went in for the Kent Festival this year,
and got two awards."

"Piano and singing," I said, simply, carrying her along. "I
know about it all. My brother is a pianist," as though that
explained everything.

"But that's not all," she said sharply, with a spark of anger,
or it may have been anguish. "You see, the head of the Royal
College of Music in London was the judge, and he asked to
speak to me afterwards. He said I had an unusual mezzo-
soprano voice, and he offered me a scholarship at his college.
Then he saw Mother and she told him we couldn't afford it.
But that didn't matter, he said, I could live in a hostel and he
would pay for that privately. So Mother said she would ask
Father to go and see him."

By now she was clinging to me as though I were a rescue
party. We had wandered off the crowded parade, and found
ourselves in one of the winding paths down the labyrinth of the
sloping gardens of the Leas, under the gloom of ilex trees and
barricades of tamarisk. The music of the band receded; the
murmur of the tide lipping at the shingle grew louder.

"And what did your father do?" I asked. I was trembling.
I knew the answer. I had already met it in my own life: the
falling of an axe.

"He wouldn't go," she said, "he wouldn't go." The repeti-
tion gave her words the weight of despair.

"Oh, don't!" I cried. It was more than I could bear. The

familiar sight of a woman struggling against some power too great for her brought back acutely my precocious knowledge. Instantly I was proprietary. Mechanically I began to make the gestures of comfort, supporting her under the arm, pressing her hand, seeking for words of endearment. I forgot that she was a stranger, whom I had first met only a few hours earlier. All the old, desperate longing to ease the pain-racked body returned, driving me to a dangerous intimacy in my effort to protect this girl from her own violent feelings. She was all women; the mothers, the victims.

"Don't!" I whispered: but my sympathy broke down her self-control, instead of aiding it. She was crying, silently, but the sobs shook her body.

"Why am I telling you all this?" she murmured. "I've been storing it up for weeks. They think I don't mind; even Elsie. You'd think she would understand. But she says it's all for the best!" She stood still, and stamped her foot in anger as she repeated, "Best!" while I supported her and wiped her tear-stained cheeks with my handkerchief.

"Father said it was wrong to be beholden to a stranger, and that London was no place for a girl to be alone in."

She began to recover, looked at me in surprise, and withdrew herself from my ministrations. "I can understand that about being in London alone. But I know how to look after myself."

I took this as a reproof.

"Who is the head of the Royal College?" I asked, returning the handkerchief to my pocket, and my impulsive emotions to the safe-keeping of memory. I had the curious illusion of turning off the detachable key of the oxygen cylinder. The hissing ceased, and, when it came again, it was only the shifting of the shingle at the sea's edge, on the beach below the Leas.

My retreat mollified her, and she grew confident again. We could not go back to quite the same formality, after this outburst.

"He is a composer too," she said. "Sir Hubert Parry. He was wonderful to me. But you know—it's another world. It frightens me a little. I can see——"

"Yes, your father meant well enough." And then I told her about my disappointment over the scholarship at Camberwell School of Art. She listened, and to my surprise took my arm as affectionately as though we were brother and sister. "Where are the others?" she asked suddenly; and with that we returned to the parade, seeking my father and Elsie.

We did not find them, however, until we got back to the little villa crouching at the foot of one of the great arches of the viaduct. Father was discoursing in the kitchen, holding his listeners spellbound by his reminiscences of cycle rides over the English counties, and his linkings-up of mutual acquaintances. Father could never meet strangers without discovering, within half an hour, that he and they had certain friends, or friends of friends, in common. Frequently the link was slender, but it was strong enough for him to haul upon, to draw present company together as jolly good fellows.

I saw the mother break from the spell when her younger daughter and I entered, blinking under the glare of the incandescent gaslight. A tiny flicker of amusement played about her anxious mouth. It comprehended us both.

CHAPTER EIGHT

On Sugarloaf Hill

I HAD FELT JUSTIFIED in bringing none of the hated swot-books with me: the digests of returns, the double-entry book-keeping, the commercial geography, the shorthand. Father had warned me that my luggage must not be too heavy, so I was content to secrete a volume of *The Faerie Queene* and Mother's copy of Milton's poems into my luggage, with Augustine Birrell's *Obiter Dicta* borrowed from Dulwich public library. One of the essays in this last book suggested that no person should call himself a bookman unless he possessed at least two thousand volumes, and that a part of literary education was to sit surrounded by one's books, absorbing them through one's skin, as sun-starved aspirants to health absorb ultra-violet rays from a lamp.

I needed little encouragement in this bibliophilic direction, for since I began to work at the Land Registry in April 1909 I had contrived to buy a cheap edition or a secondhand book every week. I still have most of them, shabby survivors, like old inhabitants of a small village that has grown into an industrial town. Augustine Birrell's sentiment was right, though in the latter-day world of close living-quarters the collection of a private library is almost impossible. Now, in the autumn of life, with the deeper and more depressing ignorances of maturity thickening like November fog in my mind, I sometimes withdraw to the library of the Athenæum, and sit there while the emanations from the walls lined from floor to ceiling with books flood over me, penetrating with a delusive warmth into my arthritic imagination. Books, in addition to their contents, have a physical symbolism, just as the sword has, and the crucifix. They are the tangible evidences of the adventure after truth.

This literary reinforcement, however, was only a minor experience, an undertone, of my adventures in life during that fortnight of holiday by the sea at Folkestone.

Before the first week-end was over, I had heard the voice toward whose education Sir Hubert Parry made so generous an offer. The Challen pianoforte was surprisingly mellow. When Father and I came down to breakfast on our first morning, Maudie was practising scales. She did not stop when I entered the front room. The sunlight flickered over the table, pronouncing a cruet of four boiled eggs, each with a tiny knitted cosy over it. Maudie's pigtail also was illuminated, and charged with bronze. I saw the left side of her face in shadow, and that, with her brooding frown of concentration over the busy hands, made her yet another person whom I must get to know, a newer stimulant to my reviving emotions.

She turned her head and smiled at me, as though to challenge any questioning of her right to be in the room and at the piano. I studied her hands. They were firm and chubby. The backs were arched, and the fingers rose and fell like the tossing heads of horses on a bearing-rein.

"Keep your wrists down," she said, and followed this axiom with a gleam of pretty teeth, and a nod of the head to indicate that she was addressing herself, in the direction of those muscular hands.

The mere sound of a piano, like the mere external appearance of books, affects me disproportionately. I have to pull myself together, as sensible people would say, in order to balance the effect, and to prevent myself from some extravagant gesture, in word or act. I am a ready subject for the fluting of the Pied Piper, or the wailing strings of those gipsies who tempted Tolstoi.

I began my breakfast, tapping the top of an egg to the rhythm of the dominant, the sub-dominant and the tonic of a minor scale, to which Maudie had just moved from the major. The shift of sound from light to dark, from outward to inward, from known to unknown, touched my chameleon senses, and I gloomed over the yolk of my egg, adding bitterness to the salt from the tiny bone spoon in my fingers. I saw my brother's beaky face glowering at me, a warning in his hooded eyes.

The spell was broken by the mother, who came bustling into the room, half amused, half angry. "Off with you, Maudie. Mr. Church will be down any minute. Time for practice when they are out."

She fluttered her apron at Maudie, as though driving hens away. The girl laughed, jumped up from the stool, and hugged her mother in passing.

"I want to hear her sing," I said, and I chattered on, confiding in our hostess while I attacked my second egg. She stood near the table, listening gravely to my story of the future that lay before me as a writer, and my present purpose of ensuring a safe livelihood by qualifying for a post in the Civil Service. She said nothing about my first part of the programme, but approved the latter, and nodded as though making a mental note of that sensible proposal.

"And is there nobody to do for you at home now?" she asked. "With all of you out at work?"

I could not reply to that. The kindness was too much. I might have wept, but fortunately Father appeared, and the landlady, after bidding him a more conventional good-morning, retreated.

"We'll explore the Elham Valley," he said. "Just the day for a ride to Canterbury and North Foreland. I'll show you round the lighthouse."

So the days of our holiday passed, and I was introduced, in detail, to the sun-burned country of Thanet, the land of light, and of flaring poppies, brassy cornfields relieved by copses of beech and evergreen oaks, the latter almost sable in contrast of foliage with the soft apple-green of the tender beech-leaves. The lanes were heavy with the amygdalic scent of wild parsley, all the perfumed umbels headed by meadow-sweet.

I lolled like an addict in the side-car, drugged in body and mind by these lascivious offerings of mother nature. I had not inhaled so much fresh air since our last holiday at Ropley two years before. But in 1908 I was only a child. Now I had been initiated into experiences so vast, so fundamental, that I felt my personal identity being bleached out of me. I tried to anchor

myself to words, to snatches of metre, jolted into the rhythm of
the road, or Father's ceaseless flow of information about the
geography of the land rushing beneath our wheels. Some of
the words stuck, and I recorded them as verses, in my notebook,
as soon as we stopped at an inn or a church. Throughout the
holiday I added my blossoms to this naïve anthology, believing
them to be evidence that would justify my claim to a special
and proud destiny as a poet.

These experiences and efforts were food to my emotions
rather than to my character. I was breaking out, not building
up; squandering, not storing. At this dangerous moment, when
discipline would have been most valuable, it was removed. I
had left school; Mother's influence was now generalised by
death, becoming merely a background; Jack's sombre monitorship was intermittent under the distraction of his new loyalty;
Father's advice was too primitive, as it had always been, to be
applied to my unique problems. His cure for an attack of
melancholia, or acute abdominal pains, or uncertainty about
an important course of action, was to cry: "Flap yourself, my
boy!" and to demonstrate his panacea by banging his arms
vigorously round his shoulders, in the manner of Dickensian
coachmen waiting in the snow.

On our return from the first day's outing, sun-soaked and
drunk with light, Father and I sat down to another high tea of
Cornish pasty, with home-made bread. Such food, so superbly
cooked, had not come my way for years. It reminded me of
our early years in the house at Battersea, when Mother was
well, and our Sunday dinners were feasts. The warmth, safety,
intimacy, of that little world came flooding back. I longed to
return to it, the feminine closeness, the endearing comfort.

Lost in that mood, I did not notice that Father had escaped
to the more cheerful company of the family in the kitchen. I
smelled the fragrance of the printer's blended tobacco. Then
I heard my Father say: "Bless her little heart! Of course, let
her go and practise. It'll be company for my *babby*! He's a
moody lad. Misses his mother, you know!"

Father's easy-going expansiveness was becoming more and
more distasteful to me. The fact that his hit-or-miss methods

so often touched the target, as in the present instance, only made me the more resentful. I scowled at the open door.

"Oh! you *do* look fierce!" said Maudie, her eyes round, her lips pursed.

"Would *you* like to be called *babby*?" I demanded.

She tittered, then became serious.

"Why, he's an old dear," she said. "And oh my, isn't he handsome, like the Duke of somewhere or other!"

"He may have a reason for that," I said darkly.

"Whatever do you mean?" she said, but without paying attention, for she was now going through the music sheets in the piano stool, a hideous piece of furniture that opened at the back, like a coal-scuttle. "Mum said you wanted to hear me sing. Well, if you'll give up being cross, I will."

And she did. Putting the keyboard cover round her shoulders, as a stole, she sang a sentimental ballad named 'Because'. The voices in the kitchen died away, except my father's, but even his was reduced to a whisper, his flow of reminiscence being punctuated by a "Bravo, Maudie" here and there, to prove that he was listening, in spite of being the victim of his own volubility.

I still sat at the tea-table, leaning over the débris of the Cornish pasty, my head in my hands. The girl's voice was a gift from God; a pure mezzo-soprano, pouring out from a full throat and strong lungs, without a trace of *vibrato* (that sympton of the mal-trained and usually ruined English singer). With a complicated irony, I accepted the banal words, "Because you sing to me, in accents sweet," bowing my head to let them pass. The thrush-throb of that voice, reduced almost to *demi-voce* in the tiny, over-furnished room, conquered me instantly. "Sing something else," I pleaded.

She half-turned, studying me with a new interest. "Didn't you like that song?"

"I liked the way you sang it. I agree with Hubert Parry."

"Huh! My word! Aren't we high and mighty!"

But she was flattered.

The next song was by Sterndale Bennett, a lyric in the manner of Mendelssohn. "Oh, refresh my aching eyelids with thy cooling drops of dew" it began, and I took the words to myself, as an intoxicant.

"That's better, isn't it?" said Maudie. But by this time I was incapable of response. The hypnosis was absolute. "Not asleep, are you?" she teased. And with that, after I had roused myself sufficiently to shake my head, she began to sing Dvoràk's "Songs my Mother Taught me."

She sang it like a child, the open notes almost breaking upon their own candour. The skill could not be that of art, for she was too young and untrained. It was the luck of youth, perhaps. Whatever the source of this perfection, it was too much for me. I left the table, and crushed myself into the corner of the room, between the wall and a cabinet, my face hidden, in an effort to control the devastating conflict of emotions: sorrow, rapture, loneliness, recognition and acceptance of pure beauty.

To my astonishment, I felt a pair of warm hands on my shoulders, drawing me away from the wall.

"You're too silly," she said. "Look! Let's for go a walk." And, with that, she kissed the tip of my ear, and fled.

That was the beginning of the renewal of my ever over-intimate relations with the world of womanhood. And, put that way, it does not mean the same as saying relations with women. Maybe it is an unfortunate difference, causing unfairness to individuals. I had begun that relationship too soon, and with too clinical an intimacy. It had given me a wrong conception of women's strength, their elemental vitality, and the feminine approach to life consequent from this. I could not, and I still cannot, put from me the instinct to be passionately protective of this fragile thing, the female human, whose anatomy and articulation I had to study so early in my life; to study, to serve, and to worship with a fervour half-religious, half sensual. It has given me understanding of the fatality between Tristan and Isolde; of the odd, domestic hypersensibility that made the boy Wagner secrete himself within his sisters' wardrobes, to caress their silken garments; of the dreadful attraction, doomed to opprobrium and disaster, between Byron and his half-sister.

Under this precocious obsession, I have never been able to condemn the follies and indulgence of lovers. On the other hand, it has made quite incomprehensible to me the hearty Englishman's attitude to women, his assumption of cool superiority, his resistance to their blandishments and caresses.

This is a naïve confession, of a state of mind not capable of being put into words. They confine it too closely; they over-simplify it. I see it being mistaken for an effort to excuse that convention which sees woman as 'the weaker vessel'; and it is nothing like that. It is passionately different. It is obsessed with the fragility, the intricacy, the ritual of beauty and fastidiousness, appertaining to the physical life of women. But to speak of the physical life as an isolated aspect is again to confine the reality. The world of woman only begins there. That is but the foundation of her variety, her perpetual surprise, her strength that is unbreakable though it has to support man's static dead-weight structure of law and politics!

Confessions, however, must always be suspect, for they carry self-consciousness with them. A return to circumstance, to the very substance of life, is nearer the truth.

What happened for the remainder of that fortnight's holiday has become, in my memory, an idyll that lasted for an eternity. Time stood still, and the round earth paused. I stood at the brink of revelation. What seems so odd, as I look back, is that I did not realise that this was taking place only three months after I had lost my mother. Again, time must have become meaningless. In the surging relativities of human life, we know how this factor of time is elastic to our states of mind and emotion. I had no sense of guilt, no remorse, no self-accusation of disloyalty to the deep, terrible love which death had cheated me of. I was in love again, and this time with a still more fore-doomed vehicle: with youth itself; with 'but a wandering voice'.

The response to my admiration was shy, charming and playful. Maudie was sixteen, pausing at the threshold of womanhood, a little frightened of what she had been told of it. The background to those fears was nonconformist and pro-vincial. Caution was the keyword to that miniature philosophy of life. Opposed to that caution was Maudie's gift, a dangerous asset, because it attracted flattery, and offered an outlet to a larger world, full of strange perils and temptations.

As we wandered along the Leas, or in the Warren between Folkestone and the Shakespeare Cliff (but not to gather samphire), I gradually learned of these fears, and how they dominated the outlook of the innocent little family, like a range of frowning mountains, and I argued that if Maudie married me, I would guide her through them to a land where art and fame shone as sun and moon in perpetually cloudless skies.

Her eyes glowed, her sturdy bosom heaved, at the prospect I painted. But when it came to demonstration, to setting a seal to my proposal, the family bugbear raised its head. Maudie agreed with me that she must devote herself wholly to the service of her God-given voice; that she must not demean it by singing rubbishy sentimental ballads at smoking-concerts, and that as soon as possible she must conquer her father's aversion to her leaving home. I was prepared to devote my life to the development of her voice. I spent our hours trying to convince her of this, and that in the process there was no immediate danger of her 'getting into trouble', a phrase which recurred again and again in her timid responses to my pleading.

I was in paradise, because once again I was in recognisable circumstances; a setting where I was already expert. The paradise was soon to be lost, by that very expertise. For the duration of the holiday, however, Maudie and I were as happy, upon the edge of exquisite pain, as Aucassin and Nicolette. Like these sweet Provençal lovers, we examined our mutual affection together, as though we had captured a rare butterfly and were fearful of smutching the down on its wings. We raised the same contention as those archetypes of young love.

"Aucassin," said she, "I doubt that thou lovest me less than thy words; and that my love is fonder than thine."

"Alack," cried Aucassin, "fair sweet friend, how can it be that thy love should be so great? Woman cannot love man as man loves woman; for woman's love is in the glance of her eye, and the blossom of her breast, and the tip of the toe of her foot, but the love of man is set deep in the hold of his heart, from whence it cannot be torn away." '

That is an ancient argument, but it appeared to be new to Maudie as I put it to her on the last morning of the holiday.

We had got up early, before six o'clock, having arranged overnight and under parental consent (for by now I was wholly trusted by those gentle-timid parents) to take a last walk together up to the Sugarloaf Hill behind the town, overlooking Cæsar's Camp.

The Saturday morning was reluctant, as though the long summer week-end promised such splendour that it was too heavy-laden to begin. I crept downstairs, my shoes in my hand, to find Maudie already in the kitchen. We greeted each other sadly, whispering together. She had just finished combing her hair, and was plaiting it. I had not before seen her with it tumbled loose over her shoulders. She lifted it and, turning her back to me, asked me to fasten the tiny hooks and eyes of her blouse. My fingers trembled a little at the task. I was at such familiar work again; all the old anxiety welled up in my heart; the compassion for such frailty; the love that cried out, in eloquent silence, to save this dear woman-flesh from its suffering.

"What's the matter, clumsy?" she whispered, half turning her head, and leaning back against me; a gesture of playful mockery.

"Such small hooks," I stammered.

The backs of my fingers touched her firm neck. It was both cool and warm; and the fragrance of her hair fountained over it, and over my hands employed there. I realised suddenly that my memory was falsifying things. Here was no sickness; nothing but young life, eager, elusive. But I could not forget the dangers, and in an access of compassion I stooped and sealed the fastening with a kiss. She shivered, but said nothing.

She remained silent as we ventured out. A sea-mist lay over the town. The viaduct loomed through it, and the top courses of brickwork stood clear against a golden-blue centre of the sky. Out in the Channel a fog-horn mourned, between spells of dead silence.

We walked away from the town, round behind the gas-works and the looming containers. The greasy smell penetrated the freshness of the sea-mist; the smell of poor quarters, of factories, of workaday life and squalid dwellings. My spirits sank. I saw this as the end of a new hope, a new sense of direction, and I felt powerless. I had promised so much; but how could I fulfil my impetuous words?

We turned off the road, to a footpath up the slope, along market gardens, and the mist dropped below us. At once the chill left the air, and I began to feel energy and confidence creeping through my veins again. I took her hand, but she was unresponsive.

"What's the matter?" I said, breaking the silence which had lasted since we left the house.

At first she did not reply, but stared ahead, dogged and obstinate. I relinquished her hand, but this gesture appeared to reassure her, and she took my arm, drawing close to me as we leaned forward to attack the increasing slope of the open hillside.

Then she began to confide in me, telling a fearful story, hesitantly, about a school friend who was 'in trouble' as a result of listening to the blandishments of a man who had come to Folkestone for the Christmas holidays.

I saw instantly that this disaster was far more real to Maudie than all the prospects of a successful career offered by her voice and urged with such eagerness by me. I was temporarily nonplussed, listening stolidly to her cautionary tale. Somehow the burden of her weight on my arm hung heavier. But this depression did not last. She was, after all, confiding in me something which she would not dare to talk about elsewhere. I began to feel a bond of union, and an added sense of responsibility. We might have been man and wife. I almost looked for the silver in her hair.

All these minor and mercurial emotions, however, were soon swept together and caught up in a larger response to the scene as we reached the top of Sugarloaf Hill. We stood there, hand in hand, and looked across the town, seeing a spire here and there, a taller roof, or a turret, sticking out of the quilting of mist. Beyond that lay the open sea, an expanse of mother-of-pearl reflecting the sun as a long sword of fire, tempered in blue and grey, that shuddered momentarily under the pulse of the tide, as though life itself were dripping from it.

Maudie forgot the troubles of her fallen friend. She stood

beside me, gazing seaward, and the sunlight caressed her freckled nose, and glistened on her lips. I watched her breathing, and wonder flooded over me. Such power, such health. It was a miracle in action. Then her lips parted, and she sang a scale, then another scale half a key higher, piling one upon another, like a lark climbing the sky. And indeed the challenge was taken up, for out of the turf not a hundred yards below us a skylark leaped up, breaking into trills and shakes as he mounted. The lyrical debate continued, until the lark was out of sight, and Maudie almost breathless: almost, but not quite, for she turned to me in an ecstasy of self-congratulation at this show of her vocal power, and hugged me so convulsively that we both laughed aloud for sheer joy of living, and collapsed to sit down on the cropped thyme and harebells, releasing the perfume of the former, and the jangling fairy silences of the latter.

There we stayed for nearly an hour, while the day opened, and the town below us woke with faint sounds of traffic, the ascent of smoke from kitchen chimneys, and thuds and clangours from the harbour. The fog-horn ceased, for summer had cleared the Channel again, and we could see the coast of France. I stared at it, in disbelief. The solid reality of Europe was beyond conception. A quick vision of those boat-trains gliding through Herne Hill Station, in the distant ages when I was a schoolboy, flashed upon my inward sight.

Maudie sat with her head on my shoulder, and I began to talk about the world that probably existed behind that faint outline on the horizon. As I enlarged on this dream-fantasy, enriching it with music and poetry, linking it up with her career and mine, I instinctively caressed her, drawing her into the innocent conspiracy.

Suddenly she drew away.

"It's time to go home," she said, coldly. "We're talking nonsense. I don't understand you. One minute you're all fairy-tales—and the next, when you touch me, you're like an old doctor."

"Doctor?" I echoed, pretending to be at a loss. But I knew what she meant. I felt as Dante must have felt when, walking in the streets of Ravenna, he heard the people claim that they saw the mark of the flames on his garments, the proof that he had walked in Hell.

I acquiesced sadly, turning over in my mind this dreadful probability, that my experience during the recent years, while nursing my mother, had marked me with the stigmata of her suffering, and that I was old before my time, no equal company for Maudie. The sweetness of that hour on Sugarloaf Hill was already tainted, as soon as I had tasted it.

CHAPTER NINE

After the Darkness, the Earthquake

EVENTS moved too quickly during the rest of that year for me to give much time to morbid comparison of the past with the present. Back at work in the Land Registry, sitting in my bay window overlooking the Gothic gateway of Lincoln's Inn, I recovered partial control of my emotions, and listened to the good counsel of my friend Arthur Sullivan, who was dismayed to find that I had done no studying during my holiday, though the next Civil Service examination for Abstractor Clerks, that low rung on the ladder of permanent service, loomed nearer and nearer.

I shared his fears, and those of all other boys on the temporary grade, of being thrown out at the age of eighteen, with small prospect of decent employment. For the business world looked upon people who had once been in the Civil Service as useless drones, habituated to dozing through a seven-hour day. And to me that unknown business world was just as impossible, and as perilous, as "the steepe Atlantick streame". I knew that I could not have survived in it for a day, because of my absent-mindedness, my inability to concentrate upon what business-men called 'facts', and my passionate distaste for competitive-ness.

It would need a psychiatrist to sort out the causes of this un-wholesome state of mind, and to explain why it should be found in a youth born into the wage-earning world, surrounded by the compulsions to bread-winning and the almost uniform examples of class humility. But here was I, making a conscious virtue of my disabilities and superstitions, assuming the point of view of a feudal seigneur toward trade and any concern with money. I believed that all people interested in the pursuit of lucre, such as bankers, stockbrokers, turf accountants, were of the same fraternity as the money-changers whom Christ whipped from the steps of the Temple. Even shopkeepers were not above suspicion. I had not the faintest conception of the part played by money in the articulating of the organism of society, from the vast international movements in the political world, to the back-street chaffering of the poorest housewife. I lived amiably in a vacuum, threatened with perpetual innocence (though I did not know it).

As against this odd point of view, which was to hold me back for many years from coming to grips with career-making, I had healthier and positive views about what was acceptable as a way of life. The most obvious was the craft of the carpenter, first, because my closest companion Jesus Christ, the mentor who now had taken even my brother Jack's place, had been a carpenter; secondly, because wood itself was something tangibly good. I could appreciate the dedication, the devotion, of a cabinet-maker, or a wainwright. All men who *made* things I placed on the side of the angels, as opposed to the keepers of the purse, the Judas Iscariots. Farmers, blacksmiths, builders, artists and musicians, all were of a kind, and at their head marched the poet against the powers of darkness, a leader because he was the historian of all their purposes and achievement, his medium of language being more significant and expressive even than wood, or metal, or the products of the soil.

Armed with this simple mythology as my equipment for making my way through the industrialised twentieth century, I was likely to find much that was contradictory, inexplicable, terrifying. I was in danger of hardening into that particular kind of lunatic who believes all the rest of human society to be mad.

Fortunately, Jack had not wholly withdrawn himself. I had an example of this in the first letter that his future wife wrote to me. It came as a surprise during the second week of my holiday at Folkestone, while I was listening to the song the sirens sang. I was chided for not having written to him. "He's so unhappy," she wrote, "and having no news of your inconsiderate self has made him still more so. You are a tiresome child."

This I accepted greedily. It shewed two strands of affection, two life-lines. I had not imagined that the writer, this cool, handsome young woman of twenty years, infinitely older than myself, had noticed my existence, except as the inevitable young brother. But this letter was evidence enough that both she and Jack had my welfare at heart, and were prepared to support my self-confidence, provided I did not betray it by idleness.

Further, the letter went on to discuss loneliness, and those solitudes of the spirit which not even the arts can fill. Nobody had spoken to me before of such matters. Jack's counsel had always been too stoical, and Mother had not been given time to speak to me in terms, and on themes, so mature. As I read the letter, between the uneasy, delirious hours in the company of the bewitching mezzo-soprano, I realised that all my adventures into the world of literature had been undertaken alone, and in silence. I was incapable of debate, or the lively discussion of abstract or æsthetic ideas, because I knew no people who were interested to practise with me in this field. The lower middle classes are a matter-of-fact folk, at least during the discouragements of their workaday lives. They lack the environment of an *academia*, where debate is an accepted vehicle of mental progress, with metaphysics as its lubricant.

Thus my excitement at receiving this letter made a permanent impression, and has endeared the writer to me for the rest of our lives. It prevented me from losing my way on Sugarloaf Hill, where otherwise I might have succumbed in sweet indulgences. In referring to the special loneliness of "the great writers and musicians" the letter must be consciously pointing at me and my brother, and on this instant assumption I accepted the writer as a wise person who could see further through a brick wall than most people. I was assured that Jack's future happiness was safe, since he would have so deep-seeing a wife. And I should bask in that happiness too, for I could not yet conceive of an existence for myself wholly separate from him.

I discovered that the writer was also an avid reader of poetry. She quoted Shelley's 'Stanzas Written in Dejection, near Naples':

"I sit upon the sands alone,
The lightning of the noontide ocean
Is flashing round me, and a tone
Arises from its measured motion.
How sweet! did any heart now share in my emotion."

The cornucopian tumble of Shelley's rhythms, index to his perfervid intellect, set me rocking like a yacht in a squall. I began to fret and crave, snatches of verse rushing through my mind, skeins of cloud preluding fiercer weather. How appropriate, I believed, were the words that followed the quotation from Shelley: "I suppose the greater a man is, the greater are his desires, and the more difficult it is for him to obtain them."

During the months that carried 1910 to its end, I lived out my seventeenth year with those words echoing around my bewildered head. The desire was rapidly gathering momentum, and sufficient of it was concentrated upon the image of that girl at Folkestone, and her lovely voice, for me to become almost overbalanced. Every afternoon I fled home, leaving the Land Registry, half-trotting through New Square, down Portugal Street and Chancery Lane, fighting my way through Fleet Street to Ludgate Hill Station, as though pursued by the Furies. I told myself that this feverish speed would give me an extra half-hour each evening to work at those dreary subjects needed for the examination (Abstractor Class): the book-keeping, the shorthand, the digest of returns, and précis, the mensuration and commercial geography. But in my heart I knew I was hurrying in the hope that I should find a letter from Folkestone, written in a childish hand, open and vacant, that would tell me nothing, reveal no longed-for secret between the lines, tantalise me and drive me frantic to bed, with no digest, no précis, no double-entry book-keeping done to keep me abreast of the correspondence course. And, to assuage the fever, I would plunge into the poetry of Keats or Shelley, only to find it to be fire-water, rather than a febrifuge.

Waiting alone at home for these letters (for my father and Jack might deliberately have been avoiding each other during those months), I sank into a paralysis of the will. At the approach of the time for the postman to deliver the evening mail, I found my mind wandering from the dreary commercial subjects on which I was working. I left my room, like a somnambulist, and crept downstairs to wait in the hall, behind the letter-box, my heart thumping, my hands sweating, my throat dry. If there was no letter, I returned to the task upstairs, trying to order my thoughts back in the same way that I commanded my limbs. And if a letter came, I read it quickly, then studied the handwriting on the envelope, re-read the few sentences, smelled the paper where that flexible hand had rested, searched cravingly between the lines for deeper meanings, finally to give up, and return as hungry as ever to the feast of dust and ashes.

In spite of this obsession, however, I sat for the examination (Abstractor Class!), spending three or four days at Burlington House, behind Piccadilly. The journey there was a sufficient adventure to make me forget the badly loaded store of pseudo-scholarship which I brought to the examination room. Motor-buses in 1910 were not guaranteed to arrive on scheduled time, for breakdown always threatened those chain-driven juggernauts. To allow for this probability, I set out hours before I needed to, and thus arrived in the lobbies of the torture-chamber with time to spare.

A crowd of other boys waited there, some bespectacled like myself, care and apprehension on their wrinkled foreheads; others vigorous, athletic and confident. Both kinds intimidated me; mere evidence of numbers was enough. How could I compete against so many; I who was consciously half-hearted in the attempt, all my interest, hope, passion, worlds away from this prospect of a premature security in the drab task of bread-winning? What was mere bread, to one who had already half-persuaded himself that his food was honeydew, and that, having been called to a special purpose, he would be fed, like Elijah, by the ravens?

Between the sessions, to escape from the shrilling of cab-whistles blown by porters outside the hotel behind Burlington House, I left the crowd of candidates, and wandered up and down the Burlington Arcade, staring at the luxury in the windows of the stylish shoplets, inhaling the atmosphere of wealth, beauty—a world fabulous to me, but here made almost tangible, to touch, to smell. I peered at great diamonds, glittering from a background of tumbled velvet. I examined the price-tickets of rings and brooches, sums that equalled two years of my father's wages. I could not believe it. Yet I *did* believe it, and for confirmation stared into those mysterious clarities of light, the diamond depths, under the same spell as I had surrendered to at the summons of that liquid mezzo-soprano at Folkestone.

But I had to break away from both, for the hour was up, and now I must return for the afternoon session, the English essay paper. Here I would be triumphant, making up marks on the losses inevitable after my bewildered efforts to deal with the arithmetic paper about water flowing into and out of tanks, and the posting up, in double entry, of items from a day-journal kept by an imaginary grocer.

I believed I was to be lucky, for one of the subjects offered for the essay was: "What is your ideal form of dress?" I wrote at fever heat, my imagination fired by this compelling theme. I conjured the pictures with which I was so intimate after my frequent lingerings in Dulwich Gallery. I saw these members of the Linley family portrayed by the lyrical genius of Gainsborough (what a contrast to the stagy, painty Reynoldses!) I strutted through my essay, as fantastic and cross-gartered as Malvolio before his mistress. That was the last paper in the examination, and I left Burlington House assured that, after all, I should scrape through, in spite of the fierce competition, by which the loss of one mark could drag the candidate down a couple of places.

I did scrape through, but not as I had expected. I got thirty-five per cent for my English essay. I was saved by the eighty-five per cent for book-keeping, and an equally high mark for shorthand, the last accomplishment being one which I have never used since I practised it in that examination room. It appears not to have been needed in the tool-kit of an Abstractor. In my quarter of a century as a Civil Servant

I never learned the meaning of that label, Abstractor. As applied to me, Abstracted Clerk would have been more appropriate.

My journey home was that of a released prisoner. I sat on the open deck of the bus to Herne Hill, giving myself up whole-heartedly to the stately blank verse of *Paradise Lost*. I need have no qualms of conscience now. I was so sure about the success of that English essay. For the rest of my life I could deliver myself to the *real* work, the task for which I, in company with one or two others of like dedication, such as Shakespeare, and Spenser, and now this newly discovered Milton (and of course my most familiar cronies, Keats and Shelley), was divinely equipped.

A lady followed me on to the bus and took the seat beside me. I had not been reading long before she addressed me in a quiet, silvery voice, asking me if I habitually read poetry.

I looked up shyly, and saw a tall, thin person with faint, corn-coloured hair, a large picture hat, and an enormous *fichu*. She smiled at me from vague, heavy-lidded eyes, looking down at my crouching figure. She must have been a middle-aged person of about twenty-five, and I answered with some confidence, feeling quite at home with elderly folk. Only with my own generation was I at a loss, with the exception of my re-dis-covered friend Bertie Bridge. My brother Jack belonged to no generation. He was an Ancient of Days.

The rest of the journey was spent in conversation. I answered her polite questions, and learned that she worked in a lending library in Dering Street, near Bond Street. That meant nothing to me, for I knew little about the West End. My excursion to Burlington House had been a geographical adventure of as much moment as the purpose for which it was undertaken. I told the lady so, and she smiled, obviously amused by my parochial innocence. .

At Herne Hill I followed her off the bus, to find that she also was walking along Half Moon Lane. So we walked together, still talking. By that time, I had betrayed my identity as a member elect of the company of Shakespeare, Spenser and Milton. To this, she asked me if I ever read books by living

authors. That was a novel idea. I felt that it was a step downwards.

We parted at the gate of the big house in Half Moon Lane
standing in its own large garden, with a drive beneath the elms
where the blackbirds and thrushes had first sung to me in 1905,
that magical spring when my family moved from Battersea to
Dulwich and I was introduced to the paradise of trees and the
period beauty of a village. I pointed across the road to the back
view of our pretty little house. She was interested, and added
that it might be good to read some contemporary literature too,
though the books were more difficult to get. She offered to lend
me some from the library where she worked. She often came to
stay with her friends at this house.

Thus began a sweet, detached friendship that was most valuable to me. It lasted through the next two years, its influence
shining over me like intermittent phases of moonlight on a
turbulent city, cool and pacific. The first book to which this
gentle person introduced me was Thomas Hardy's *Tess of the
Durbervilles*. I cannot forget the impact of that poet's sad,
negatively sensuous work on me. I suspect that it has permanently tinctured the colour, the flavour of my own verse and
prose. At the age of seventeen the human sapling is too pliable
for heavy handling. And Hardy's sombre genius, saturated in
nostalgia for an ever-vanishing past, flowed into my character,
through channels already prepared by my childhood experiences, which were happy enough, but conditioned frequently by
morbid health, first my own, and later my mother's.

I have never quite shaken off the emotional influence of
Thomas Hardy, though technically, in the verbal fabric of my
work, I have not been affected by him. But in what might be
called æsthetic tone, in temperamental attitude, I have not
escaped. The only other writers near my own generation who
are equally if not more indebted to the same monitor are Siegfried Sassoon and Cecil Day-Lewis, whose poetry has, in consequence, given me more pleasure than that of most of our
contemporaries.

Another novel that moved me deeply during those autumnal
months was Henry James's *Roderick Hudson*. It may be no exag-

geration to believe that the encounter with the tall, slow-speaking lady on the omnibus, during my return from the examination rooms of the Civil Service Commission, was to introduce a compensating element into my life, that should balance the somewhat sulky depression caused by uncongenial drudgery at commercial subjects, and the increasing estrangement between my father and his sons.

Some touch of pride, or intuition of the fitness of things, prevented me from telling this new friend about affairs at home. Still less could I confide in her the secret of my infatuation for the Kentish mezzo-soprano, though at that time I was completely enslaved by it, almost to the point of mental instability, as was poor Hector Berlioz at the time of his first, overwhelming love for Harriet Smithson, when after one rebuff from her he rushed out of Paris and buried himself in the snow, and had to be dug out by a distinguished search party which included Chopin, who caught a bad cold in the process. My new friend learned of Mother's death earlier in the year, and about my brother, his music, his character, and his betrothal.

Apart from those confidences, we talked of books, and the fundamental mysteries, our discussions being followed invariably by the loan of a book from the Dering Street library, to have some bearing upon a recent conversation. The books were usually novels, whose authors, in addition to Hardy and Henry James, were Jane Austen (the lady's favourite), George Moore, Edith Wharton, and other novelists of that calibre, all of them artists whose manner was as valuable as the matter of their work. What I owe, therefore, to that unaccountable friendship, and to the gentle person who moved like a comet into, and out of, the orbit of my life at that stage, is a debt which I have not yet summed up, because it is probably still accumulating.

She disappeared, after two years, as suddenly as we had met. At the end, having missed her for several weeks, I went up to Dering Street, and found that the library too had gone, the half-circular windows of its office now stacked with cardboard boxes containing, I suspected, nothing heavier than millinery. Why she vanished, I have never been able to understand. The gentleness between us had never been broken, or even ruffled.

Sometimes she had taken my arm, and on one of these more personal approaches I had observed that the long, thin hand which lay so lightly on my sleeve was roughened with a patch of eczema. She saw that I had noticed it, and explained its nature, quaintly adding: "Do you mind?" And soon after that, after another meeting, she stooped and kissed my cheek at parting. I never saw her again.

Before this inexplicable severance, however, I suggested one Saturday afternoon that she might like to come in and meet my brother and his fiancée before going to her friend's house across the road. I explained that I knew they would be at home, because Father had asked us all three to be there, as he was coming home too, with a surprise for us. I did not add that nowadays it was a sufficient surprise that he should appear at home on a Saturday afternoon. For the last few months of the year, Jack and I had scarcely seen him. Both he and his motor-cycle, with side-car, were out. He had taken to housing the combination away from home, to obviate, as he said, the labour of uncoupling the cycle from the bath-chair late at night, and persuading them into the narrow verandah at the back of the house.

I was apprehensive, in spite of my eagerness to introduce my brother to the lady. I feared that Father might welcome her too effusively, and she was not likely to appreciate that. Further, he might also have something to say about the romantic attachment between his 'babby' and the mezzo-soprano at Folke-stone, a connection of which he was emphatically in favour, his belief being that every male needed what he called "a little affection in his life".

Neither Jack nor I had questioned this, for we knew that the effort to pin Father down in an argument was as futile as tethering a rainbow. This characteristic had increased alarm-ingly since Mother's influence was removed, nearly nine months ago. He was now as elusive physically, in day-to-day life, as he was in mind. But though Jack and I were uneasy, and touched with a vague sense of foreboding, we missed him sadly. Like the rainbow, he was also compounded of the qualities of light, and Jack in particular needed these prismatic touches to open out the sombre caverns of his nature. Father was also the tangible relic of our unique family life, its innocence, compactness, utter self-sufficiency. Jack and I were breaking out of that too; but we cherished the fragments.

I introduced my librarian friend by the front door, and invited her to sit in the drawing-room, where the two floor-to-ceiling mirrors at once attracted her attention. She saw the diminishing and fading reflections of herself, the picture hat, the *fichu*, the tall languor of her figure dominated by the corn-coloured coiffure and the pale, quizzical face. After explaining the origin of the mirrors, and apologising for her being exposed to the scrutiny of a public that consisted of herself multiplied to infinity, I retreated, to seek out my family.

I could hear Father whistling upstairs. I knew that sign; the dawdling, timeless tone. He was uneasy. Again the sense of foreboding seized me. Jack had not yet arrived. I knew this by the quality of the silence. Whenever Jack was present, silence became more concentrated, more significant. The house was now merely silently silent, an indication of emptiness, except for Father's nervous fluting upstairs, to the broken time of 'Marching with the Deathless Army'.

But I was mistaken. As I passed the kitchen door, on my way to the kettle, the tap, and the gas stove, I looked in. Sitting under the window of frosted glass was a living creature, a woman in deep mourning. The light rushed past her, leaving her as a mere silhouette. I saw only a shadowed face, an empty moon. She sat on a wooden kitchen chair, her hands in her lap.

Instantly I knew. For a moment I hesitated, my throat convulsed. Then the fatal mechanism began to work. I felt my body rise from the floor, and I was out of sight of the stranger. The sink pressed against my stomach, cooling the blood that pulsed there. I groped for the kettle, filled it, lit the gas under it. During this interminable process, I tried to gather my scattered wits together, and to do something that would not be too extravagant or ill-natured.

I heard the mourner cough; a little, rasping cough. She too was in difficulties. Father's fugue continued to filter down the stairs, airy and indifferent. On legs of leaden weight, I turned and entered the kitchen.

The stranger was evidently paralysed by embarrassment, for she began to rise, then relapsed on to the chair, her hands fumbling in her black handbag for a handkerchief, which was quickly twisted into a rope between her dead-white fingers. Her face was dead-white too, a flat, inexpressive oval poised on a high, boned collar, that rose from sloping shoulders and a flat bosom, all encased in black. Her eyes were two jet beads, flickering with fear. "He shouldn't have left me!" she said. "It's not right, it's not right!"

The voice was as flat and toneless as the features and the figure. It came out of a world of depression. There were no mountains in it; not even a hillock. Even the near-hysteria through which she spoke could not lift it.

Such supine helplessness made me both sorry for her and hostile. This must be an inhabitant of another planet. My hostility was remote, passive. A dull anger began to nudge the forefront of my mind, not against this pathetic intruder, but toward the self-conscious whistling that corkscrewed its way down the stairs.

Then, as I stood in the kitchen doorway, listening to that complaintive outcry, there flashed into my consciousness the image of the little cushion which I used to set behind Mother's head when she leaned back, exhausted after a bout of coughing. I saw it now on the floor of the side-car, flattened, faded, dusty.

"Did you put your feet on it?"

I heard myself say it, and felt the dagger-thrust go through that helpless body. I had stabbed a ghost. But we were a company of ghosts. None of this was real.

Then she spoke again, my words having been unintelligible to her, and probably not heard. "Please fetch your father. It's for him to explain."

With that, the twisted handkerchief went to her eyes. She was weeping. I returned to earth, and to some recognition of responsibility. "Please," I said, accepting her as human, "I've brought a guest too. Will you come and meet her?"

She was still helpless. Waving the wet handkerchief before her face, she repudiated my suggestion.

"No! No! Not before he has introduced me. I shouldn't have come. But he persuaded me. He said it was time and that you were prepared."

"We're always prepared," I said bitterly. "But I will fetch him."

As I reached the foot of the staircase, the front door opened, and Jack entered behind his fiancée. Both were serious, ready to face an ordeal. That promise of a 'surprise', Father's only reference to a proposed change, had warned them.

At the same moment, my guest, puzzled by being left so long alone in the drawing-room, came out to the hall. I stumbled over an introduction, and added in a panic-stricken whisper: "There's a strange woman crying in the kitchen. I'll fetch Father. She wants me to."

Jack, ivory-pale and calm, guided the two young women into the drawing-room. "When Father comes down we'll go out and get tea," he said. "I see no need for excitement."

My guest and my future sister-in-law drew together and sat on the sofa at the far end, in front of the Klingmann pianoforte, gules of coloured light through the stained glass of the french doors falling about them, neutralising the blonde and the brunette. The elder was composed, as usual, and quickly removed all constraint and embarrassment.

Jack took me aside, putting a hand on my arm.

"Keep calm now," he muttered. "Grace is nervous and I don't want her disturbed. You and I will discuss later. It's quite all right. I've been expecting it. Grace's mother warned us. She's a realist."

I had no need to go upstairs and summon Father. He had heard the assembling below, and while Jack was admonishing me for my odd behaviour, I counted the firm footsteps treading the stairs, one to thirteen, of the lower flight. Voices came from the kitchen, and I heard the caressive words "Old girl!"

Then they appeared.

The stranger was still shaken by distress. The jet-dark eyes glanced around furtively, seeking a means of escape. The white hands still clutched the handkerchief with the handle of her bag. Her mourning gown reached to her feet, making her all of a piece, a figure on the chess-board.

Father took her arm, and with a jocular shove urged her forward.

"Here we are," he cried. "A family gathering again! We had to do something, eh, Jack, my son? This is your new mother. Known her since we were children in Sunday school at St. Luke's, Chelsea, long before I met your mother. Now for some good, old-fashioned buttered toast. And then we'll have a sing-song, to get to know each other."

I took that opportunity to introduce my guest. Her detachment and calm nature had a catalytic effect upon the tensions and strains. Father took to her at once, and thanked her for encouraging his boy with his reading, though urging her to persuade him not to forget the needs of the Service, and a healthy mind in a healthy body—by which he meant that I had neglected my bicycle of late.

We had the buttered toast, and a large cake which the stranger brought (as Father explained). Round the dining-table we sat, and darkness came down. The gaslight from under the huge crimson silk shade, lined with white, made a greenish-pink pool over the table, outside which the six figures, three male, three female, receded into a half-shadow, unreal, unrelated, making perfunctory remarks; all except Father, who was himself again, eloquent with jocularities about young love, the future generation, and the unquenchable delights of the open road.

CHAPTER TEN

"Tomorrow to Fresh Woods"

THAT UNEASY TEA-PARTY marked the beginning of the
final stages of the uprooting. The last of the aspen trees along
Ruskin Walk was down. As Christmas approached, another
gang of men, vanguard of the builder's team, began to root out
the stumps, a job done by hand-labour. The old fence over
which I had watched the pensioned horse, and the processions
of sunsets blazing over Herne Hill Station, was removed, preparatory to widening the walk into a suburban road. Foundations of villas were already being flushed in along the edge of
the paddock; tiny lozenges suitable more for dolls' houses than
for humans' dwellings. Soon our home would no longer stand
overlooking the old farm buildings by the pond, the paddocks
and trees "where late the sweet birds sang". It would be lost in
a regiment of villas.

But no matter, I thought, we shall be gone: foolish to tease
my affections, to torment myself further over the discovery that
what seemed so changeless, so permanent, was nothing but
flotsam on the flood of time. I had sufficient to occupy my
moods, without mourning over the dismantling of my little
room, and the rest of the house, where every piece of furniture
rested eloquently in its place, contributing by its static solidity
to the illusion that all is certain and set into an assured pattern
of continuity.

Homes are no less than that to children, and probably to
many adults also. I know that for me the precise placing of the
furniture demonstrates a philosophy of living, a faith in the
harmony latent in one's surroundings. That is a concept surviving from the placid comforts of eighteenth- and nineteenth-
century English life, when all was parochial, and a change

"from the pink room to the blue" a recordable event, as Gold-smith noted in *The Vicar of Wakefield*.

Perhaps the violent character of the twentieth century, in those last days of its first decade, was already beginning to dominate the field of history by breaking down our home life in Dulwich before lifting its bludgeon against the fabric of Europe, the last of Greco-Roman culture, and the Christian faith.

During the rapid days that followed the tea-party, Father more openly hinted at his intentions. We could not be clear about them, for he spoke in generalities, but we gathered that what he had in mind was an amalgamation of two stricken households. The widow with whom he proposed to effect this union was also but lately bereaved.

She had been left with three children, the eldest a daughter of my age. In order to keep them, she had returned to her pre-marital training, and now ran a dress-making establishment in Putney, where a spinster sister also inhabited, to act as fore-woman of a team of seamstresses.

Jack and I did not, of course, learn of this directly, and in a single explanation. Father was more tentative. He waved a hand airily when Jack asked him to come down to facts. "A fine opportunity," he said, "and a lane at the back to put up a garage." And at another attempt by my brother, a demon for accuracy, to pin him down, Father expounded the theory that we should be able to benefit from the profits of a very sound business, and that so far as he was concerned, with the spinster in the house, he would have the advantage of a *ménage* with as good as two wives. It would be to our advantage also, because we should gain a young brother and a pair of sisters. And he looked at us sadly as he added this attractive prospect, to reflect that he had always regretted the lack of sisters for us in the old days, happy though they had been.

Jack was more surgical than I in our response. He cut through the rosy speculation mercilessly, and I could have felt sorry for Father had I not already hardened into an intolerant scepticism toward him since his refusal to allow me to take up the Art Scholarship, and after his jocular remarks about my aim to devote myself to the art of poetry.

A tiny, irrelevant factor, like a butcher's thumb, touched the balance against him at this moment. It was a recollection, harboured unconsciously by me since a Christmas morning in one of the years of infancy at Battersea, those serene and ever-lasting years. I recalled, as I stood watching him moved by his own sly rhetoric, how in the dusk of that Christmas morning, sitting up in bed surrounded by the joys and débris of the un-packed stocking, I was playing with a toy crane, that made a loud clicking noise as the ratchet leapt back between the cogs of the safety-wheel. Suddenly Father appeared from the parental bedroom, tousled and angry, and cried: "Stop wind-ing that infernal thing, I'm dead with sleep!" At the time I had understood, because for three weeks before Christmas we had hardly seen Father, and were told again and again by Mother how he was working day and night at the Post Office, to earn enough overtime wages to buy our presents, and to help pay off the mortgage on the house. Not until this moment, across the widening rift, did I feel any resentment toward him over that incident.

Anything would serve now, however, to foster the conspiracy between Jack and me against our father. We were so blinded by our fears, and those quixotic loyalties which make youth un-accountable in its behaviour, that we did not appreciate his generosity when he agreed that we should take what furniture and household needs we required to equip rooms for ourselves. This he did after Jack's blunt refusal to have anything to do with the proposal to join the dress-making household at Putney. Our anger prevented us also from detecting an element of relief in his gesture. We had solved a problem which was too com-plicated for him, one which had called out the evasiveness and incurable immaturity of his character.

Merciless in resolution, we lost no time in making the break. I have already described in a previous book, *Over the Bridge*, how we went about this desperate task, blindly plunging for the first time into the unknown world outside the walls of home, where neither Father nor Mother stood to support the four corners of the universe on their hands. With an issue of *Dalton's*

Weekly in Jack's pocket we set out one Saturday afternoon together, Jack grimly morose, his neat figure gliding along, distaste and boredom carried in his features, as though he were disposing of a plate whose rancid contents were contaminating the neighbourhood.

Again the miraculous protection of chance moved with us. The first address we chose was of a double-fronted, but not detached, house at the bottom of a steep street leading down from the top of Dog Kennel Hill, one of the minor heights on the northern side overlooking the plain of Dulwich Village. The network of streets, houses built in the 1870s, was a gloomy, featureless quarter; but it was near the romantic charm of Camberwell Grove, and only five minutes' walk from Champion Hill, the pass to Dulwich where lay most of my previous happiness and enchantment: the Gallery, the Shakespearean associations, the school, the glory of ancient elms, and the woods up the ascent to the Crystal Palace.

That would have weighed sufficiently for me to favour this lodging: but there was more concrete persuasion in the nature of the married couple who owned the house, and now received us. I saw them as middle-aged, staid people, somewhat reserved, if not taken aback, as they studied the applicants for the four rooms advertised at 12/- a week.

They were candid people. They told us about themselves, how she was twenty-nine and he thirty-five. That sounded very mature to me, as also did the solemnity of his work as a King's Tax Collector. They were Anglo-Catholics, and the symbols of their decorative religion adorned their long drawing-room, which ran from front to back of one side of the house, the french doors at the back opening into a tiny conservatory, made subaqueous with greenery. The room was austere in comparison with our over-crowded, Victorian home. Prints of Botticelli, and primitive madonnas and saints, hung on white walls. Two sets of shelves from floor to ceiling were filled with books.

I stared hungrily, and my sharp-featured host saw my interest. He had a rasping voice, rough with eagerness, its rhythms accented with tiny nervous coughs; and at each of these inter-

ruptions his eyes blinked behind powerful pebble lenses. Sometimes his small figure gave a leap up on to its toes, rocketed by
mental excitement, in which state he lived perpetually. He was
a natural saint; but a saint with an intellectual sword forever
bared in his hand. His mind was to be revealed to me as never
being at rest. It darted like a dragon-fly over the landscape of
ideas, religious faith, passing events political, social and cultural.
If an Aztec tomb were uncovered in Mexico, he had spotted the
news in *The Times* before breakfast, and I would find the copy,
folded back and marked in red pencil, thrust between the
balusters on the stairs, for me to read when I came home at tea-
time.

His work, done by contract, appeared not to occupy him
oppressively, for he was always rushing in or out of the house,
at all times of day, with half a dozen library books under his
arm, and one being read in his hands. How he was not killed
by passing traffic, or by tripping on kerbs or other stumbling-
blocks, I could never understand. His powers of concentration
were only exceeded by his allusiveness. The two together gave
him the deadliness of a jumping cracker; but a good-humoured,
wholly generous and benevolent deadliness. I lived for over
four years in that house, and never once did I see him angry or
self-interested. Distress and embarrassment sent him tiptoeing,
his voice raised to breaking-point in banter or gentle admoni-
tion. As a disciple of the beatific St. Thomas Aquinas, he
read the works of his master assiduously, and practised the
precepts.

As our landlord was a natural saint, so his wife was a natural
Madonna. She was tall, and moved serenely. Fair hair parted
over a long, oval face with full chin. She wore boned collars,
and this gave her a stiffness of head movement that accentuated
the sweet deliberation of her character. She tended to say little,
perhaps from lack of opportunity, but she was an eloquent
listener, who invited confidence. Her husband's conversation
showered round her, like rain over a fresh-leaved tree, and she
emerged out of it more simple, more personally fecund than
ever. And when I, after the shy overtures of settling in, offered
my occasional outbursts of perfervid enthusiasm, she absorbed

these too, as contributions to her foliage and its ever-deepening shadows of sympathy.

What is so remarkable is that the couple revealed all this latent wealth of personality at that first interview, though Jack and I were half-anæsthetised by nervous depression and fear at the step we were taking in leaving Father and home.

After a few days, we were installed, and on the Saturday afternoon Jack and I sat in our upstairs room, contemplating the stacks of our books on the floor, the petrified forest of organ pipes, the open and empty fabric of the organ, the eight-foot Erard grand pianoforte that half-filled the room. This noble instrument had been found by Jack's devotee, the piano-tuner who looked like a game-keeper. Jack exchanged the Klingmann for it, and also received a sum of money sufficient to pay for the move and the purchase of a few utensils for our kitchen.

We were exhausted and apprehensive, for a minor disaster had attended the moving-in. The organ-case was wider than the stairs, and the men had been forced to lift it high in the air. The weight caused them to lower it to rest on the balusters for a moment. They collapsed, with a sound of rending wood, and out darted our landlord from the kitchen, dancing on his toes and almost singing in an ecstasy of concern—but on our behalf: "No hap! No hap!" he cried. "Not a bone broken!"

This kindness, augury of a happy relationship to come, only added to our sense of guilt, and now, after the event, Jack and I sat alone in a strange world, with this immediate intimidation of circumstance to flavour our adventure with foreboding. We might have sunk into misery, had not a gentle knock at the door been followed by a deep, contralto voice, inviting us to partake of a light supper downstairs. We dared not refuse, and once again we entered that long, semi-ecclesiastical drawing-room, to see a round table set for a meal, in front of a low, upright piano, heavily ornate and thus conspicuous in the austerely furnished room.

Jack's gloomy eye examined it. His mouth moved and froze again, and a cold hand rose, to mould and modulate his lips. Then he spoke; one word only, in soliloquy:

"Bord!"

The power, the knowledge behind that ejaculation acted like the prod of a spear on our landlord. He appeared to leap into the air as he cried:

"Exactly! A *Bord*, from Paris. Try it, my dear sir, before we sit down to the feast of welcome!"

Jack studied him for a moment, and the sardonic lips twitched in amusement. He approached the French piano as though stalking a sitting hare (it was the colour of a hare), sat down, pulled the stool closer, and began to play the Chopin Prelude No. 17, which has an ominous bell-note in the bass. It came out on the instrument like the distant sound of a woodman's axe at the bole of a hollow tree. At each punctuation by these muffled bell-notes, a tiny wrinkling of the skin at the corner of Jack's eyes was to be observed. I, who could read that epidermal script, knew what the wincing meant.

The performance was followed by several moments of complete silence, during which the grim mask over Jack's face readjusted itself, while his fingers fastidiously moved among the several albums of music on the stand. Before any comment could be made by our host, Jack found, and began to play, the charming lyrical piece by Grieg, 'To Spring'. The delicacy of this, and the oppressive melancholy of the Chopin *étude*, evidently convinced our host and hostess that they were entertaining a *maestro*, for from that moment, until the day he left to get married, they approached Jack with awe, and a shyness that canalised their good nature rather more in my direction.

CHAPTER ELEVEN

A Picture of Billingsgate

MY TRANSLATION from the temporary status of a Boy Clerk to the permanence and safety of an Abstractorship carried me away from the Land Registry Office in Lincoln's Inn Fields, centre of a Dickensian quarter of London's heart which I was not to haunt again until, twenty-five years later, I went to live in chambers in Old Square, adjoining those of Sir Frederick Pollock, authority on international law and the philosophic system of Spinoza, that divine luminary who has shone steadily over my personal landscape, flooding it with light.

I was directed by the Civil Service Commission (again under the signature of J. L. le B. Hammond) to present myself at the Government Laboratory, Custom House Branch, Billingsgate. This was unvisited territory, but my imagination had already peopled it with figures out of Rowlandson drawings; and when I got there I found I was not far wrong. Diving down the slope past the Monument, I returned to the roughness, the brutality, the stench, of the picturesque eighteenth century.

I find it difficult to describe what awaited me in the Laboratory, for I have already drawn upon these experiences, and those scenes, for material to furnish the first of a trilogy of novels, published twenty years ago. Its title, *The Porch*, may have indicated to perceptive readers that this triptych was intended to present the British Civil Service as a corps trained and dedicated to Stoicism, in the Roman manner. The title of that first volume had a more concrete reference, for it indicated also the entrance to my career through the grim doorway of the Custom House, against whose step the tide of fishmongery lapped, slimy and malodorous, from the small hours of the morning until after midday, to be followed by flushings from hosepipes, whose jets of water were laced with carbolic.

Above this alternation of smells, I was to spend the next nine years of my official life, between the hours of nine and four, amid a company as kind and eccentric as any misfit individual has ever found. Dickens moaned about the few months which he spent in his cousin's blacking factory under Hungerford Stairs, and he made much of the humiliations he was submitted to there. I can only look back with gratitude, and some degree of incredulous wonder, at my nine years among the chemists and young Excise officers with whom I consorted from the age of eighteen. They were to be my university; the older chemists my professors and tutors, the Excisemen my fellow-under-graduates.

I went there as a more or less isolated and friendless barbarian, trained in a reclusive home to an oysterlike ignorance of social and academic contacts and graces. I had to spend my days in close association with this small college of men between the ages of twenty and sixty, the chemists being permanent, the Excise-men a moving body who spent two or three years there as part of their experience in assessing revenue from imports, according to the dutiable ingredients. The chemists were professional men of graduate standard, some of them interested in other cultures than those found in test-tubes and retorts. The young Excise officers came from all parts of the British Isles (a large pro-portion from Ireland, where the convent schools turned out a regular army of well-educated competitors for Civil Service posts). They were a fair cross-section of the grammar school and secondary school population of the country, and as soon as I joined them I found myself sadly inadequate in school-book knowledge.

Leaving the elementary school at the age of fifteen, to be left to my own educational devices (except for the worthless disci-pline of the correspondence course for the Civil Service examina-tion), and to have met this lack of direction at a time of abnormal emotional and practical stress while I was nursing my mother, had congealed my young mind into a habit of fantasies, such as the insane ideas about money which I have already described.

Self-continent under the shaping of those odd circumstances,

I was by nature prone to outbursts of gaiety, a kind of lyrical capering, that lacked all forethought and caution. Between these extremes of reserve and recklessness, there was little opportunity for building up a political sense that should give me the armoury of forethought in my relations with people, or cool judgment in moments of crisis. I must be either a child or a god, a zany or a prophet. Mature manhood, the good citizen, were rôles still to be learned, and it was my new colleagues in the Government Laboratory who were to teach me, or at least to attempt the dangerously belated task.

In the teens of the century the Civil Service was not what it has since become, a vast and efficient machine in close contact with the public, trained to administer the Welfare State, its personnel indistinguishable from that of any other large organisation. The ghosts of Charles Lamb, Thomas Love Peacock, Anthony Trollope and Austin Dobson still haunted its corridors. A living novelist lurked in its inner shrine, the Treasury, and a young poet in the Board of Trade, both of them to rise later to eminence in the hierarchy of the administration. Dramatic critics, black-and-white artists, longshore writers, roosted in the Government departments, pretending to ignore the larger reputations which they were making in the outside world. Indeed the Civil Service was recognised as a shelter for younger sons, cranks, eccentrics, misfits, and persons with a vocation; members incapable of holding their own, and unwilling to compete, in an increasingly commercial and industrial world.

I joined this brotherhood at the age of sixteen, and was to remain with it for twenty-four years before I could claim to be a truly healthy member of society; that is, a person who makes his living at the work which is his whole life and purpose. There is perennial controversy about this matter of professionalism and amateurism, in the arts. The problem will never be solved. The artist, whatever his medium, is always in an equivocal relationship with the community because he deals in matters of taste, his contribution being æsthetic, even though expressed in some concrete and commissioned form. Thus, until his work has become familiar and accepted as authoritative, he will never be assured of bread and butter and the respect of the man in the street. Even then, should he come to a position where he commands a sufficient income as a contributor to the sum of civil life, he remains slightly suspect, as a dealer in cobwebs.

I can illustrate this by an incident which took place only a summer or two ago. My wife and I were sitting on the terrace before our house in Kent, taking tea in the shade of a yew hedge that enclosed us from the farm-lane dropping down the hill. Two labourers from the farm came trudging up, pushing their bicycles, their day's work done. The hedge hid us from them, and them from us. As they drew abreast of the terrace, a bucolic voice growled, grudgingly: "Seems a bloody funny way ter make yer living, writing books!" No answer. The heavy clob, clob of boots, while this observation by Bully Bottom sank into the consciousness of Snout. Then, more grudging still, the reply drifted back down the lane: "Seems ter do bloody well out of it, anyway!"

That has long been the Anglo-Saxon attitude toward the arts, shared not infrequently by the artists themselves. Shakespeare retired in early middle age from his craft of playwright, to become a country gentleman in his native town. His gesture was self-defensive, for nobody is encouraged to persist in a way of life, or a profession, which his neighbours refuse to respect. Actors, scribblers, daubers are treated still as idlers and vagabonds in Britain and America, unless they chance to make a substantial income from their queer activities. It is not surprising that the less confident practitioners of the arts should begin to agree with the philistine majority, and try to cover up their work by some pseudo-profession, driven to it as much by wounded pride as by the need for bread and butter. The only alternative is to live abroad, in France or Italy, where the arts are at least revered, even if not remunerated.

My criticism of my own countrymen, however, is somewhat behind the times, for thirty years of radio has brought æsthetic reality into millions of isolated Englishmen's castles where formerly nothing penetrated; no ideas, no music, no books. The awakening has been a powerful renaissance, as effective as that which followed the dispersal of the libraries of Constanti-

nople in the middle of the fifteenth century. But for this modern
awakening renaissance is a wrong description, for the bringing
of knowledge and culture by the instrument of radio has not
displaced a senescent scholarship and social philosophy; it has
irradiated a strange barbarism, the condition due to a sudden
increase of population wherever industrialisation has spored
factory-fodder, masses of people living removed from nature,
with neither craft nor folklore to give them roots in a coherent
tradition. Now, in the mid-twentieth century, we see the fruits
of this whispering, incessant instruction from the radio; a wide
interest in music that has transformed the gramophone industry;
a passion for pictures that has overcrowded the public galleries,
so that they are no longer trysting-places for lovers seeking
solitude; a demand for books so vast that new publishers have
sprung up like mushrooms (and vanished as quickly), while the
efficient producers of books have built up a turn-over that defies
general inflation and the degrading of our educational system
to suit the material needs of mechanisation.

Fifty years ago, in the teens of the twentieth century, it was
still the fashion for citizens to wear clothes indicative of their
occupation: the farm-worker his smock, the navvy his buckled
corduroy trousers, the carpenter his paper cap, the stockbroker
and banker their silk toppers.

The fish porters of Billingsgate had a picturesque uniform.
Over their jackets they sported a long grey linen garment like
a frock-coat, and on their heads they wore a wooden helmet
with a platform top, for carrying heavy burdens. The pressure
of a box full of mackerel would ram the helmet down, causing
the flesh on the skull beneath to wrinkle, and pass on that
wrinkling down the forehead and temples, giving the porter's
face a distortion that resembled rage, incredible grief, or an
imbecile mirth, according to the basic cast of the features it
had to work upon.

Both overalls and helmets were saturated by fish-slime, a
dreadful, glutinous fluid that pervaded the market, its buildings, its pavements, hanging in viscous skeins through the grids
of its gutters, and from the edges of boxes being carried at a
slow trot by the porters, whom it festooned in a hideous travesty

of bridal veiling, the very reverse of aphrodisiac in its fœtid stench, which can only be likened to the odour of the lowest dregs of Davy Jones's locker.

I, too, was orthodox in my garments. Having found my *métier* as a poet, I wore my hair long, and sported a deep-green velvet coat, with a loose bow tie of wide black ribbon. This costume, suitable for the part of Rudolph in *La Bohème*, made its way that first morning, with me inside it as a nervous ghost, over London Bridge, down past the Monument, and through Billingsgate Market at the busiest hour.

From every doorway in the labyrinth of wholesalers' premises laden porters dashed, their heads thrown back to support the weight of their malodorous and dripping burdens of fish. Shouts, cries, imprecations, related to prices, enquiries as to the whereabouts of retailers' vans and barrows; jokes and blasphemous ribaldry; all filled the air, if so contaminated an atmosphere could be called air, with an almost solid confusion, bewildering and crushing to the nerves of an intruder.

I, the unwitting Rudolph, picked my way with half-apologetic disgust through this marine traffic, my eyes furtive in an effort to avoid collision with a weight-entranced porter, or contact with one of the myriad independently floating skeins of fish-slime. My nostrils, the long nostrils of the dedicated Apollonian or Dionysiac, quivered with revolt against the asafœtid air which they had so reluctantly to inhale. I was tempted to escape by exercising my secret faculty of rising from the ground and soaring above the contamination, but to do so I should have to breathe deeply; and that would make contamination worse contaminated, filth within as well as without. I was trapped. I had to walk on through the fishmarket as though I were an ordinary human being, risking the danger that threatened my singing robes.

So intent was I upon my self-protective advance down the slippery slope past the Monument that disaster was bound to overtake me. Suddenly, out of a doorway, there burst a gigantic porter, balancing a barrel upright on his helmet. He was bawling the name of the retailer, linking it with ornaments of blasphemous design, to maintain the continuity of his enquiry.

His bloated face was contused by pressure of blood from the top of his head, this sculpturing so affecting his features that his eyes protruded like headlamps of hate, and his mouth sagged open under the expulsion of his angry monologue. He was of the wretches writhing in one of the more repulsive lakes of Dante's *Inferno*.

This dreadful force coincided with my feather-weight in the middle of the treacherous pavement. I put out a hand and shut my eyes. I felt a mountainous, warm body, as though I were caressing Moby Dick. I heard a sliding sound, followed by a cry, a crash, and a long, slow rustle, as of shingle being lured back into the relapse of a sea-wave.

I opened my eyes, to see my hand still outstretched; beyond it, the porter sprawling in the gutter; beyond him, the barrel; out of the barrel, a gentle flow of winkles, whose semi-hollow shells were the source of this sweet, mermaid music which had followed the crash.

Then silence fell. Billingsgate Market came to a standstill, to watch, and to listen. It saw the fallen Goliath, and the oblation of winkles. It stared at the fairy-like figure, the figment from opera, in green velvet coat and flowing tie. It waited for the kill.

I too waited. I could do nothing else. I could not turn and run, for I was hemmed in by the army of porters and the floating bondage of fish-slime. Besides, I had to report, on my first morning, at 9 a.m. at the Government Laboratory, as instructed by J. L. le B. Hammond of the Civil Service Commission, and it has always been my oddity to have a dread of ever being late for an appointment. This is so instinctive a habit that, willy-nilly, I arrive on the minute at railway stations and other rendezvous. Only recently, I set out by car from the Wortersee in Austria, to drive over the Julian Alps to keep an appointment at 3 p.m. with a nun and her schoolboy nephew in a convent in Udine. It was a long, picturesque drive beside opposed rivers, through mountain passes, on an unknown route. My attention was given throughout the day to the wonder and beauty of the scene. I drew up at the convent in the centre of Udine at one minute to three.

Goliath sat for a moment or two. Then he straightened his helmet on his head, rose to his feet, contemplated the half-empty barrel and the long, oyster-coloured tongue of winkles protruding from it along the pavement and the gutter. Slowly, he turned to me, and looked me up and down. He scrutinised the velvet coat, the flowing tie, the bohemia of hair.

Billingsgate Market sighed. It knew what was coming: the raised sword of imprecation, long, heavy, sharp with every cruel and blasphemous invective that had ever been forged in ships and further whetted in Cockneydom.

One or two of the forefront spectators shuffled half a pace nearer, morbid to witness the annihilation of this ephemerid with the green body and the now helpless, invisible wings. The skeins of fish-slime, that had been streaming horizontally, now hung vertical during the momentary inaction. Gnarled hands supported the boxes on their heads, caryatid-fashion. My eyes saw all these elements in the glaucous auditorium with the vision of a martyr about to be executed.

Goliath's scrutiny at last settled on my face. He looked me in the eye, his great loose lips contorted, and he spoke.

"*Now* you've done it!" he said.

Billingsgate gasped, woke, and resumed its traffic. The cries redoubled, the jog-trot took a quicker urge, the wisps of slime floated out to the horizontal once more. Shaken, and still incredulous, I muttered an apology, and resumed my way, with a few minutes to spare.

CHAPTER TWELVE

The Stoics' Threshold

ALL HOPE ABANDONED, after the shock of that humiliating incident, I stood before the western door of the Custom House. The building, of grey and sooted stone, stretched between the river and Lower Thames Street. Legend said that it was a quarter of a mile long, though architects and statisticians will know better. It looked even longer to my timid eye. It stood like a rampart, cutting off the fishmarket from the healthy light of day and from the open space of Tower Hill. A spear-rank of iron railings stood immediately at its feet, a few inches from the stone courses. Into that interstice were gathered waste paper, rags, and half-recognisable fragments of horror. Fish porters' overalls, odd or broken boxes, helmets and billy-cans, hung on the spikes of the railings, which made a convenient wardrobe for this outcast community, neither seamen nor landsmen.

The windows facing the darkened street were blind with grime. They might have been glazed with thin laminæ of the same stone as the walls. This lack of intelligence in its windows gave the Custom House an inscrutability, an ancient indifference. It squatted there, ageless, timeless.

I stared at it, from end to end: the near abutment against the market, the distant perspective where peristyle met ground level. Round me, as I stood hesitant, the piscine traffic roared, miraculously leaving me untouched, unsmeared. Nausea rumbled in my stomach, a double sickness induced by apprehension and by physical disgust for the stench of the fishmarket. But nine o'clock was sounding from the bells of the City churches, which sprinkled their Jacobean music like sweet-scented herbs over old London. It could not deodorise Billingsgate.

I crossed the road, pushed one of the grimy double doors beneath the stone lintel, and entered the Custom House. Semi-darkness and silence covered me. After a moment or two, I made out the shape of a stone staircase, that wound upward, flight upon flight, with a dreary sameness; a gleam of dusty electric light at each landing. Approaching the first ascent, I entered near the end of the main ground-floor corridor, which ran, to my left hand, away to infinity and increasing gloom. Along it drifted the body-odour of Billingsgate, a miasma that hung like fog round the electric bulbs, reducing their light to a torpid glow.

In front of me stood an open door, and an iron bar that came down to rail off entrance to an open-cage lift. A huge man, in dungarees and a peaked cap thrust to the back of his head, was trolleying a packing-case aboard the lift. There being no less intimidating mortal about, I enquired of him where I could find the Government Laboratory. He grinned, and wiped the sweat from his face with the back of a meaty hand.

"That's where I'm bound for with this!" he exclaimed, giving the crate a hearty smack. "Come aboard!" And with the same hand he almost carried me on to the platform of the lift, having first flung up the iron bar, which locked itself with a clang into a clip on the wall.

My nausea still not dispelled, I observed that the floor of the lift had a plank missing, and that the wire protection stood up only about a foot from the floor. The ascent was outside the wall of the building, up an inner well, the bottom of which was ripe for the archæologist, for it could not have been disturbed by human foot or hand since the Custom House was built. Cast-outs from the interior lay rotting there, with bits of machinery, building materials, broken crates and destaved barrels, coils of rope and unrecognisable parts of tools. Over this rough terrain time had sifted down veil after veil of grime, a geological chronology that would have given an expert the exact age of the deposit.

But now my companion and I, with the packing-case, began to rise from that level. Again the meaty hand took charge, pulling on a thick rope that ran from floor to ceiling of the cage, disappearing at the top through an irregularly worn eyelet. Far above, the sound of water tumbling in a cistern revealed the source of power by which we were being rocked and jerked up outside the building, to the top floor. I peered through the gap in the floor, and instantly averted my gaze, while a contracting sensation seized my genitals. With a last lunge, we halted, but restively, at the top of the Custom House, in what seemed a world of light.

"You the new clerk?" asked the mariner, as he flung up another iron bar, and let me pass to the firm stone footing of a corridor. But I was, by now, too nervous and shaken to be capable of speech. I nodded, in such a way as also to thank him for the lift, and followed the indication of his finger, as he directed me to go round the two right-angles of the corridor at the end of the building, where I would find the door labelled 'Sample Room'.

I found this door, and observed that outside it stood an ice-box, six feet long, out of which an elfin figure was forlornly chipping pieces of ice and collecting them, with a blue, trembling hand, into a bowl held against his hip. His body quivered too, and from a long nose there hung a dewdrop which was surely in process of becoming an icicle. He looked up at me sadly, like a mouse detected by the cat, and a smile began to form over his bowed features, when suddenly the door marked 'Sample Room' burst open, and out darted the cat, which an instant later proved to be a tightly buttoned figure in grey, wearing a flat black stock. His head was grizzled, with a short beard to match, and from this hairy cranium peered two vivid black eyes, sparkling even in this dim corner of the corridor, set close with a fire of mirth and malice.

"Ah! Sapristi! Glasgow, where have you been?" he cried. "Run to earth at last!"

The little figure almost dropped the bowl of ice, so violently had his body accelerated its congenital tremble. His mouth opened and shut, but no words issued.

"Explain, man, explain!" cried the miniature and feline Mephistopheles. "Here are these young men craving for ice for their refractometers, while the King's time is squandered because of a wrong temperature. What is this Christian faith of yours if it cannot speed you to normal movement? What use are your prayers if——"

But he suddenly saw me, an auditor of so odd and unexpected appearance that he stared with gimlet closeness at me for several moments, before switching his oratory from the pigmy to the newcomer.

"Ah! I perceive! You are the new clerk? Pardonable, pardonable on the first day! But take note, young man, take note! Five minutes past nine o'clock. Five minutes stolen from the Crown; ruinous, ruinous and wreckage! Bear it in mind! You lost your way; you had to enquire? Granted! Granted! And did you sign the book in the vestibule? No? Sapristi, this is treason, disaster! Come, my friend, come!"

And he set off in front of me, while I followed him back round the two angles of the corridor to a tiny room beside the lift, containing a table, and on the table an open attendance book where, under his supervision, I signed my name for the first time as an established Civil Servant, at the bottom of a list of some thirty others, and put the time against it: 9.6. "Come, young man!" he said, after that initiation. And I followed him again round the corridor to the door marked 'Sample Room', which he flung open, to usher me in.

I was confronted at once by a counter, with a drop leaf as in any village shop. The counter was filled with sample bottles, tins of fruit, small packages of every shape and appearance. A confusion of smells rushed at my nostrils, which would take time, and more serenity of my senses, to identify: but overriding was a powerful odour of rancid butter, of bad feet. It hit me like an invisible fist, or the hand of the Plague. I had no freedom, however, to react to it, for my sinister yet strangely attractive guide was leading me by the arm through the gap in the counter and introducing me with some ceremony to a person whose appearance instantly commanded all my attention.

He had a large but cadaverous face, with a long, pointed nose slightly off-true. A long mane of golden hair, brushed back and falling to his sloping shoulders, at once proclaimed a character unlike the conventional Civil Servant. I thought of Alice in Wonderland, as drawn by Tenniel; but this man, a little older than I, was powerfully built, very much a male. He looked at me out of clear grey eyes, smiled, and grasped my hand in a vice.

"Feather!" exclaimed Mephistopheles, clacking his hands together like castanets, and bobbing from his waist, to and fro, to and fro. "I suspect birds of a feather! Mr. Bembridge, young man, is espoused to Saint Cecilia."

"No, it's moss at present," said Mr. Bembridge. And he followed this Lewis Carroll-like remark with a long, throaty chuckle that split his face horizontally, and heaved his torso up and down with some violence.

The small, grey figure suddenly shrank, frowned, and stepped back to the outer side of the counter. "Well, man, initiate him! Initiate him! Make him one of the team. And remember, nine o'clock sharp, *on the second*!"

With that, he backed against the door, which opened behind him. I saw him glance up and down the corridor, heard him mutter "Gone! Gone! Elusive!" as the door closed. Another chuckle shook Mr. Bembridge, and while I waited for his anatomy to reassemble, I studied the scene around me. The room was narrow, dimly lit at the window end because that window was a small square near the ceiling set behind a thick stone balustrade, the ornament that ran along the top of the Custom House, above the architrave.

This weak combination of daylight and lamplight (from the bulb over the counter) revealed a picturesque interior: one wall lined with lockers, once painted in chocolate brown, now smoked and blistered. A fireplace with a high basket-stove, on which stood a dinner plate full of damp moss. Gleaming at its foot lay a Georgian copper coal-scuttle, which gave me a friendly sensation.

Rapidly observing these features, I next noticed that Mr. Bembridge, now fully recomposed and contemplating me with a kindly smile, was standing ankle-deep in straw, before two packing-cases similar to that which I had accompanied up the Custom House wall. Both stood open, their lids bent back against the lockers, and straw appeared to be foaming out of them.

"You could help me unpack this laboratory glass," said Mr. Bembridge. "I keep the stores, and number the incoming samples: child's play, but you need to be careful, first, not to run out of apparatus, and, second, not to forget to put down the last number of your sampling; otherwise, two or more samples will get the same numbers, and then there's hell to pay, for the results would go out all wrong to the docks and wharves. You'd have *him* on your neck like a scorpion!" And his leonine head nodded toward the door.

By this time the flutterings in my stomach had begun to subside. One touch of friendliness was sufficient sedative. I took my place, shuffling through the straw, and imitated Mr. Bembridge, who plunged his arms into the froth of straw still in the packing-case, and drew out glassware of all sorts and shapes: beakers, test-tubes, dock-glasses, long-necked flasks, elaborately made condensers like transparent bodies with equally transparent intestines winding round inside the fragile carcase. Lengths of glass tubing had to be drawn out with care, for fear it should be snapped asunder.

Gradually, as we worked, the glassware began to fill the table, the long dresser-shelf under the lockers, the two or three chairs, the open shelves behind us. It gleamed in the cross-light with a dusty warmth, still sleepy from the merchants' store-rooms. My spirits rose, for the tangibility of these objects pleased me, though my fingers handled them with distaste because they were rough with dust.

During our labour, Mr. Bembridge talked freely, with a large, generous impersonality. He asked me nothing about myself. I was accepted as part of a world which, obviously, he found vastly entertaining, subject for mirth (the disembowelling chuckle frequently shattered his monologue), and removed from dangerous contact with himself because of the two garments of enthusiasm which he wore so easily and candidly. I was shewn them. The one was the music of Bach, which he studied in microscopic detail from the scores; the other was British mosses, which he collected and studied similarly, enter-

ing his observations, by pin-point handwriting of exquisite
precision, in large black quarto notebooks an inch thick. He
shewed me one of them, lying open under a camouflage of
blotting paper and sample-sheets, to which he returned intermittently with his official work. And if he had no moss to work
on (using a spare microscope from store), or if he preferred his
other protective garment, the blotter would conceal a music
score, or notation-paper on which he was transcribing back into
the original a string quartette from the works of Vivaldi which
Bach had adapted for the harpsichord.

Mr. Bembridge shewed no surprise that I knew something of
this matter, though nothing of his specialised botany. Both
were everyday nourishment for him, and he was wholly unself-
conscious about these activities, just as he was about his long
mane of golden hair, which gleamed on his head like Siegfried's
Tarnhelm.

The fact that within an hour of our introduction he was confiding in me about these unusual pursuits wholly restored my
confidence. I was again the person, both present and future,
whom I believed myself to be, and I could not decently disguise
my royalty from one who had been so forthcoming.

He accepted my pretensions as naturally as he had offered
his very solid accomplishments, and the morning passed
happily; I began to feel at home, standing in this twilit, im-
provised manger, on the attic floor of the grimy old Custom
House, thrown so unexpectedly into contact with a bird of my
own feather. This, I told myself, was surely another demonstration of the special protective interest of the gods in my
unique and endowed person. Just as they had selected my
brother and my first landlord and landlady to urge me with
monitoring hand, so now I was introduced, in the most un-
likely place, to this musician and natural philosopher, hardly
disguised as a clerk in the Government Laboratory, where I
might have been condemned by fate to serve utterly incognito,
through days, months, years of seven-hourly exile, "at the mill,
with slaves".

That first morning was not spent wholly alone with my
fellow clerk. Other men, all of them older, wandered in, some

by the door to the corridor, others by an inner door leading I
knew not where. They were merely stage figures to me, and
my only remark of them was to notice how different they were
from each other. One was old, with a grey walrus moustache
and a strong Scottish accent. He smiled at me severely, shyly.
Several ignored me completely. Another, a stiff-bodied man,
wearing a double-breasted marine coat with brass buttons
stamped with the crown, and a naval peaked cap, stayed and
chatted with Bembridge, his curiosity in my green velvet coat
and Symbolist bow-tie causing his eyes to wrinkle as though he
were a sailor seeking landfall, while his long, lean jaws opened
and shut as in a sort of intermediary flexing between the words.
I was intrigued by his intrigue, returning his curiosity two-fold,
because I could not understand why he should be in this
subfusc marine uniform, and wearing a cap indoors.

He had got to the point of quoting a verse of Kipling, when
a small man of demure manner entered from the inner room,
with a motion as of skating. This was due to both his feet being
wrapped in towels. He saw my amazement, and explained
simply, and in still broader Scots than that of the elder with the
grey moustache, how he was testing hydrometers in the next
room against the standard, master instrument, "an' I no wish
to splash me shoes with the alcohol!"

Also, during the course of the morning, the man who had
brought me, with the crate, up on the moving platform, by
hydraulic power, looked into the Sample Room. Two other
men, turn and turn about, shared this routine with him. One
was bearded, exactly like the sailor whose head is portrayed on
the packets of Player's cigarettes. The third was a foxy individual, with narrow face and cross-eyes. All three were ex-
sailors, my giant with the meaty hand having also served in the
London Police.

These men, and the elfin Glasgow, were called 'watchers',
and they did the dirty work: washing apparatus, disposing of
used samples, portering, and generally serving the staff. Their
habits and manners, when not Shakespearean, were Dickensian.
They were always grousing, yet they were always cheerful;
always macabre, yet always comic. Their work was dirty, for

the cleaning of apparatus was frequently a filthy process; the samples analysed included the raw materials used in every kind of industry: dye-stuffs, egg-yolks from China (long matured), butyric acid (the origin of the skunk-like smell which lingered during my first morning in the Sample Room), black molasses, crude sugars, oils, varnishes, all fiercely adherent to the glass walls of beakers, test-tubes, or any other container.

There was compensation, however. The largest room in the Laboratory, called the Wine Room, tested imports and exports only for alcoholic strength. In and out of this room flowed hundreds of pint samples of every kind of drink ever conceived by Bacchus: wines from France, Germany, Italy, Spain and Portugal, lager beers from Pilsen, Munich and Denmark, spirits and liqueurs from all over the world. The ruling in the Customs Code Book was that all samples sent for test to the Laboratory should be destroyed, as they were taken before duty was paid. The methods of destruction were not specified, and all members of the staff, assisted by the watchers, showed great discretion in this matter.

During my years at the Laboratory, therefore, I cultivated a nice palate for wines, a doubtful accomplishment for a clerk in the lowest ranks of the Civil Service whose maximum salary was never to exceed £150 a year. At the time, this access to samples of drink and food helped me to keep myself alive; tea, coffee, cocoa, chocolate, tinned fruits, malt extract in unlimited quantity, crude sugar, condensed milk, patent foods and cereals, all were meted out for 'destruction' to the individual members of the staff. With this auxiliary, I was able to save money, and to continue to buy books.

Thus, after two years, when my brother had married and left me alone in the Camberwell rooms, I had £8 by me, with which I bought a Collard & Collard grand piano, a vintage instrument, bi-chord only, but in sufficient though veteran voice for me to struggle through the Bach 'Forty-Eight', the Vivaldi concertos, the Haydn, Mozart and early Beethoven sonatas; a stumbling progress without my brother's disciplinary support. The nocturnes of Field and Chopin, odd and irrelevant pickings from the vast field of pianoforte music that flourished during the nineteenth century after Schumann and Liszt began to explore the possibilities of the iron-framed instrument, all were open to me, the only restriction being my ten thumbs and the aged body of my instrument.

Free access to used samples of wine and spirits was not without its risks. One young Excise officer, fresh and innocent from a monastic school in the west of Ireland, took to the possibilities immoderately. When he came to the Laboratory, he was a tall, dark and fiery-eyed young prophet, with a brogue that baffled his Saxon colleagues. He had not been with us many months before his disposal of wine samples was begun early in the morning; and this led him to other excesses. He arrived an hour late one day, tousled and savage-tempered, wearing one of his own shoes, and one woman's shoe. It must have belonged to a magnificent specimen of her sex. On another occasion, he became obstreperous at an untoward moment when the Laboratory was being inspected by Treasury officials. Fortunately, he fell asleep just before they were conducted by the Superintending Analyst round the laboratories, including the watchers' kitchens and packing-room. They did not probe too closely into the last, that dim quarter where the helpless Irishman now slept securely nailed down in a coffin-shaped packing-case.

This romantic fellow's last official adventure followed soon after. He went out one lunch-time and climbed up the Hanoverian statue which stands looking from the entrance of King William Street along London Bridge. There he sat, riding pillion-fashion, defying the police. After some time they got him down, and, discovering a King's Commission in his pocket, brought him discreetly back to the Custom House.

The variety and oddity of the men who served in the Laboratory were unlimited. Analysts were permanently placed there, a few of them going to, and being replaced from, the parent laboratory in Clement's Inn, near the Law Courts, a gloomy mass of brickwork close by the little coffee-house where my former colleague Arthur Sullivan and I had eaten so many steak puddings at fivepence a head, before rushing down to the Strand to spend the rest of our lunch-hour listening to organ recitals in St. Clement Danes Church.

I have already drawn upon my experiences and contacts at the Billingsgate Laboratory, to furnish *The Porch*, a novel written in middle life. It would be interesting, but also it might be tedious, to recapitulate some of the real-life adventures and compare them with the fictions in that novel. Critics are never weary of examining the processes of creative writing, of tracing sources and influences. To expect the writer himself to do so is to ask the rose, or the cabbage, to botanise.

I hope that in the novel I gave a sufficiently commodious picture of the characters, and their habits, the scene and period of a singular corner of the British Civil Service. I know that I have not shown how much I am still indebted to that fantastic brotherhood, my only university. Almost every member played a part in educating me toward a wider view of life. Some helped by an almost contemptuous indifference to my pretensions. Not only had they no use for my poetry (I had not then descended to writing prose): they scorned that of Shelley and Keats. This seemed like blasphemy, and I was comforted by being able to write these philistines off as mere lay figures, stage properties, in the drama of life: an insolent reaction which I find is common amongst all specialists. It becomes an ingrained, self-protective habit, and is not easy to shake off. It inspired some of Matthew Arnold's criticism, and most exclusive artistic fashions are based on it.

I quickly became one of a group of these young Excise officers who used to meet others of their own kidney working elsewhere in the Custom House or neighbouring Revenue stations. They met in the Customs Club, a canteen on the top floor at the eastern end of the vast building. There a tiny art-quarter established itself, and I sat in the midst, learning for the first time in my life that I was not alone in my enthusiasm and discoveries in the arts. Painters, musicians, fellow-poets, revealed themselves, and I had to exert myself to debate with them to justify my curiously isolated manias, to display and protect my juvenile verse-making. These contests and encouragements heaped fuel on my inward fire. I could afford to eat at the Club only once or twice a week, and I had to hurry back, my cheeks flaming, my mind incandescent after the holocaust of words, often to be caught by the Deputy Chief Analyst, that stickler for punctuality and rational conduct; to be caught, stopped, harangued for being a minute and a half late. His threats were of the bastinado, the scourge, the cat-o'-nine-tails. He cracked his fingers, he twitched his own nose and pulled his own beard, to demonstrate the tortures deserved by young clerks who neglected their official duties for a minute and a half, to squander that stolen time upon the Muses.

I soon discovered that this intimidating figure, so like a pantomime cat in appearance, hirsute and sparsely sinister, was no philistine. He was married to a painter, the daughter of a Royal Academician, was a keen student of Compte and other rationalist philosophers, ranged widely over the literature of France and England of the eighteenth century, and was powered by a large and generous heart.

One day, after I had begun to feel a little too much at home in the Laboratory, and had been impudently marching out of step just to show how different I was from the rest of mankind, he gave me his usual imaginary flagellation with bastinado and other instruments in his torture-chamber. Suddenly he dropped his attack, looked at me in silence, then said, in tones pitiful and distressed: "You know, my boy, with a head like that, you should use your brains more responsibly. If you would only think more, only think more, and talk less extravagantly, you might go far."

A spasm of fear at my own weaknesses, so many and unknown yet suspected, shook me as I heard these words. I recalled that they repeated the warning given by my headmaster when I left Dulwich Hamlet School. And indeed they summed up my brother's attitude toward me, which was implicit with this criticism. How was I to follow this austere counsel, to curb my grandiose impulses of word and deed, to turn the vitality wasted thus toward a strengthening of my mind and body, so that in the end I could justify my pretensions, and replace them by solid, patient work and achievement?

The question hung round my neck like the albatross that weighed upon the Ancient Mariner, whose adventures I was sharing at that time, having come to Coleridge and Wordsworth during those first months at the Laboratory, because the poetry of Keats and Shelley was temporarily too painful, too near the bone, during my infatuation for the mezzo-soprano at Folkestone.

CHAPTER THIRTEEN

More of the Tree of Knowledge

IF I HAVE SUGGESTED that my infatuation for that clear, girlish voice, and for the robust figure which generated it, was no more than a background to my emotional life, then I have been false to facts.

The kindness of this girl, combined with her reticent shyness, and even with her turns of frightened hostility, had fastened upon my hungry imagination and drawn me to the verge of mania. What is so odd is that this vivid direction of my vitality did not lead me away from my other premature bias. Indeed it fed my preoccupation with words, illuminating the pages of my dictionary and grammar-books, as religious joy and misery drove the hands of medieval monks to the fiery intricacies of initial letters during the scribing of their love-story of Christ's passion.

Ceaselessly, at the edge of my consciousness, I heard the whispering of shingle on the beach below the Leas at Folke-stone; the obbligato to that deep-throated voice which I could see vibrating behind the little necklace and the cross which I had dared once to kiss, pressing it back into the warm flesh, to the terror of us both.

Her letters were no appeasement. They fed the fever, which raged in my veins like the initial symptoms of a consuming disease. Mind and body ached with it. The heightened sensibility, after weeks of torpor following my mother's death, made me realise how intricately the feminine half of life had woven itself into my nature; emotional, mental, physical. I was lost, hungry, crippled in a world of men, because I could find no contact there, to use my experience, my tender, manipulative responsibility, the quick intuitions and almost hypnotic craft, developed during the nursing of my mother.

This force was different from calf-love, which would have been more normal, and perhaps more healthy, in a boy of eighteen. I was physiologically experienced, a precocious young doctor, in the articulations, the troubles of womankind. It was a dangerous knowledge, beginning so soon to affect my freedom, as a foretaste of further enslavement as the craving toward this morbid ministry took deeper root in my nature.

It was inevitable that my brother's influence should wane. Though we lived together in our four little rooms, nested in an atmosphere of friendship under the roof of our Anglo-Catholic landlord and lady, we went our separate ways, increasingly reluctant to encroach on each other's privacy of mind.

Jack too was in the bondage of passion, sombrely translating it into terms of his melancholy spirit, and expressing the result through an ever greater musical authority and definition. But this took most of his time and will, and fed upon his vitality. His features grew more pronounced: the powerful nose, the cheek-bones, the delicate chin and nervous lips. The light of day, shining upon his ears and those filbert-tipped hands, touched them to shell-like transparency. He began to be looked upon by friends and colleagues with an increasing awe, because of this wrapped-away quality of person and character. From saying little, he now said less, but that with more effectuality; sardonic, grim, yet with a penetrating tenderness saturated in laconic humour.

About this time he turned to fresh fields of music, especially the French: Debussy, Gabriel Fauré, Franck and his pupil Chausson, and Maurice Ravel. He played the pianoforte works of these masters in the new, impressionist idiom, and found others such as Scriabine, Liadov, Cyril Scott and Arnold Bax, whose delicacy and disturbing sonorities became subscriptive to his own personality, as he shaped the beauty of their work on the Erard piano, under his subtle hands, causing passers-by to pause in the street, and our landlord and landlady to desist from their occupations, to come out and sit at the foot of the stairs, to listen, huddled together like love-birds.

Sometimes I had misgivings about the safety of our sitting-room floor, as the heavy tonnage of Handel or Beethoven rolled out of that eight-foot Erard, making the windows shake so that the view through them became a palsied scene. Even the one or two neighbours who halted to the command of this powerful music stood trembling through the deception of the panes, as with ague.

The weight of the piano, combined with that of Park Walk Chapel organ, which Jack's devoted tuner had reassembled, pipe by pipe from eight-foot wooden diapasons to tiny metal flutes hardly bigger than a toothpick, caused the floor to sag like a hammock. As the months passed, my regular accumulation of new and second-hand books added to the peril. I mentioned my fears to our landlord, but he only tut-tutted, rose and sank on his toes, and assured me that the music was worth the risk. So I said no more, and was content to pump the organ from time to time, when Jack wanted to play something too complicated for him to sequester one foot for working the smaller pumping-pedal himself. Thus, I had a close-up acquaintance with the organ music of composers such as Franck, Max Reger and Karg-Elert (whose *Pastels from Lake Constance* reduced my brother to even more oyster-like silence than usual; always a sign of deep feeling in that too-expressive body and soul).

So the months passed, timeless like all the seasons of youth. Jack and I settled into our rooms, gradually losing the sense of chill and strangeness. The furniture which we had brought from the old home shared in the conspiracy, deceiving itself, as we deceived ourselves, into the assumption that we were once again at the centre of a static, changeless universe.

But our shocked instincts knew otherwise. Certainties had vanished, following Mother into the unknown. New influences had broken through the gaps. I saw Jack building hopes and anticipations upon his love for the calm and gentle betrothed to whom he had fastened himself with such consuming intensity.

I was no more safe than he, for my absence from the little brown nightingale of Folkestone only augmented my passion. Day and night I conjured that marvellous *demi-voce* (the sign of a real singer), taking its inward, brooding tone into my heart, as an addict inhales hashish. It kept me in a state of waking coma, half impervious to the nudgings and knocks of my immediate surroundings at home, in the public libraries, in the Government Laboratory, or out in the near hills of Kent where I went cycling.

Even the personality of Dulwich Village, so dear to me because there I had wakened to a primitive knowledge of myself, and there had claimed a hand in my own destiny, grasping the weapon of poetry—even Dulwich was now seen through the veils and steams of this heated condition, induced by young love, treacherous ally to the art to which my vows had already been made. Part of my torment was that I recognised myself as a defaulter from these vows. The puritan in me (twisted outer roots from the Woburn subsoil) persisted in this dreadful and destructive belief that love and art were rival forces.

This Manicheism was not to be rooted out of my nature for many years. Circumstances were to favour its doctrine of the hated dualism. That is not surprising, as all artists and other dedicated people know, when, having given themselves to a non-materialist vocation, they fall in love and marry, to find a competitive way of life forced upon them. Where there is marriage, there must be money. And where there has to be money, there must be secretiveness and the closed fist, instead of innocence, candour and the open hand. This fact is at least a superficial argument in favour of a belief in moral dualism: but it is not really so. It is no more than a demonstration of our human limitations, the close terms of our vitality, the small scope of our faith.

Yet at that time I believed my faith was boundless. How else could I have gone forward, a boy of scanty and elementary education, meagre health, petty suburban environment, content to settle into an imprisoning and so-called safe occupation in the lowest ranks of the Civil Service; how else could I have been justified in my certain belief that I was travelling through life incognito, endowed with this significant faculty for rising from the ground, removing myself or appearing at will, according as my inner self was threatened or evoked, and that inner self a prince of poets?

These were problems of which at that time I was instinctively aware, rather than fully conscious. My pretensions could not have made me unpleasant to other people, who were almost unanimous in their kindness, and even acquiescence. The artistic set in the Custom House fed me with encouragement, applause, admiration. One young Exciseman from Edinburgh, an amateur painter, made an illustrated and illuminated manuscript booklet of a dozen of my sonnets. Another, a black-and-white draughtsman from Devon, kept up a running series of caricatures of me in the Laboratory house-magazine, representing me as a long figure, in a black alpaca overall like a priest's soutane, surmounted by a fulsome black bow, an emaciated visage pronounced by an inquisitive nose and spectacles, under a crown of carelessly parted hair that tended to stream out in the wake of my habitually eager and express method of walking from room to room or round the corridors of the Laboratory. These caricatures must have been approximate, because I was always apologising to people with whom I collided at corners, in my urgent passage from one place to another under the impulse of the fierce internal engine whose power grew more and more irresistible as I stoked it with lavish experience, moment by moment, and the equally inflammable material from books.

Books and life! By this time, there was no difference between their reality. I remember sitting on the top deck of a tram one winter morning, on my way to the Custom House. Cold and fog congealed like chlorine gas, green upon the glass. Tobacco smoke thickened the semi-darkness on the deck. The tram lunged and swayed like a Channel steamer, causing nausea to contract my ever-sensitive stomach-muscle, so that I felt a knot of numbness round the solar plexus. Half on, half off the seat, which I shared with a body twice as large as my own, I drew a copy of W. B. Yeats's play *The Land of Heart's Desire* out of my fibre despatch-case, and began to read my way along the Walworth Road. The elusive beauty of the verse (I had recently fallen under Yeats's spell) worked upon me with increasing

magic, so much so that when I reached the fairy-song that
ends:

> "When the wind has laughed and murmured and sung
> The lonely of heart is withered away!"

I could read no more.

Everybody knows that contradictory state into which we fall
at the very brink of ecstasy. The moment of final bliss approaches, is perceived, even felt, by the antennæ of our nerves,
as we listen to Mozart, or contend mentally with a paragraph
from Plato's *Banquet*, or the more divine Spinoza; or as we try
to comprehend a vast stretch of landscape, or the diminishing
perspective of the depths of a star-filled sky, or maybe merely
the design and perfume of a sprig of honeysuckle; all is about
to be revealed to us under this vast or microscopic persuasion—
and suddenly, unreasonably, we can bear no more, and have to
break away from the spell, angry and frustrated, to fall into the
humiliation of our inadequacy.

I let the open book lie on my lap, bowed my head, and burst
into tears, sobbing so violently that my spectacles slid down my
nose, and I had to snatch them off and grope for my handkerchief. I felt the large body beside me draw away in alarm and
embarrassment, and for very shame I fought to control myself,
to put away the agony of beauty, the words, the situation so
much more tangible than the actuality of the Walworth Road,
the tram-top, the winter morning, the prospect of a day
frittered away in the Government Laboratory with its meaningless discipline and futile tasks.

The spasm did not last long, for I was quickly aware of
averted faces, some distasteful, others sympathetic. Somebody
said, in a stage whisper: "Poor boy, he's in trouble!" But I
wasn't. I was at the threshold of heaven. It is ironic now to
recall that only a few pages further back in the play a character
named Father Hart says:

> "You should not fill your head with foolish dreams.
> What are you reading?"

Now that I had relieved myself of the worry of cramming for the Civil Service examination, and of the spectre of starvation which I believed to be the only alternative to a Government post, I was able, wilfully and certainly prematurely, to give all my time and interest to reading. I set myself campaigns of block-reading round subjects, authors, any nucleus upon which my imagination fastened as being a corner-stone of knowledge.

My mental hunger was so fierce that it gnawed into my bones, and drove me to a watchful excess in all I did. The small daily occupations were affected by it. I washed up our breakfast cups at double speed, fastening upon the task a symbolism that brought it into my scheme of personal enlargement. The eagerness made me rush through the streets almost at a jog-trot, my limbs throbbing, my stomach on fire with this double-distilled desire. Unable to reach the unreachable quickly enough, I indulged more freely in my dubious practice of drawing a deep breath and lifting myself from the ground, gliding like an owl through the streets. A kind of shamed gratitude lay at the bottom of my consciousness, in acknowledgment of what I believed to be this unique physical faculty. I never questioned its actuality, for it was part of my daily life, my very being. By its use I made my way, morning and afternoon, through the dreary and humiliating rush-hour traffic, winging over the close-packed phalanx of office-fodder on London Bridge at nine o'clock, and flitting unscathed through the horrors of the fishmarket.

It helped me, too, to master those eight flights of the stone staircase in the Custom House, that grimy and dusty shaft where the stench gathered and staled into a dank semi-solidity. Every afternoon, in spite of a day relieved by the encouragement and help of men older and better educated than myself, I fled toward home, driven headlong by a contradictory emotion of despairing hope, always on the brink of some new revelation, yet maddened by the loss of another seven precious hours that could have been spent in seizing the universe and dragging it into the scheme of my authority as a poet, whose commission I had now more fully assumed after reading Shelley's essay, Wordsworth's Prefaces, the turgid *Biographia*

Literaria of Coleridge, and, above all, the letters of John Keats.

With my fibre satchel in one hand, in which was the book currently being consumed, and one or two ex-samples of a nourishing kind, such as condensed milk and malt extract, I would pause for a moment of sighing relief and anticipation at the top of the landing, by the cabinet where the attendance-book was enshrined. Then, drawing that magic breath, feeling it penetrate, a stream of cold fire, down into my ever-fluttering stomach, I felt my body grow lighter, with an intoxicated sense of freedom and ease. The free hand rose, like that of a violinist with his bow to the strings, touched the balustrade, and instantly I was launched downward. In this process, I must have been invisible, for nobody ever remarked upon so un-orthodox a method of descending the Custom House stairs; yet in my flight I passed many plodding up or down under the burden of mediocrity.

What with this hunger after knowledge, exultation in my sense of poetic mission, and the passionate longing for the mezzo-soprano at Folkestone, my days and nights were filled and overflowing with mental and emotional fervour. I aged under the welter of experience, and collapsed into bed every night utterly exhausted, only to find myself rejuvenated in the morning, the fires unslaked, though burning in a stiff and tired body.

To counteract this physical weakness, I changed my noc-turnal posture. My bed enabled me to experiment in this matter because it was a doctor's consultant-couch of wood and wicker, given me by my aunt in Wakefield, when it was thrown out of her husband's surgery. I could raise it in the middle, at the head or at the feet. I tried sleeping with my feet raised a few inches and my head on one thin pillow. This was done on Jack's advice, who had his own nocturnal difficulties. He had always to sleep with a heavy cushion on his feet, to counteract the sensation that they were rising and thus converting the bed-clothes into a draughty tent.

Our domestic régime in the flat was a useful discipline. It pegged us down to actuality. Jack was fastidious and tidy. His music albums and sheets were methodically arranged; his drawing and painting materials stored in boxes. Our rooms did not permit of his other activities: the carpentering, metal work, and the minor handicraft involved in the building of gramophones. I was less methodical, and frequently irritated him by leaving books open on chairs, and shedding small manuscripts like leaves from an autumn tree. Yet he tolerated my more outrageous caprices, as when, driven by moods of exasperation or restlessness, I tried to vent them on the furniture.

In one of these aberrations, I turned out his oil-paints and, using the tubes direct, squeezed out upon the yellow door of a cheap wardrobe that stood in the kitchen a diabolical face. There it remained for the four years of my tenancy, shunned by my landlady as a manifest of something anti-Christian. It glowered at us as we sat, every morning, at our breakfast of baked bananas, bread and butter and tea, I memorising a fable by La Fontaine, or a list of words noted in my little pocket-book during the previous day as newcomers to my vocabulary; French or English, according to my reading.

Jack, meanwhile, would sit passively, his face sombre, his whole person withdrawn behind a luminous cloud of thought. He was seldom without that emanation of silent expressiveness. It caused everybody in his presence to wait, with expectancy, for something revelatory, authoritative. He kept them waiting. Only in his music, or in the water-colour painting which he was now practising more and more, or in his rare outbursts of uncontrollable emotion, did this power reveal itself with decision. Those pronouncements, usually through his art, sometimes directly personal, permitted of no contradiction. They bore the signature of assurance, and were accepted.

After these monastic breakfasts together, we usually saw little of each other until bed-time, for Jack's habit was to go direct from school to 'over the hill', his future mother-in-law being convinced that we were both starved and chilled to the bone in our bachelor rooms. She was not going to have her daughter marry a skeleton. So Jack's evenings were spent brooding, working and yearning, so near and yet so far, in that other household, where he was to be fatted up against the wedding day soon to be fixed.

I got home from work by five o'clock and, after restoring myself with a pot of tea, set to work regularly on an evening's reading, following up the uninhabited territories of knowledge which I was mapping so naïvely yet picturesquely, as medieval geographers planned their circumnavigation of the globe by the aid of charts ornamented with figures of Aeolus and Boreas blowing blasts of storm, with mermaids and tritons sporting in the main, where galleons stood in full sail. I was such a galleon, self-navigated, trusting vaguely to a craving for order, and never losing faith in my own intuitions toward the unknown shore.

Much of my reading was drudgery, because my school years had not sufficiently broken me in to impersonal mental gymnastics. I found it hard to think clearly and continuously. I trusted too much to flashes of insight, to the momentary vision, to the mystical sense of rightness. What I needed was more grammar, more logic, more mathematics. I tried to school myself to that tripartite exercise, and sat night after night, holding passion at bay, while I puzzled over Euclid's propositions, and Nesfield's *Grammar*, carried over this rocky ground only by the hope that in this direction lay the approach to the masters of philosophic method.

All such abstract thought, however, was alien to me. I could proceed only in terms of warm humanity, by the means of image and symbol. Most congenial, therefore, was historical reading. It has remained so. What coherence of mind, what singleness and balance of vision, I have found in life, have come from my reading of history, the seeking of a sense of tradition.

"History maketh the man wise," said Francis Bacon, "mathematics maketh the man subtle." I have, in my dangerously isolated adventures in the country of the mind, tended to look upon subtlety as a device for use in the market-place and in political life, of dubious and short-term value. Wisdom has been more distinct as the embodiment of simplicity of purpose, openness of character, and that quiet, faithful self-confidence without which no work in the arts can be substantial and wholly sane, set above all fashions and the acids of time.

For by now, after a year or more in our rooms, and fixed in the routine of work and contacts at the Laboratory, I was firmly assured of my vocation as a poet. At that stage, the mission seemed hierophantic, with no need for prose, which in my youthful Excelsiorism I regarded as the mere foot-hills of literature. When I was not studying, I was drugging myself by the reading and writing of verse, practising in every measure, even such forms foreign to English as the hexameter and the hendecasyllable; a strange excursion for a boy with *no* Latin and less Greek! I cannot understand why I did not apply myself at that time of apprenticeship to the study of these two languages, sometimes called 'dead'; so necessary, I have always imagined, toward a chromatic command of English, if the writer is to explore and reveal the etymological significance, the depths of meaning, in his use of words.

That belief has been shaken, perhaps, as I have gone through life and met so many classical scholars who, in spite of their knowledge of these root languages, manage only to write English that is lustreless, otiose and arthritic. I think I must have had some kind of resentment because Latin and Greek were not taught at the elementary schools at the time when a child's memory works mechanically. Resentment breeds fear and inhibition, and thus I have prevented myself from first-hand communion with the gods of Olympus, and the literature which is still so large a part of "the glory that was Greece, and the grandeur that was Rome".

I have had to peer over the railings by standing on Lemprière's and Smith's Classical Dictionaries, and the translations offered by Loeb's Library, under the guidance of such interpreters as Dr. Gilbert Murray and Lowes Dickinson. Dr. Murray's little book *Religio Grammatici* and his *Seven Stages of Greek Religion* have been two unflickering lanterns to help me on my way backwards, yet forwards, into that Golden Age. Even so, I still have the illusion that I could have worked wonders with my native language, had I but possessed the mastery of Greek and Latin, as a demonstration of roots and an exemplar of style.

While Jack still commanded my clumsy pair of hands for an occasional bout of duet-playing on the Erard, his habitual absences also withdrew much of his music. To compensate, my friendship with Bertie Bridge developed. Here was a different kind of musician: a practical and professional instrumentalist whose simple nature was content to pasture on the art, from stave to stave. It was his bread and butter, but he followed the craft with the almost mystical fervour of a medieval guildsman. It was his whole life, and the vehicle of his childlike religious faith. Its light shone out from his person; the slight figure, the handsome oval face and large brown eyes, the wavy hair worn somewhat long, the slow, hesitant speech, trembling always on the brink of kindness.

I persuaded him to buy a bicycle, so that occasionally we could ride together, on a Saturday afternoon, over the Dulwich hill and out to West Wickham, at that time a country spot, or further into the hills to Titsey, or Woldingham. He cycled timidly, sitting stiffly on the machine as though he were attempting to balance his double bass upon his back. His gentleness, his good looks, his tentative manner of approach, endeared him wherever he went. When we stopped at a cottage for tea, he would instantly be mothered by the good woman. Younger females hovered round him like moths round a sanctuary candle.

He had no intellectual curiosity, apart from his musical life and its demands. As our friendship ripened and settled into the slippered stage, I often submitted him to harangues, making him the strop on which I sharpened my own wits. My prejudices, my enthusiasms (which were limitless) in literature and music, and my naïve attempts to bring these wonders to some coherent shape to fit into the house of philosophy flowed over his shapely head.

He smiled at my fervour, encouraging me with gentle but vague appreciation. Even in musical matters he seldom intervened, allowing my theories with a tolerant smile, probably because he didn't know what I was talking about. Had he been an old man, and had he not been a professional, I should liken him to Anthony Trollope's Warden, that gentle spirit who in moments of agitation began to play an imaginary 'cello. Bertie, in such a crisis of nerves, would have hastened to play a *real* double bass.

It was not possible to see him frequently, because when I was free he was at work in the orchestral pit of Covent Garden, or playing in Beecham's Symphony Orchestra, or deputising at a concert of chamber music. He was able, however, to smuggle me into Covent Garden during some rehearsals at the height of the opera season, when the repertory was so full that the usual morning rehearsals overflowed the midday break. I rushed up to Bow Street from Billingsgate, inquired for Bertie at the stage door, and was passed on by the stage-door keeper (all such people being devotees of my friend) along small corridors like passages in a coalmine, and finally deposited, awed and apprehensive, in the vast, darkened but still royal auditorium, among a dozen or so other shrouded human beings, probably creatures from another planet.

Thus, in these odd circumstances, I had close-up views of some world-famous figures: Chaliapin lolling back with his arms spread wide over the adjacent seats, an enormous hat thrust on the south-west corner of his head, a pair of eyes glittering like fire-balls in the semi-darkness.

Coming out, furtively, from the stage door with Bertie after one of these sessions, I saw the tenor Martinelli hand Dame Nellie Melba into a taxi, with an operatic gesture of hand, and an heroic pose of his whole body that struck me to the heart because of its grandeur and aplomb. The demonstration of perfect rhythm, wherever I observe it, has always affected me in the most embarrassing way. I become the rabbit before the weasel. A cat washing itself, a woman brushing her hair, the tiny muscles rippling under the skin of her inner arm, a horse galloping, smoke billowing up from a bonfire, waves running up a beach, speech-periods exfoliating in matched team-work from the brain and throat of an orator; all such, amid the million forms of perfect motion in everyday life, have kept me in a state of worshipping expectancy. No doubt, to an observer, my attitude gives me the semblance of a village idiot daftly gazing at thistledown.

I know that this habit affects my judgments upon works of art. Where I see this same outpouring of rhythmic freedom, this insouciance, unfettered by theory or second thoughts, there

I recognise a master-hand at work. It may be in major or minor degree, but it is the living testimony. Rhythm is recognisable instantly, and it is the presence of God, of the Creator of all things. The most blessed spirits reveal it in all they do: Mozart, Schubert, Milton, Racine, Eric Coates, Dvořák, Edith Evans, Victoria de los Angeles, Clifford Curzon, Augustus John; these I name as pure artists by the possession of lyrical grace and ease, based upon an instinctive sense of rhythm which formulates, pronounces and disposes of all they do or make. Timing is all.

My consciousness of these things was sharpened during those stowaway half-hours in Covent Garden opera house, and during the performances for which Bertie frequently gave me tickets. I fed avidly upon these experiences in the world of music, which through opera I was able to link up with my own world of letters, and the production of the human voice in speech and song, the adjuncts of poetry which England poets have tended to neglect. I believe that a poet, unless he is physically handi-capped, should make it part of the mastery of his art to learn to speak his verse with the utmost distinction and grace, so that its qualities of meaning and music become embodied in per-formance that is man's highest form of communication.

Slipping off to Folkestone, by the help of a 3/6d. ticket issued by the National Sunday League, I was able to meet my mezzo-soprano, and to pour out before her my gleanings from so rich a field. I told her about my friend, his character and skill as a musician, the Sunday evening quartette-playing at his home, my reflections thereon, my own practice in the making of poetry, my plans toward future conquest. I urged her to share all this with me, and to work at her singing with like enterprise and ambition.

She listened, and her little freckled nose wrinkled with laughter. Half-indulgent of my fervour, and encouraged by her mother, who had in mind that safe post in the Civil Service, she allowed me to pay my tempestuous court.

Between these walks together, during which my dialectics carried us along almost at trotting pace, we sat in the little house under the arches of the railway viaduct, the meal-times punctuated by the rumble of trains on their way to the harbour.

One or two of my current poems (and the current was rapid) would be read to the family. On one occasion the quiet little father, smoking his fragrant tobacco mixture at the head of the table, amid the débris of a huge Sunday dinner, remarked solemnly: "A future Kipling!" This I took badly, for I had no liking or even respect for Kipling's verse at that stage in my cloud-capped career. I felt wholly misunderstood, and retreated into my incognito, a garment by now beginning to be somewhat rubbed at the elbows and frayed at the cuffs.

Returning from these amorous excursions to Cythera, at 3/6d. a time, I lay exhausted in the train, my brain throbbing, my stomach pulsing, under the stress of recapitulation, over the day's events, and non-events. Exalted, yet frustrated, I summoned that girlish form, heard her pure, strong voice, savoured the warm home-life again in all its innocence and closeness, and realised that I was retreating, or advancing, further and further from so normal and healthy a mode of life, to venture on "strange seas of thought, alone", seeking the further shore of those Indies of the mind, thus making the same mistake as Columbus.

CHAPTER FOURTEEN

When Greek Meets Greek

DURING this enlargement of our lives, Jack and I had not wholly deserted our father. We kept our resentment, and ignorantly accused him of being the breaker of our home and our sense of security. Our compassion mortified by his secrecy, we were unable to realise how troubled he must have been by his own decision to break new domestic ground. We could only see him as an elderly widower (he was then forty-three!), long past emotional entanglements, 'all passion spent', who would henceforth feed upon memories for the short autumn of his life.

This view of him was quickly dispelled, for me, by the purchase of the Humber motor-bicycle three weeks after Mother's death. The minor disloyalty to her wishes hurt me, but I forced myself to forget it and persuade my conscience that, after all, Father *must* have some means of consoling himself after the cruel blow so recently dealt him. Further, I shared, in a small degree, his enthusiasm for the open road, for bicycles, and for the new forms of locomotion so rapidly being introduced by the use of the internal combustion engine.

But Father's obtuseness in taking Mother's small cushion, where her poor racked head had rested after the bouts of asthma, and flaunting it in open weather over the English countryside, brought back to my mind his obduracy over my Art Scholarship, and his total lack of appreciation of the fact that I had been called to the vocation of poetry with the finality of a young zealot to the cloister. He had not even discussed the matter with me. It was dismissed as an argument wholly outside his comprehension, spoken in a foreign language.

Throughout the future forty-five years of his prolonged autumn of life, he was to show this same bland indifference. I made it a practice always to give him a copy of every book I wrote, and he received them with a casual word of thanks. Some he kept, in a bookcase among his road-maps, and books with such titles as *Awheel in Lowland Scotland*, or *The Road Westward*. Others would be passed on to acquaintances met in the bars where he went habitually for a glass of ale before his midday meal. He had an old-fashioned, aristocratic dislike for the intellectual life and the scribbler. Both in appearance and personality he was a soldier, loyal to the regiment and his comrades.

Later that summer, after I, too, had tumbled headlong into an emotional future, I was not so preoccupied that I failed to notice how the little cushion was fading, and that it was frequently flattened on the seat of the side-car. I dared not allow myself to wonder what this meant. I told myself that it could only be that Father was taking some of his office colleagues on his rides, to fill the gap left by death and the increasing coldness of his sons' estrangement.

Then the crash came. From that moment, time and space, life and human relationships, lost all coherence. The universe began to plunge and fall. Alternations of numbness and violent emotions robbed me of a balanced outlook. I now had my own problems, especially those arising from improved physical health and need. I was beginning to warm more than "both hands before the fire of life", a fire rapidly growing beyond control. New environment, new acquaintance, roared about me like a burning forest.

That is why Father's affairs, though eventful enough, had receded to the background. Following the departure of his sons, he lost no time in escaping from the condition which he most dreaded—solitude. He shut up the house, advertised it for sale, and married the widow. After this rapid course of action, Jack and I communicated with him only by letter for some twelve months, during which he sold the house, repaid the mortgage, and generously sent us ten pounds each. I bought myself an all-black bicycle with this windfall, a handsome New Hudson tourer with three-speed gear and oil-bath. It was to be a good friend for many years. I had to keep it in our upstairs kitchen, stalled against one wall, its headlamp turned at half-glance toward the demon's head with green and vermilion eye-balls which I had painted in Gauguin-like mood on the door of my wardrobe. Once a week I groomed my sable beauty, and sometimes I mounted it, to sit there in the saddle, reading for hours at a time, or writing verse in the little black notebook which I always carried in my pocket, to record words, and their etymologies, new to me.

On several occasions my landlady, knocking at the kitchen door to offer me a round of jam tart or a pot of home-made marmalade, or perhaps to invite me downstairs to a tête-à-tête with her husband or to a small party, discovered me thus astride my bicycle, balanced with one foot on a chair, with book or pen in hand. She never commented, but I was cunning enough —already touched with that self-awareness from which the artist cannot escape, since he is a mirror of himself as well as of the rest of the universe—to see a smile flicker round her large, mobile mouth.

It was at one of these parties, toward the end of 1911, that I first met a professional writer, with awe and envy. He was George Bishop, at that time dramatic critic on *The Era*, and later on the *Daily Telegraph*. I recall a tall, severe figure, who stooped over me benevolently while I gazed in reverence, and an irrational urge to make a few prophecies on my own behalf in this matter of professional activity. I have always coveted the life of a journalist, just as I have aspired to that of a physician. I was held back by my morbid dread of an un-certain income from following the former, and by lack of capital from the latter.

Eleven years were to pass before I began to practise literary journalism, beginning in 1922 on the *Spectator*: but eleven years at that time of life is a vast continent of time, and I was to flounder in many deserts before I crossed it.

The intolerance and youthful cruelty which had driven Jack and me to such high-handed action in breaking away from Father gradually subsided as the months piled experience after experience between us and our boyhood. But Father's open invitation to visit him went unheeded until the Christmas of

1911 came with its spirit of reconciliation and its now poignant reminder of those intimate family joys in the Battersea and Dulwich homes.

I was at a loss what to do with myself over the few days of the Christmas holiday. Its power is too great to be ignored, and private habit, no matter how solemn and dedicated, has to be abandoned. Jack was concerned about me, for though I had been invited with him to spend the Christmas Day 'over the hill', he felt that this would be an imposition upon that tiny, compact household, where he already owed so much in hospitality.

On Christmas morning, therefore, we nervously presented ourselves at Father's new home. Jack hardly spoke a word during the journey to Putney Bridge. He was paler than usual, and the bony ridge of his Savonarolean nose shone like ivory. His eyes flickered with apprehension under the heavy lids, in which tiny veins criss-crossed, giving them a leaden hue. He sat on the bus, his head drooping, his shoulders hunched, an inexpressible boredom masking his face, half-concealing the dread and distaste in his soul.

I was more expressive, excited as always by new adventure, and venting my tense mood through a running commentary of speculation and fantasy. Half-sick with this nervous forecasting, and with the motion of the bus, I badgered my brother intolerably. He ignored me, except for an occasional flicker of irritated amusement, or a sardonic remark.

One of these last referred to my appearance. I was wearing a cutaway morning-coat, vintage about 1895, with tails and tiny lapels, which I had been given by Jack's future mother-in-law, one of many examples of her resolution to save me from what she predicted as an early death from starvation or exposure. The coat produced an austere effect, aided by a black silk cravat wound twice round a single, stiff collar and tied in a bow. I might have stepped out of a George Cruikshank illustration in *David Copperfield*.

"Why do you have to look like a demented undertaker?" Jack said, as we approached the house near Putney Bridge. "The whole situation is insane enough, isn't it?"

But we were at the door, and I could not reply. One of us knocked. Whose hand it was, his or mine, I cannot recall, for all mental process was suspended during the next few minutes.

Nothing happened, and, as I remember vividly, it was I who lifted the highly polished brass knocker for the second time, because my hand was still raised when the door opened, and a young woman, struggling with anger which she tried in vain to conceal, stood confronting us.

"I'm sorry," she said. "Your father is unable to come to the door."

Then, seeing that we were also uncomfortable, she smiled, stood aside, and invited us in.

That momentary picture stamped itself upon my memory. The pathos of this stranger striving to hide some powerful feeling, and to greet us with conventional good manners, opened me at once to sympathy. I was instantly alert. I noticed the tremor of distaste with which she spoke the words 'your father'. I saw the flush in her dairymaid cheeks. She was fair, with a central parting, and the hair carried down over her ears. A little pulse beat in her creamy neck, and it kept time with her foot, which was nervously, or savagely, tapping the oilcloth beyond the front-door mat.

She was nearly as tall as I, and firmly built, with an elaborately made dress tight across her bust. She stood like a statue, the violence of her emotion incongruous with so sculptured a figure.

"You are Jack and Dick?" she said. "You can imagine, we've heard a lot about you since your father came to live here a year ago."

Her voice had a slight break and a tremor, that made Jack wince. He studied her severely, and I detected fear in her eyes. They were clear, candid eyes, incapable of dissimulation. I turned to Jack, longing to signal to him, to urge him to switch off that dreadful, authoritative scrutiny. But of course it was unconscious, and I could do nothing except assume more cordiality than I really felt.

"He's cleaning his motor-bicycle out in the yard," said the young woman, "and he's covered in oil."

She led us past a kitchen tray that lay on the floor of the narrow passage, its pattern half obscured by a mess of black grease. She saw me glance with curiosity at this, and she spoke again with a bitterness that made her voice break harshly.

"He insists on keeping it here, in the hall. That's what the tray's for, to catch some of the dirt."

Jack and I were now in a front sitting-room, in which we recognised a china cabinet, one or two pictures, two armchairs, diluted with other furniture of a similar kind, but meaningless and alien to us. "He's still at it!" said Jack, nodding grimly toward the passage. I knew what he meant: the tray, the motor-bicycle. I saw the cycle-shed on its eight legs in the yard of our Battersea home, and Father tuning up the new tandems on Christmas morning, while Mother cooked the aitch-bone of beef. It was now inexpressibly sad: most sad of all, the impenetrability of Father's nature. The innocent people, perhaps, are the cruellest, because they cannot be changed or turned aside from their simplicity of purpose.

"What do we do now?" said Jack. "One would think we'd come to collect the rent!"

Then we heard voices at the back of the house, one of which I half-recognised by its dead flatness. It said: "They're your sons. It's for you to meet them first."

Jack was right. Father was at it again. Here was a difficult situation which he wanted to dodge. But now he had to deal with a household of women. The odds were against him.

We heard the familiar whistle, with its carefree assumption of ease. I knew the song. 'I am Waiting for thee, Asthore.' He had been waiting for this for over a year.

"Well, my lads," he cried, his face alight with fatherly affection, while he wiped his hands on a towel. "Come to share the Festive Season? Welcome home!"

He kissed us both, and I heard a reference to his 'babbies'. Jack remained unflinching, his eyes hooded, a deep melancholy regathering round him, like mist on a limestone peak. I found myself quite at a loss, bewildered by my own lack of feeling. Something within me had died. I was not even hostile. A cold scepticism, too old for my years, had frosted my love for Father.

Indifference was something new to me, and I was afraid of it. This could not be added to my scheme of things. It brought nothing positive to my philosophy; there was no poetry lurking in it, no movement. It was flaccid, inert. And I blamed Father, staring at him warily, with distrust.

"Come and meet the family, poor souls. Think of them, left fatherless, just when your mother——! But there, we won't talk of that!"

He led the way, and we followed to a long room at the back, where trestle tables, piled with dressmaking materials and tools, had been pushed against the wall, and a dining-table laid in the middle, for the Christmas feast.

And there stood the family. The mother, now no longer in mourning, but still with that flat, sallow face and black-irised eyes; another woman of about the same age, but lighter, simpering on the verge of tears; a young boy and a younger girl, nondescript in Sunday clothes.

"There we are!" said Father, sitting on the edge of a work-table and swinging his legs. "My new young family! 'Pon my soul, what with one and another, I don't know where I am! Eh, Auntie Polly? I said at the time that I couldn't make up my mind which one of you to marry!"

"Oh, go along with you," said that simple soul, her soft lips trembling; a movement which never ceased.

As Jack made no overture, I forced myself to shake our step-mother by the hand, and to wish everybody a merry Christmas. And as I did so, I heard an oven door slam in the near-by kitchen. Then the young woman reappeared, her face flushed, an oven-cloth in her hands. "Ah!" cried Father, "our young housekeeper and cook; always smiling!"

She ignored this, and poured two glasses of ginger wine, which she offered us. I could feel, behind her discomfort, a personality quite unused to such complicated problems as Father's and Jack's characters offered. Jack obviously frightened her, and he did nothing to help her. Indeed, every time she laughed, in the course of the day, I saw him wince as though he had bitten on an open-nerved tooth. The harsh note that sometimes broke through her speaking voice emerged with startling force when she laughed. It was a kind of indrawn scream, that stabbed and stabbed again, causing her to raise her magnificent shoulders and jerk her head forward in an oddly remarkable way. Such a gesture, coming from so basically calm and statuesque a figure, was disconcerting. It was, however, a blemish that appealed to my protectiveness. I found myself anxious to shield her from Jack's deadly criticism.

As the Christmas party proceeded through the well-cooked meal to the *bonbon* stage, and the somnolent afternoon following the washing-up and the almonds and raisins, I found more need for me to extend that protectiveness between this young woman, whom the family addressed as 'Car', and my father. It became obvious that here was real enmity, real hatred, mutual and sword-drawn. I had never met a force like this before, and I was terrified. I found myself being drawn into it, to take sides. Knowing Father, his imperviousness, his cavalier yet schoolboy attitude toward women, regardless of their physical and emotional capabilities and needs, my bias was not in his direction.

On our way home, Jack and I were silent for some time. The friendliness of these strangers had defeated us.

"We must keep clear of that," said Jack, as we walked through the leafless tunnel of Camberwell Grove, in a deserted world, on the quietest night of the human year. We were passing the house of the local hermit, who lived alone behind a high barricade of corrugated iron, sharpened to spear-points at the top and penetrated through a cut-out doorway doubly padlocked.

"Better to live like *that* poor old lunatic," said Jack, indicating the Georgian villa hidden behind its fortifications, "than to be dissolved in Dad's treacly, philistine, sentimental huggermugger. That girl! Did you hear that laugh? It broke through G sharp; nearly split my skull!"

"The Old Man has got on the wrong side of her too!" I said, dryly. "I expect she feels much about her father as we feel about Mother. And she's got to stick it there."

"Maybe; but you keep away from it, my boy. That kind of life doesn't go with what you're after."

"Good Lord, what *are* you talking about?" I cried, offended.

Then we dropped down the other side of the hill, toward midnight, our footsteps crisp but weary. A heavy frost was settling over the world. I felt its touch in my bones, and shivered with dread.

CHAPTER FIFTEEN

Holy Communion

FOR A WEEK OR TWO after that first visit to Father's home
I moved about in a world darkened by melancholy. The
winter struck hard, heavy frost gripped the earth. It touched
me too. I have never been able to escape the sense of foreboding and even despair which cold weather conjures upon me.
Even in summer, should the wind veer north or east, fear comes
down. I feel myself to be dogged by conspiracy, a menace from
which there is no escape. No wisdom, slowly gathered over a
lifetime of generous experience, and strengthened by religious
reality and the quiet faith that works through meditation, has
been able to banish these primeval moods lurking and prowl-
ing in blood and bone.

I recall that only recently, during a tour round Italy, where
I was giving readings of my poetry to the Italo-English clubs,
and being fêted and lauded with all the honours customarily
given to writers in the Latin countries, I reached Ravenna, and
was there overtaken by a sudden break in the serene autumn
weather. A bitter wind, with rain flapping sordidly across the
Adriatic, howled round Dante's tomb and the mausoleum of
Theodoric the Visigoth.

My joyous excitement at being able to study the ninth-
century mosaics in the famous churches was instantly obliterated.
The chill hit me, my stomach contracted and communicated its
stiffness to my legs, and its obstinacy to my brain. The sense of
conspiracy, of impending and world-wide disaster, fulminated
once more, like the fumes of an opiate within my mind. Only
by a resolute act of will, and the tonic encouragement of my
companion, who had spent thirty years combating these
meteorological seizures, was I able to face the audience.

It is a humbling thought—and therefore salutary—that a drop in temperature can thus interrupt the articulation of a mature human organism built up slowly over the years with some degree of philosophic effort and hope, under the manipulation of experiences that never cease, waking or sleeping.

If, however, I pause to examine every mood which memory so vividly recalls, I shall fall into a Proustian *adagio* movement, and fail to finish my narrative of the story of a decade. But these moods are the beads on the rosary of every human consciousness, and in telling over the adventure of living and our combat with Time we have to touch them, as reminders of the tricks played by that life-long enemy, who, in the end, turns out to be wholly benevolent, with the last gift of peace.

In that New Year of 1912 I could not shake off the immediate foreboding. I was haunted by Father's acceptance of that alien domestic setting, in a home without a book or a musical instrument, where the only pictures were framed enlargements of photographs, hung sky-high near the rail.

It was a religious household, yet a matter-of-fact one. It was attached to the small-club life of the local Congregational chapel, an amiable sodality, but not likely to further my father's happiness. I could see that the obstinate side of him, with its wilful perverseness that could suddenly sharpen into cruelty, was already showing itself through his insistence on keeping his motor-bicycle in the narrow passage, inside the front door of the house.

This was a declaration of war against his step-daughter, a Martha who worked from morning to night cleaning, running the house and catering for the family and the team of seamstresses who came in during the day. The place was kept like a man-o'-war; everything scoured and polished, under a back-breaking routine of duty, whose rigour might have warned Father that he was pitting himself against a formidable opponent, armed with simple honesty and candour likely to survive his subtle devices.

I was to observe all this on further visits, for I found no excuse for a complete break with Father. He insisted on his devotion to us, his 'babbies', and we were haunted by the half-sincere, half-shy reproachfulness with which he greeted and parted from us, at our infrequent meetings.

He rarely came to our rooms. On those visits, I heard the *honk-honk* of his motor horn outside our living-room window. Looking out, my vision blurred by reading, I saw the vague shape of his motor-cycle, with or without the side-car, and Father sitting in the saddle, looking up in boyish eagerness, waving his hand, gesturing toward the open road in the direction of the Crystal Palace, and Kent beyond. I knew what he meant, on these summer evenings or Saturday afternoons. He was lonely, and wanted a companion who would share his old campaigner's passion for the wind on the heath, under the open sky. He was not finding that comradeship, with its pagan sympathies, amongst the members of his household at Putney Bridge.

He was reluctant to come up to our rooms. Perhaps he was saddened to recognise furniture from the old home. Certainly he found our landlord and landlady too scholastic and ritualistic. "All those books! And bowing and scraping!" he commented. Again the puritanism, a double streak, of Bedfordshire farming stock and the intolerant whiggish Woburn strain, manifested itself. His pale grey eyes glinted, hard as granite, and he planted himself foursquare in a posture of obduracy, erect as a guardsman, and as unimaginative.

"Are you stretching that chest?" he would say, after a hostile glance at my bookshelves, to which Jack added from time to time, as my regular book-hunting in the twopenny stalls and boxes brought home a dusty harvest. "Ozone, my boy, is what you need!"

He did not say much about his life and relationships at Putney Bridge. Once, after he had inspected my new bicycle in the kitchen and pointed out a streak of dust on the gearcase, I reminded him that Jack and I did not have the feminine attention which he could now command, and that all our housework had to be done by ourselves; the cleaning, floor and furniture polishing, bed-making and washing-up, and as for the cooking—— But he interrupted me impatiently:

"Too many women around! Can't be master in my own

house!" he exclaimed. I did not point out that he never had been, or that his present house was also maintained on a fifty-fifty basis, a policy which gave him more financial freedom to follow his particular fancy, now transferred from pedal to power-driven bicycles.

Since the one outburst of bitter anger against him, which I still remembered to my shame, when he had scoffed at my declared intention to devote my life to poetry, I had never contended with him. But that incident had cauterised my mind, leaving an insensitive scar upon my affection for my father. I was unable to talk freely with him, except on the surface mechanisms of life and his enthusiasm for touring. I never mentioned my own interests, my hopes and fears, the absorbing and wonderful pleasures which I found in books, in music, in the very air I breathed. I was removed to another continent from his, and he was so far away that I could not study his distress. I did not appreciate that to a man of his nature my aloofness, reserve and indifference were a poison that corroded his virtue, shrinking it from a fine, cocky boyish-ness into an obstinate core, wilful and perverse. From time to time an ugly streak showed itself, as though he were being cornered by life, and forced to take on the responsibilities which hitherto he had carried so lightly, if at all.

This sinister side found an ally in his old mother, whom he brought to live in the household of women at Putney Bridge, when his step-father died. At this time, in her eighties, she was more witchlike than ever, with hair still jet-black, her hands still idle. Whenever I visited there, I found her peering out of the window. The view was limited to the length of the suburban garden, but her hooded eyes searched vast distances, with an upward glance. "I see my blessed Saviour," she would say, "carrying His Cross up Calvary Hill."

This mystical flight of imagination was wholly unintelligible to the other women, who by now were inclined to believe both mother and son to be a little odd, or even wicked. Father's religious experience was less concrete than that of his mother. Every Sunday morning the family went to chapel, after a quick rush round the house and much activity in dressing (the elaborate and smart coats and skirts having been made on the premises). Father's wife always asked, in a flat, defeatist tone, if he proposed to come with them. His answer was invariable. "I go to worship my Maker in my own way! The road, the sky, the hills and dales, the little wild flowers!" This oration was accompanied by a derisive gesture, and a malicious twinkle in those now cruelly grey eyes. And off he went on his motor-bicycle, backing it out of the front door, holding up his hand to take the feel of the weather, and disappearing for the rest of the holy day, to return late at night, white with dust or dripping wet, to drag his travel-stained 'old faithful' (as he called it) back into the immaculate hall, which had been cleaned up during his absence.

I learned all this about Father's new life and environment only gradually, and as a distant spectacle in which I was but half-interested. Jack rarely went over to Putney Bridge. That G-sharp laugh was too much for him. He was intolerant, too, of the small, material interests, the incurious matter-of-fact outlook of the *ménage*. Even so, I think Father was more fond of him, and felt more at ease with him, than with me. Jack might savage him occasionally, with one of those deadly, Spanish glances and an excoriating remark, but he remained, whenever Father mentioned him, as '*our* Jack', spoken with a tremor of tenderness, which I suspected to be assumed. But I was wrong, as the young are so frequently about their elders.

Jack had written off Father and his affairs as a bad debt. After Jack married and shared a household with his parents-in-law, Father occasionally drove over to see him. Jack would receive him calmly enough, but quickly to disappear up to his music room, having passed Father on to the mother-in-law, who would take him into her semi-basement morning-room, give him a rum-and-egg noggin (all men being utterly feckless, helpless and on the verge of starvation) and engage in a knock-about dialogue that would have put them both at the head of the bill had they conducted it on the music-hall stage, she the sceptic, he the dodger.

Meantime, in those budding years, I went my own way too, dividing my life between the Government Laboratory, that eccentric university where I was so rapidly absorbing a miscellany of conflicting instruction, my daily sessions of reading, my friendship with Bertie Bridge, my excursions to Folkestone, where I enjoyed more and more exquisite suffering at the hands and mocking eyes of the mezzo-soprano.

She was willing to accept my adulation for her voice and my prophecies about her future, but kept me at arm's length when I ventured to minister more intimately, in the only way in which I believed men should handle women, lest they be damaged by the rough contacts of daily life and their fragility shattered.

Tortured by her distrust, enraptured by her voice and occasional moods of affectionate approach, I went to Folkestone whenever I could afford the Sunday excursion fare. Her mother encouraged me. We fully understood each other. I recognised all the familiar qualities in this patient housewife: the gentle, self-sacrificing personality, the fierce undercurrent of protective ambition, the strain of anxiety over the weekly budget, the dim striving after something larger, more civilised, in a way of life that would be more promising for her children. I was treated with a prodigality that probably did me an ill-favour with my mezzo-soprano. I noticed that whenever the mother showed me a particular kindness, the daughter became hesitant, elusive, a Daphne changing into laurel.

My visits to Folkestone, therefore, gave me small happiness, and no assurance of that close association with a woman which my oddly warped nature demanded. Without the tenderness, the revealing secrecy, the infinite surprises of beauty, wildness, and the vagaries between dependence and passionate protectiveness that I had known during the years with my mother, I felt as though the half of my emotional self had been amputated. I stumbled uncertainly in the world of men, chilled by its impersonal relationships, its formality and legalism, its pedantry and lack of quick insight. This demanded a technique I had still to learn.

My reading of poetry, with the close study of words and their precise handling, was too much my own self in action, too male an activity, to fill the gap. Already I had discovered that poetry was something more deep-seated even than emotion. It was a distillation of human feeling through the cooling condenser of language, that frozen history, and pre-history, vast, deep, terrible in its implication, a racial experience tortured and stilled in its roots.

I must seek some comfort about which I could be content to know less, since it was not so closely involved in my destiny, and therefore was less disciplinary and merciless in its demand upon my mind. Music had always served me in this way, and I turned to it now with feverish appeal. It affected me just as instantly and as subtly as all the things, qualities, powers that comprise the world of woman; the dangers and the joys, the element of demonic, primeval force, that logic of the instincts both more and less than rational, that sensual purity which combines worship and appetite.

This craving drew me to an even closer understanding with my brother; but he had less time and attention to give than formerly, and I veered aside, to seek my friend Bertie Bridge. Here was a simpler relationship, and at that stage one more acceptable to my vanity and self-groping. His busy, professional attitude toward music was rather that of the industrious apprentice than of the mystic or the voluptuary. My outpourings about music, a vehemence that was a substitute for love-making, amused him. They also impressed him, for by this time I had, half-consciously, developed a faculty for making other people share my enthusiasms, or at least acquiesce in them. That was why I had gathered a group of men around me in the Custom House, several of whom began to write, one or two to paint, and others to join me in this erotic adventure into music. Six of us shared a season ticket for Henry Wood's seasons of promenade concerts at the Queen's Hall, each member going once a week, the purists such as my colleague Bembridge taking a miniature score of the Bach, Mozart or Beethoven work, in order to see the bones beneath the too seductive flesh.

Sunday after Sunday, I went alone, or occasionally with Jack, to the Bridges' home on Clapham Common, to share that family sweetness and innocence—so heartrendingly reminiscent of our lost home-life—and to listen to chamber music. I learned much. I learned how ingenious and fecund an inventor was Haydn, and what a vast amount Mozart and Beethoven owed to his experiments. Schubert, Schumann and Brahms were intimates of this suburban home, cavalierly treated by Uncle Charlie Bridge, who was not a respecter of idols, and would rap his own favourites, with a sharp tap of his violin bow on the reading desk, if he disapproved of a musical phrase or a resolution which he found abrupt. For him, music was a matter of good manners. That was why he hated Wagner, whose heated outpourings he pronounced to be nothing less than copulating in public. "Always after the women," as he said.

My clandestine attendances at Covent Garden, during rehearsals, were also instructive, though I could not allow myself to become too closely involved. Instinct told me that I must keep my 'mental strife' (as Blake called it) for my own art in the medium of words, a still more demanding vocation, in spite of Schopenhauer's belief that literature is always approximating to music, and is therefore inferior to it. He said this in weariness of mind about his own field of work, the study of meaning. And what words mean, through their etymological roots, brings to their right use, their poetic use, depth beyond depth of historic undertone, so that the utterance of an individual poet can carry these chromatics in a capacity that holds the human race.

At one of these Saturday lunch-hour intrusions into Covent Garden, I suggested to Bertie Bridge that after the performance of *Tosca* that night he should come over on his bicycle, sleep in my rooms (Jack being away for the week-end), and that we should set off early on Sunday morning for Westerham, twenty miles into Kent, and there take Holy Communion in the squat old village church.

I had a particular liking for this church, because of an incident there during boyhood years when Jack and I, on one of our Saturday cycle rides, entered the church, to find the organ console open. What followed, I have described in a book called *Kent*. We left the church, and were about to ride on, when Jack remarked:

"Did you notice the score of Fauré's *Requiem Mass* on the desk?"

I knew what was coming, and I did not reply. "I'd like to try that over. There's nobody about."

So we abandoned our bicycles again, and crept back to the empty church, where all was silent except for the *tick-tock, tick-tack*, of the ancient clock, that occasional shifting of vowel sound serving to make the silence almost visible.

Then Jack switched on the pump, and began to play, while I sat, summer-sleepy, in a pew, listening. I was half-way down the nave, lost in daydream and the welter of beautiful sound. The wooden beams of the roof curved above me, framing the music with their shapely solidity.

Suddenly I was aware that somebody had entered the church, and was tiptoeing toward the pew where I sat cuddled over my own arms, which were clasped round my stomach to prevent it from fluttering too violently under the emotional stress caused by the music. Then the intruder sat down beside me, ignoring my presence. There we were, side by side, listening to my brother's skilful foot-and-hand work. At last it ended, the sadly serene beauty thinning out into echoes round the building, picking up the latent, historical melancholy of the old church, to add to its own.

The vicar looked at me over his clerical collar. "Who is that?" he said, severely.

"My brother," I replied. "He saw the Fauré on the desk and could not resist it." Now I quote from my book on Kent: "Then something happened which I shall never forget. The vicar got up, put his hand on my shoulder, and said very quietly: 'Thank your brother for me, my boy,' and walked out of the church." That escapade, with its happy ending, had endeared the place to me.

Westerham itself, and the Kentish countryside of downland and weald, became more familiar as the years passed, and I was able to explore during summer week-ends, riding out over the Dulwich and Sydenham hills, sometimes with Jack, frequently alone, my mind and body urgent with that sense of impending adventure which stirs in the veins of boy and girl on the brink of adolescence, when every moment is dramatic, and even boredom is a smouldering fire.

Bertie eagerly accepted my suggestion. So I went home in the early afternoon, buying a large smoked haddock at the fishmonger's on Camberwell Green. I prepared the sitting-room to receive my friend. First, I polished Jack's Erard pianoforte. Then I sprinkled a handful of cumin under the rugs, to sweeten the air; and I made up the bed in Jack's room.

There were many hours to wait, and I knew that Bertie would be late, for he had little time-sense. He was always being waylaid by people with a tale to tell, seeking his sympathy or help. And he was so gentle that he could never break away, even from a garrulous stranger. He would listen to the longest and most self-centred story, nodding seriously, murmuring "Yes, yes!", a sweet but absent-minded smile lighting his handsome face, as though he were on the point of apologising for he knew not what. And that would always delay him, so that he came hurrying to every appointment, with yet another anxious smile and a spoken apology that had no bearing whatever on the real cause of the delay.

Knowing that he would not arrive until midnight, I warned my landlady, and told her that I had arranged for him to give a low whistle from the street, the opening bar of Beethoven's Fifth Symphony (hackneyed during World War Two as a Victory sign), so that she and neighbours would not be disturbed. She entered into the conspiracy with characteristic kindness, and said that she would leave a jug of cocoa and milk on the little shelf in the angle of the staircase.

Then I settled down to work, which meant an hour or two at history or French, memorising a list of words, or tackling Browning's *Ring and the Book*, which I was then reading for the first time, having tried and failed to make headway with *Sordello*, in spite of my hero-worship for this poet from Peckham, so near at hand.

The summer day was hot, but I forced myself to read on, because no work would be done next day. At eighteen life was short. Had not Keats died at twenty-five? But I anticipated living on far longer than that, and reaching at least to thirty, Shelley's span. That surely would give me time enough to ensure my immortality! I did not enquire too particularly into

what I meant by immortality. Sufficient that it was a warmth,
a luminosity, burning but unconsuming, its fuel the powerful
poetry which I was yet to write during the coming eleven years.
All must be sacrificed for this purpose. Why, I did not ask
myself. That again was a superb generalisation, a premonition
of sunrise.

I was expecting a letter from Folkestone, and toward the
hour of the last delivery I found my attention wandering from
the noble sentiments of 'The Pope's Book' in Browning's epic
novel. Nausea and nervous pains began to rumble in my
stomach. My head burned, my vision lost the power to focus,
and an irrational anxiety robbed everything else of value.

The postman passed the house. I watched him from my
window where I stood in the bay, with the volume of Browning's poem closed on my forefinger. Shamed by my weakness,
determined not to give way to a sudden desire for sleep consequent upon the emotional exhaustion, I stood myself against
the door, bolt upright, and forced my mind to return to the
Pope's soliloquy.

While I was thus in penitential stance, a gentle knock at the
panel of the door hardly penetrated to my consciousness. The
door slowly opened and I stumbled forward. My landlady's
head peered in. "Whatever . . .?" she said: but she was never
wholly surprised. She took life as it came, and people's idiosyncrasies as a part of this world's unimportance.

"I was on the rack," I said, in explanation.

"I've put the cocoa there, and some marmite sandwiches,"
she said, "so don't go starving."

Midnight came, but not Bertie. The suburban world of
Camberwell closed into its respectable sleep. I looked out from
time to time, emerging from the tiny pool of my reading-lamp
to stand at the window and watch the chalky moonlight on the
roofs. I saw the pallid reflection in a window across the road,
and gradually the full moon passed across one pane, and across
the next. Then it began its artificial waning as it left the
window, and was half-gibbous before Bertie came down the
road, his brakes creaking and rasping in the silence of the night.
I saw the moonlight on his dress-shirt front. He was carrying a

small suitcase across the handlebars, and had ridden in this discomfort from Covent Garden. His hat was on the back of his head, and the moonlight glittered on his hair, changing it to silver and making him venerable. He saw me at the window, and gave the low whistle.

"Here we are, old man," he whispered, as I let him in. His voice quavered, breaking on its own gentleness. It was two o'clock before we went to bed. Three hours later, I got up, heated the pot of cocoa, and roused Bertie. At six we set off, making no sound, though the summer morning had already opened out and Dulwich Village was full of the chorus of bird-song.

We had not slept long enough to feel the usual morning lethargy. A false alertness drove us on, and we pedalled fiercely, knowing that we had to cover the twenty miles to Westerham in two hours, if we were to be in time for eight o'clock Communion.

Nothing is more promissory than early morning in summer, "when half the world a bridegroom is, and half the world a bride". The sunlight comes slanting out of a liquid sky, uncertain, flickering, yet with the pressure of a caress, rousing the colour, the texture, the form of every tree, flower, clod, until these attributes of beauty become more than the human eye can receive, so limited is our power of appreciation. This quality of the morning world is even more elusive than that of evening, when sunset throws a last sulky gesture of passion over earth and sky. The morning light is spiritual by comparison, timid and shy. It hesitates; and in that uncertainty it makes every object seem illusory. Some it magnifies, others it diminishes. It has a virginity in its approach, and comes veiled.

Dulwich Village was touched with this magic as we rode through it that Sunday morning; not even a milkman about. Our tyres made tracks on the dewy macadam, as I noticed when I looked back to point out the creeper hanging like sea-weed over the windows of Beech House.

From the great elm trees on the grass verges of College Road (these remnants of Saxon common grazing ground) song-thrushes and blackbirds shouted in jubilation, though the confused dawn chorus of miscellaneous bird-song had died down. So harmonious was our friendship that Bertie and I had no need to comment on this music, pouring out a broken passacaglia to send us on our way. We merely looked at each other, and by an eye-glance indicated that we were sharing this bounty.

Up Fountains Road and over Sydenham Hill, skirting the water-chute tank in the grounds of the Crystal Palace; down into the depression of Penge; out through the labyrinth of Elmers End, gradually shedding suburbia, and coming to premonitions of the true countryside of Kent, which in 1912 began at the four cross-roads below West Wickham church: on we rode, pedalling against time.

But before tackling the cross-country climb along by-lanes, up past the church and the mansion where Henry VIII slept on his way from Greenwich to Hever Castle, to visit Ann Boleyn, we had to pause for me to recover my wind. I have never been able to keep going on an empty stomach, and without a little food at three-hourly intervals my muscles fall slack, my mind wanders, and moral collapse threatens.

"Is it all right if I eat one of our marmite sandwiches *now*?" I asked of Bertie. This was a doctrinal problem, for we both accepted the principle that no food must be taken before receiving the sacrament of Communion.

The dilemma caused Bertie to wrinkle up his forehead and rest his head on his shoulder; a family habit so marked in his brother, the 'cellist. "Oh," he began, drawing the exclamation out on a long note, bending over it too, as though fingering it on the E-string of his double bass and pulling it forth with the bow, vibrant and resinous, "considering that you're not too strong and inclined to be poorly, old man, I'm sure it will be all right."

Then with characteristic, generous second thought he leaned across his bicycle, and looked closely into my eyes, his own alight with compassion.

"Look here, old boy. I'll tell you what! I'll have one with you, so if there's anything wrong about it . . . you know!"

The one small sandwich acted instantly on my absurdly mercurial constitution. With vitality restored, I mounted my New Hudson, and led the way up into the no-man's-land over the downs, past 'The White Bear', and ultimately to the top of Titsey Hill, where one of the most expansive views in the south of England breaks upon the traveller.

By then I was beginning to tire again, but there was only half an hour before the service began, and I must not eat again. Further, the rest of the way was down Westerham Hill, an easy free-wheel. This we did at such speed that I was stiff with cold when we reached the village, and with trembling hands I leaned my bicycle against the wall of the old inn outside the church gate, at the top of the sloping green. The landlord was up, shaking the doormat and sweeping out the doorway, so we told him of our intention to go in to the service (for which the bell was ringing). We arranged to come to the inn for breakfast.

We entered the church, adding two to the dozen or more of the congregation. There was the organ which years ago, in those remote schooldays, had been the centre of that alarming escapade. I led the way to what I calculated was the pew where the vicar had joined me. I looked guiltily now at the vicar as he came in from the vestry, wearing his surplice, but I could not recall his features. I had been so embarrassed, even frightened, on that other occasion, that I had not dared to look up, half expecting him to hand us over to the police.

This fear of the police is dormant in all people whose childhood has been spent in the streets of large cities. The policeman was the threat, the deterrent, in the background of my days in Battersea. Even now, late in life, I find myself amusedly observing faint recurrences of that fear when I enter a big store, a bank, or any place in which there is a possibility of being accused of felonious intent. I keep my arms rigidly to my sides, my hands in my pockets, finally to escape with a sigh of relief.

Kneeling at the altar rail, I forgot the fast broken by the minor sin of the sandwich eaten at West Wickham. There were larger omissions and commissions to confess: the pride, the vanity of ambition which tempted me to think more of fame than of the work itself; the greed of my passion for the mezzo-soprano, at that moment twenty miles nearer to me than when I was yearning for her, and craving for her unsatisfying letters, on Denmark Hill; my still surviving hostility to my father; and, above all, my mental laziness.

This last was a constant source of shame and mortification. Now that I was in contact with men, and young fellows of my own age, I marvelled at their intellectual vitality. They absorbed knowledge so massively and so permanently: in science, in politics, in the goings-on of daily life. I compared myself with them, and saw a butterfly—not even a respectable honey-bee—flitting from flower to flower, sipping the sweet dews ingrained with pollen-dust, which was no sooner in my system than I exgurgitated it again, but half-digested, in the form of poetry.

Worried by this self-indulgence, this moral slackness, I read Keats's letters and tried to excuse myself by accepting his proposition that the poet moved amongst men, in human society, with a difference; solely as a mirror, his own personality and character nothing but negatives. Keats's wonderful phrase of 'negative capability' for the poet's instincts, intellectual method, the whole bag of tricks comprising his nature with its prophetic claims, its dodging of the queue, its usurping of the laurels, was used by me as an ointment to my wounded conscience.

But this could not disguise the fact that my mental equipment was perfunctory in performance and limited in scope. I wanted to grasp the universe in both hands, to observe it, to master its workings, to relate one detail with another, so that my conclusions on the nature of things could be untainted by the hated dualism, the departmental view of life, which keeps men from a full understanding of each other and of their vast inheritance. Already Spinoza, that divine guide to Wordsworth, as Virgil was to Dante, had drawn me too by a natural affinity.

But, to my chagrin and humiliation, I found that my reason and memory were too feeble to fulfil the vision which my imagination was continuously enlarging. This drawback has dogged me all my life, and still today I find myself working on in ignorance and faith, rather than in knowledge and confidence. The old saying that you can't make a silk purse out of a sow's ear has had to be applied in reverse to my own problem. I have coveted the firm, gristly sow's ear, the massive intellectual equipment of the true scholar, the man of affairs, the powerful legalist, knowing that poetry is a hard vocation, needing the accuracy of the grammarian, the authority and cunning of the statesman, the sense of proportionate order of the judge.

This consciousness of my needs was already alive at that time, lurking like banks of storm-cloud on the horizons of my youth. The misgivings took immediate form in the details of my efforts. I had to fight against this weariness of mind day by day in my unguided studies. I made ambitious schemes of work, with strategic systems of reading to be done, in philosophy, history, and the leeway in mathematics that had to be made up. The *idea* of mathematics filled me with a feverish excitement. I stood at night looking up at the Euclidean order of the stars; I seized on a poem to Number by the French naturalist, J. H. Fabre, its opening lines sticking like the writing on the wall:

"Nombre! Regulateur des effets et des causes,
    Qui me donne le comment et le pourquoi des choses,
    Que me veux-tu, Nombre Imposant?"

It was characteristic of my undisciplined brain that I should seek to know more about this godhead, this 'Word that was in the Beginning', this 'Nombre Imposant', by going not to a textbook of elementary mathematics, but to the *Revelation* of St. John, where the Chaldean fixation upon the number seven was given such picturesque expression.

So, in that eternity of inward strife which rends us during those few moments when we kneel to receive first the bread, and then, another eternity later, the wine, before the altar of conscience and that passionate craving which is the basis of all religious faith, I struggled that morning at Westerham, my friend beside me, active too in his own universe.

As we came out of the church into the sunlight, I found it blinding and hot. Faintness overcame me, and I staggered, groped toward a tombstone, and subsided upon it.

I felt Bertie's arm round me, and heard his gentle, trembling voice saying: "Come along, old man, come along," just as his mother spoke when vainly urging her family to the supper-table between one movement and another of a Haydn quartette, "You want your breakfast, old boy."

Shivering in the heat, I was glad of the support of his arm as I crept into the bar of the inn. I heard the landlord bolt the door behind us, and I accepted the thimbleful of brandy which he brought as a prelude to the substantial breakfast of bacon and eggs, home-made bread and butter, and hot tea which raced into my body like a siege-raising army.

CHAPTER SIXTEEN

Chain-links of Routine

DAYS, WEEKS, MONTHS PASSED, with the uneventfulness of those dangerously quiet years before the First World War, when people moved along the social grooves without questioning. It did not occur to me, for example, to envy the lot of those youths of my own age who were able to give themselves, the whole day long, to study at Cambridge or Oxford. If I thought of them at all, it was as fabulous creatures from another planet, just as I had stared, in boyhood, through the railings of the playing-fields of Dulwich College, at the beings of a larger growth, mentally and physically, than me and my kind.

All that summer my routine went on unbroken; I was up at five o'clock, stupid with sleep but driven by the purpose that burned, like a watchman's dark lantern, within me. A draught of cold water, a lump or two of sugar, roused me sufficiently for me to begin my reading. I made history the keel of my ship of knowledge, being convinced that the historical approach to every field of enquiry was likely to reveal cause and effect, and to give me a sense of proportion.

This I needed to counterbalance the impetuous enthusiasm with which I naturally reacted to experience. Something seen, heard, smelled out of doors; a face or a gesture; a new idea from a textbook; or even the etymology of a word looked up in the dictionary, could turn me from steady intellectual ploughing to an ecstasy of imagination or fancy, and I would stop work, in order to follow this violent impulse, and take it in a net of verse. Then, shame-faced, I returned to my horn-book and the pedestrian task of acquiring the elements of academic scholarship.

At seven o'clock I roused Jack, and we breakfasted, to desultory conversation. School-mastering had already begun to irk him, and his physical idiosyncrasies were more marked than ever. I often studied him covertly as he sat at the kitchen-table in that bare room, as dark and clean-cut as my all-black bicycle against the wall behind him. His nose protruded cliff-like, his eyes were hooded by the discoloured lids, his sensitive mouth articulated through a sardonic pattern of sceptical amusement. He leaned over the table, and I could observe that the thin, silken figure was now smaller than mine. The hands, with their filbert nails, were more fragile and transparent than ever. His distaste for noise, violent demonstrations, every form of crude emphasis, was growing almost into an eccentricity.

Every morning, soon after eight o'clock, we walked over Denmark Hill to Camberwell Green, where we parted, he to Vauxhall, where he was teaching in a slum-school, I to the 'Elephant and Castle'. I would watch him: the fastidious, in-drawn figure, deliberate and grave, picking its way in a crude, over-fecund world. A spasm of fear sometimes gripped me. He seemed always to be departing momentously, on a long journey; not just going off to his day's work.

Having fought my way on to the tram, I resumed my read-ing, usually something that had to be memorised, a stanza from *The Faerie Queene*, or a list of the new words encountered in yesterday's reading, or another fable by La Fontaine.

The day in the Custom House was coloured by the company there. I sat at my desk in the largest of the laboratories, sur-rounded by leather-bound registers into which I entered the results of analysis of samples of tea, coffee, cocoa, chocolates. I helped the analysts to lay out hundreds of little sample-tins of tea, each with a tiny cup and lid before it, into which we put a pinch of tea, then poured boiling water on it.

All this mechanical work I did indifferently, my mind else-where. Often I sat dreaming, or composing verses to be written down later, while round me the murmur of conversation flowed; the musical tinkle of liquids leaping in the flasks over Bunsen flames, distilling through condensers; the tiny roar of a muffle-furnace; a sudden, exquisite assailing of the senses as an essential oil, jasmine or attar of roses, was being tested;

all these externals congealed around me like amber round a bee.

I received much encouragement there, some of it unacceptable because too astringent. There was a division of opinion about me. One half of the staff thought I was in need of discipline, and that I should be broken in to the stoical team-spirit of the Service, and forced to study for an examination to take me to higher rank and salary—the Customs and Excise, or the Second Division. The other half treated me as an exotic, a special case, who had to be shielded from the harsh winds of reality, which blew unintermittently through Billingsgate, Eastcheap, and Tower Hill. Toward the end of my nine years at the Laboratory the latter school of thought prevailed, and I was thoroughly spoiled.

Even the Superintending Analyst, a formidable figure of angry mien, dreadful in his morning-coat, who sometimes walked through the rooms, his hands clasped under his tails, his eyes cold and magnified behind huge gold-rimmed spectacles—even this fierce inquisitor relented, forgave my inattentive half-service, my imbecile mistakes, and was known to enquire after my bouts of sickness, or to encourage me with the gift of a book. As for his Mephistophelian Deputy, this personality, who at first had terrified me by his dragon-fly dartings round the Laboratory, quickly began to show an interest in my literary progress.

My immediate chief in the Tea Laboratory was a middle-aged analyst with a nervous awe toward authority. When the bell from the Superintending Analyst's sanctum rang, to summon him into the presence, his bald head immediately began to steam, and his eyes and cheeks to be suffused with a moisture which he had to subdue with a handkerchief, while he gathered up the papers and material which he knew would be needed. For he always was prepared for criticism, or other official 'trouble', and worked to forestall it.

Another analyst in the Tea Laboratory interested me because he came from Stratford-on-Avon. He was a short, plump, square-headed chemist, wholly sceptical, derisive, and disillusioned by life. One of his aphorisms was that "all women

are the same from the neck downwards". He had no use even
for his immortal fellow-townsman. Yet he befriended me, in a
fatherly way, and once gave me a set of Victorian miniature
volumes of poetry, printed in diamond-size type, the little silk-
bound books three and a half by two inches: Milton, Wordsworth, Scott and Tom Hood.

At infrequent intervals a tiny bearded man, dressed as a
Customs Watcher in plain uniform and peaked cap, appeared
in the Laboratory from the vast floors below. He sold books at
cost price. I was soon singled out, and one by one I bought the
Oxford editions of the English poets. Sometimes he would
place a book on my desk and whisper that it had already been
paid for "by some of the gentlemen", a generalising phrase that
covered both my embarrassment and my gratitude.

At four o'clock I left the Laboratory, my fibre case heavy
with its load of books and nourishing samples of black treacle,
or condensed milk, or a sadly jostled *vin ordinaire*. I was not
aware that I was smuggling contraband into the country. Had
I been arrested, with a punctured tin of full-cream milk or half
a packet of Lindt & Springli's chocolate in my bag, I might
have pleaded, "Thou shalt not muzzle the ox that treads the
corn," though this bovine plea from a youth weighing under
eight stone, his neck resembling a stick of washed celery, might
have been unconvincing.

My light weight was an advantage, however, in aiding me to
get home with the speed of Ariel. Having floated down those
sinister flights of stone stairs in the Custom House, I abandoned
myself, in the empty well-flushed Market, to the free air. I felt
myself being picked up by the force of my own mental excitement and carried along past mere pedestrians. Up by the
Monument, my bag banging against my thighs, over London
Bridge, past Chaucer's 'Tabard Inn' to St. George's Church or
the 'Elephant and Castle', I was borne at the speed of an owl
gliding over stubble and hedgerow, unheard music and a sense
of glory following me and preceding me, lighting up Newington
Butts. The young Coleridge, 'swimming the Hellespont' along
Fleet Street, could not have been more realistically propelled
than I. I was on my way to another session with the masters at

whose feet I now sat, but with whom, before I matured and ceased round about the age of thirty, I was determined to fraternise on an equal footing.

One hot summer afternoon, after a day of fierce internal excitement at the Laboratory, sitting at my desk amid the familiar sounds, pondering over the symbolism and beauty of Plato's *Banquet*, I was accompanied to the 'Elephant' by an Exciseman, a gigantic, red-haired Welshman from Fishguard, fierce and blasphemous of speech. He strode out like a Viking, and I had to keep pace, but it seemed slow and irksome to me, who could not indulge in my secret method of flight, learned from the winged creatures of Parnassus.

The conflict of these two speeds must have had a grinding effect on my internal organs, as of a motor-car gear being clumsily changed. Suddenly, half-way across London Bridge, I felt a wave of heat flood over my brain, rising up from stomach and chest. I stumbled against my companion, and knew no more, until I found myself standing shakily, at the 'Elephant and Castle', with the giant Welshman's arm round me. He had picked me up and carried me for half a mile through Newington Butts.

"Now, young bugger," he said, handing my case to me brusquely, "you'll have to fend for yourself, for I go off to Wandsworth!"

He waited awhile, for me to assure him that I was back to normal, and he hoisted me on to a tram, with a hand that covered my shoulder-blades. I made my way home, trembling and mentally deflated. The sense of exalted anticipation, by which I habitually lived from moment to moment, had collapsed like a pricked balloon.

I crept up the stairs, and into the kitchen. The house was dead; everybody out. Despair gripped me. I stood by the table, one hand on the saddle of my bicycle, fighting this black mood.

Then I heard a small sound amongst the paper and kitchen rubbish in the kettle-shaped coal-scuttle. I stared, my heart beating, and saw a beady eye. A mouse was moving round and round, alarmed by my coming. Its impotence was too like my own. Rage seized me; I snatched the poker, and with the knob-end beat the poor little mortal to death.

The silence of the empty house closed round me again, after the din I had raised. I was sweating violently, the salty beads running into my eyes and over my lips. I found myself praying, wordlessly, dumb with horror. This was the end of my day at Plato's *Banquet*, and the fall was too much.

I forced myself to grope amongst the rubbish in the scuttle. I picked up the mouse in the tongs and carried it to the W.C., and, having thus disposed of it, I was violently sick.

After this expiation, I lay on my bed, shivering in the hot room, until Jack appeared.

"Idiot!" he said. "What have you been eating? And you didn't see the letters on the mat. There's one for you." He handed it to me, saying that he would make a pot of tea, and that I had better not work that evening. He was staying at home, so we would have some music.

The letter was from Bertie Bridge, to tell me that next week at the end of the Covent Garden season he was going with a small orchestra to play at Folkestone, in one of the big hotels, until the end of the summer. He suggested that I should take a few days' leave and spend them there, as he would be free for most of the day.

The mere idea revived me, and after an hour's sleep I got up and joined my brother. Our landlord and landlady still being out, we settled down at the Erard, with a volume of Robert Volkmann's pianoforte duets. I struggled at the bass, my hands still not fully under control, and my stomach rumbling and throbbing with the pains which I had almost forgotten, so long ago was the childhood which they had overshadowed.

CHAPTER SEVENTEEN

The Embarkation for Cythera

I COULD NOT GET a week's leave until the end of August, and the intervening dog-days dragged slowly, partly because I continued to feel physically exhausted, partly because I was looking forward so eagerly to joining my mezzo-soprano, and introducing that gifted voice to my friend Bertie Bridge. He might share my enthusiasm and be able to help her toward a professional start, in a wider field than the small-town musical circle of Folkestone, where she did nothing but teach children the rudiments of pianoforte-playing (being herself hardly more than a beginner) and singing at local conversaziones.

Circumstances forestalled me, for Bertie had not been at Folkestone for more than a week when I had a letter from him, to tell me that he had met my paragon, and shared my belief in her future. She had sung at the hotel, and had handled 'An Old English Love Song', by Francis Allitsen, with real musical understanding. He was not sure that she might be trained at present as an operatic singer, because he suspected that her voice would deepen into contralto as she matured to womanhood.

I was exalted by this confirmation of my judgment. My demands from the arts, and from their practitioners, were by now becoming more boldly defined. I hated obscurity, confusion, muddle. I was beginning even to question Browning's difficult verse, no longer wholly blaming myself, my narrow wits and ignorance, for my inability to understand much of it. Francis Thompson, at the height of poetic fashion in 1912, was also one of my principal intoxicants. But now I found the poems of his master Coventry Patmore, and the suspicion cooled my mind that this poet of a more sedate idiom might be the greater of the two.

Simplicity began to attract me as the highest aim of all

artists, in every medium: cleanness of line, firmness of structure. But I could not relinquish the grandeurs. I read the letters of Hector Berlioz, and the two-volume autobiography of Wagner (which I had bought second-hand, to give to Jack for a wedding present, in addition to a life of Michelangelo), and I rolled myself like a drunken god on the luminous clouds of their theories and billowing self-confidence. Yet I was turning from Coleridge to Wordsworth, and finding myself in company more of my own kind. Directness of statement, in language, stone or pencil, now struck me into awe-inspired recognition, as the quality which I must seek to command. It would be my purpose to write poems deceptively simple, in which the depth and universality of feeling and thought would be almost naively expressed, as in folksong, and therefore diamond-hard, as unforgettable as the form was unfashionable.

I was innocently unaware of the formidable task to which I had set myself, and how unwelcome candour of statement can be to fashionable critics who thrive upon the vanities of experimental and often meretricious forms. I was already veering away from the artistic tendencies of the age, the revolt against tradition and historical roots, which were to dominate the first half of the twentieth century, as a reflection of the social, moral and political break-up of the structure of the human family throughout the world.

I was not even aware of these tendencies at that time, for it was not until a year later, during the period of desperate loneliness following Jack's marriage, that I found the French Symbolist poets, and the English Imagist group, to recognise with some dismay that I was destined to plough a lonely furrow of my own, which would be kicked aside as out of line, by the pundits. But I went my own way.

My landlord at this time gave me a copy of Chapman's Homer, of which I knew only through Keats's sonnet. I read it just a century later than that prodigious boy, and was likewise transported to "the realms of gold" where "a new planet swam into my ken". Here was an art wholly unself-conscious, muscular, supple, ready for all human, and indeed superhuman, purposes.

My landlord also lent me a little book of verses by W. H. Davies, at that time still sensationally stigmatised as 'the Tramp Poet' because he had been a hobo in America, and had published his first book from a doss-house in Lambeth. Other than Yeats and Masefield, Davies was the only contemporary poet whose work I found, and it delighted me by its simplicity. I saw that this book, called *Nature Poems* (a sad misnomer), was published by one A. C. Fifield at 13 Cliffords Inn in London, where formerly Samuel Butler had lived in chambers.

If Davies could put out a collection of songs, why could not I? Within a few days I poured out some fifty poems from the top of my cornucopia, and sent them to this Mr. A. C. Fifield. I did not even tell Jack about this, for I knew what his comment would be.

Jack came to Charing Cross to see me off to Folkestone. The late summer weather was set fair, and we stood on the platform looking up-river at the blaze of light on the water. The world was on fire. It lit up even the hollow caverns of my brother's personality. I looked down at him from the railway carriage. He was smiling grimly, for once at peace with noisy humanity. He wore a new tweed hat, and had a woodland look. But no matter how countrified his clothes, he gave the impression of being concise, scrupulously groomed, fastidious. And there was, too, a touch of frailty about him.

I saw then, as I had noticed suddenly only a few months before, that this frailty was more pronounced of late. He was burning himself like a torch, in his exploration of the lover's road toward marriage. What he hoped to find I dared not conjecture; I could not, for my own ignorance and eagerness were almost as great as his, though his goal was fixed and mine uncertain. "Good-bye," he said, as the train began to move. "Don't commit yourself. Don't let yourself be cheated."

He stood near the water-crane, at the end of the platform, his features fixed in a nervous spasm of affection, his thin hand raised with the fingers stretched, close and shapely, as though he were hushing an orchestra to a pianissimo. I watched him grow smaller, and saw him as a concentration of all my earlier life, the close family love, the loss of Mother, the defection of

Father, the new and terrible freemasonry of the arts into which this obstinate pioneer, my monitor, had led the way.

Then he was gone, and I closed the carriage window, sinking back on the seat, unaccountably sad, to face the joyous days ahead.

I had written to the little house under the arch of the viaduct, to bespeak a room, and to ask Maudie to meet me at Folkestone Station. The anticipation of this coming together, after weeks of unsatisfactory correspondence (most of it mine), made me restless, and I could not read. Nor could I enjoy, as usual, the scene of the Kentish countryside; the North Downs, the patchwork of the Weald, the woods, orchards and hop gardens, these last already coloured with pickers, who looked up from their bins to wave at the passing train. The serenity of mind, the interested detachment, toward which my studies and my instinct directed me, were broken like the surface of a pond into which a stone is flung.

I was not unhappy. Indeed, I pictured the warm, nightingale-throated mezzo-soprano waiting for me at the end of the journey, and a pulse of joy beat in my temples, making my head ache by its violence.

By the time the train drew into Folkestone Station, my eagerness had driven me out of the compartment into the corridor, where I stood, holding my body down to the floor by an effort of will. I dared not breathe, lest an anxious inhalation should lift me. The platform approached, slid alongside the train, and my eyes tried to single out the one figure amongst the crowd.

She was not there. The train stopped, doors opened, voices broke into the music of greeting and welcome, and I stepped down alone into the indifferent multitude. Chilled by misgiving, I looked around once more, but the difficulty of finding her from within the tumult made me give up.

Not daring, for the moment, to wonder why she had not come, I passed through the wicket, still searching incredulously, the rhythm of disappointment beating up through my heels as I trod the ground, thudding in my brain.

I left the station, to find dusk settling over the happy little seaside town. The last light touched the flower-beds at the

junction of roads, and the blooms burned with a sombre introspection that caught even my distracted eye. Then two
shadowy figures approached, and before I could fully recognise
them I knew who they were. Maudie walked with that lighter-
than-air motion, part of the qualities of her voice, which gave
her girlishness an almost inappropriate manner, an authority, a
distinction which led one to expect too much from her. I heard
her laugh, and the familiarity of that deep-throated gaiety,
a kind of animal immediacy, took me too by the throat. I
stood still, waiting for it to mean more than it possibly could
mean.

The other figure was Bertie Bridge. They had come together
to meet me, in a conjunction of friendship. The warmth of it,
following the chill of disappointment, flooded over me, and I
stood irresolute, waiting for them, unable to speak, my bag on
the pavement in front of me.

"There you are, old man," said Bertie, his voice trembling as
usual. "You've got here safely."

"He hasn't come from the North Pole," laughed Maudie.

I detected a coldness not only in the idea, but in the way she
spoke. She was critical of me, though it was not I who had
suggested that the journey might have been long or arduous.
But she relented, and I found myself walking between them,
she taking my arm with an ingratiating display of affection,
somewhat overdoing it, leaning forward and examining my
features, laughing into my eyes, over-excited, pouring out a
flood of questions to which she wanted, and expected, no
answer.

Bertie insisted on carrying my bag.

"I'm used to lumping a big instrument about," he said.
"Besides, you're looking a bit done up, old man."

His solicitude was characteristic; but just a little more emphasised than usual.

I walked between them, finding little to say. My silence
must have chilled the air, for Maudie suddenly shivered, and
withdrew her arm from mine. Bertie leaned forward, speaking
across me. "Are you cold, Maudie? Wrap your throat up,
now, my dear."

Maudie obeyed, tucking a gauzy scarf closer round her full neck and bust.

"Oh dear, why are we so gloomy?" she said. "Won't somebody say something?"

"What would you like us to say?" I replied.

The rest of the holiday proved to be cross-grained. Triangles are conspicuous by their sharp points. I found myself frequently alone, a familiar state, but not what I had anticipated during this week of release from my routine habits. In the company either of Bertie or Maudie, I found them absent-minded, distrait. Bertie was incapable of being cruel, and he tried hard to make me enjoy myself. His effort was the most unkind cut of all.

We spent the mornings together, while Maudie was giving piano lessons to local urchins. I met Bertie after the first session of his quartette, at the gates of the huge hotel. One afternoon he introduced me to Mr. Ketelbey, the composer of 'In a Monastery Garden', and we stood at the bar in a public-house, drinking tankards of beer, while I listened to musical shop-talk, in the course of which Mr. Ketelbey frequently tapped my friend on the shirt-front with a massive forefinger and addressed him as 'Bertie, my boy'. It was most impressive, and healthily down-to-earth. I was to find it typical of the conversation of professional musicians, a matter-of-fact brotherhood. One of Bertie's colleagues, perhaps the most distinguished bass-player in the country, appeared to have no interest in anything except the small cutter which he kept on the Thames, and to which he devoted a celibate love.

I was interested—for who but a mental invalid can be bored in this perpetually astounding world?—but I had the sensation of taking part in a game of blind man's buff. The marvels and rewards of the holiday began to shrink. Even the whisper of the tide on the shingle below the Leas lost some of its fairyland illimitability. I sat for hours at a time listening to it, but the rhythm had lost its magic. I was restless, disturbed.

Then, on the Saturday, the first of a September heatwave, we set off for a boating picnic on the Hythe Military Canal; Maudie and her elder sister, Bertie and I. We carried a wicker hamper of food in the manner of *Three Men in a Boat*. I wore a blazer and a straw hat. Bertie was elegant as usual, in his little black bow-tie, white shirt (ready for quick-change into evening uniform) and his large-lapelled coat. His auburn hair rebelled against all headgear, so that hats always receded to the back of his head. The girls wore filmy home-made frocks, and wide-brimmed hats trimmed with scarves, an outfit that gave them the appearance of water-colour sketches by Sargent or Strang, rather than of flesh-and-blood young women. But they were real enough, with their warmth enhanced by the fumes of eau-de-Cologne.

We started off from the end of the canal, pulling out from the tree-shaded boat-house into the sunlight, which hit the girls' white dresses and nearly blinded the oarsmen. A long day lay before us. There was no need to hurry, for we had been told by the boat-keeper that the canal was silting up with weed and neglect, and that we should not be able to reach more than a few miles westward toward Romney.

Even so, I began to pull vigorously, urged on by a perverse demon. I was frightened. The fear had been looming up, darker and darker, all the week. I was struggling against a storm, a new experience so violent, unexpected and complex that my confidence was threatened. I had been through the break-up of our home. I had seen Father and Jack fasten themselves to other loyalties. A year at the Custom House, under the team-discipline of the Civil Service and the semi-satiric interest of older colleagues, had given me an inkling of the ways of the world. I was no longer sure of my concise, book-made certainties, and had already begun to suspect abstract principles and theories, and the words that expressed them. But I had not hitherto lost my confidence in my steersmanship. The universe hitherto had been a boat with my hand at the helm.

The story of any individual's disillusionment about the fantasies surrounding youth is of small interest to other people. It is of the same kind as fishermen's tales, and war-time bomb-stories, heavily discountable and only too familiar. But it is real enough. It is as real as Dante's *Divine Comedy*, with its dreadful disclosures of hell, its uncertain purgatories, its elusive and in-expressible moments of heavenly revelation.

That glorious morning on the Hythe Military Canal, I was rowing the boat toward hell. It would be morbid to try to describe that hell. There is no question of degree in the recog-nition of wickedness in one's own heart. Pride comes tumbling down with Satanic grandeur—Milton's Satan. I could not believe in this murder within myself. It was too fierce, too destructive of every value which my life had hitherto built up under the shelter of my home, my family, my reading. I had but lately entered the serene estate of Spinoza and Words-worth, the philosopher and his poet of compassion working always toward unity; a true universe. I was on the threshold of that recognition, which was to give my whole life a firmness and balance. I was indeed already assuring myself that a poet must have an anchorage in the harbour of a philosopher whose system is healthily protective of his particular creative impulse. Such schemes of life and work, in their gradual deployment, have to be based on moral mood as much as on thought or con-sciousness. They are climatic, founded on the weather of the soul, the trade winds of compassion, sensitive recognitions, deep, gentle currents of understanding.

Now here was I, with one scull for murder, the other for hatred, rowing the holiday boat toward destruction.

None heeded the danger. The elder sister sat with a hand skimming the water, a bracelet of green water-weed gathering round her white wrist. She was lost in a pretended soliloquy, gazing into the distance over my head, to the wooded slopes that fell toward the marsh, from Appledore to Romney, once a sea-coast and now an inland rampart, overlooking flocks of sheep instead of fleets of ships, a dream back-cloth to a dream stage.

Bertie, rowing stroke, sat with his back to me. He was an un-trained oarsman, and at last I had to suggest that he might do better to ship his sculls and leave the job to me. He assented with the greatest good-humour, and proposed that he should hum the accompaniment of Schubert's boat-song, '*Auf dem Wasser*', while Maudie sang the melody. It appeared that he had taken her repertoire in hand, replacing such pieces as 'Because', 'Kashmiri Song', and 'Two Eyes of Grey', by *lieder* chosen to draw out and confirm the quality of Maudie's singing voice.

I stopped rowing as she sang. I leaned over the sculls, my head heavy with the tumult of this conflict. Bertie beat time with one hand, his blunt-ended fingers flashing in the sun. His humming accompaniment was so deep-toned that the sides of the boat vibrated. The blue sky above us, with a dappled cloudlet here and there; the sleeping hills to the north, and the sleeping pastures around us; the green willows posting the canal, shuddering under the heat of the sunlight; Maudie's pure voice, effortless and ravishing; and death, and hatred, and murder in my heart.

Within that eternity I fought my battle. It is impossible to express the horror with which I observed this second overthrow of my world. For two years I had been at work, building up from the ruins after Mother's death. I had survived that, and its consequences, gaining day by day some insight into my own consciousness, and testing that tiny increase of authority against the widening experiences that poured into my life, from people, places, the arts, and the mysterious concretions that follow after the processes of thought, ceaseless demonstrations of the way in which all life, all substance began.

This had been the reward of merely being alive and young, part of the wonder of the commonplace, the signature of a Creator toward whom I was beginning to look with certainty, as my Master in life and the poetry that must be its clean mirror and epitomiser; concave, reductive, and therefore clarifying.

But to achieve this relationship—a logical advance upon that childhood vision of Christ which had carried me through sickness, pain, and the wild ecstasies of my early reading and contemplation, while in Battersea and Dulwich—I had learned that stillness of mind, calmness of spirit, must be found, and held.

It had been a gradual recognition: but now, at the age of nineteen, approaching manhood, I was constantly and clearly aware of this necessity, and determined to fulfil it. How could I possibly know what I was undertaking, or how little I had yet under my command?

At that moment, leaning over the sculls in the boat, pressing their butts into my chest in order to add to my torture, a counter to the pain within, I was breaking through to a further, a deeper realisation.

For two years I had made this girl, this lovely voice so appropriately embodied in sweet flesh and blood, the symbol of my aims and faith. I had tried to tell her so, not only by words, but by touch, expressive silences, intimacies almost occult in their penetrative suggestion. It had come to nothing. She had responded hesitantly, and her mother had tried to break down her reluctance, but she had always been afraid. She continued to look upon me as 'an old doctor', as she had said at the beginning.

And now I could see what was happening.

> "Soon as she was gone from me,
> A traveller came by,
> Silently, invisibly;
> He took her with a sigh."

The melody of Schubert's song floated out from that powerful throat. I glanced up, out of the Pit, and saw the smooth muscles of her neck, the perfect teeth and the moulding of her mouth. Then I dropped my gaze again, for I had seen something else, something to accuse me. She was looking into Bertie's eyes, with adoration. She was singing to him, and under his instructing guidance.

I had to recognise his handiwork. Within a few weeks he had brought out the latent qualities of her voice. I had detected them two years ago, but all my theorising, my worship and caressive persuasion had failed. His was the master's hand, and his the true love. I had to acknowledge both, before that day was over.

The purity and simplicity of Maudie's singing finally roused me from the despair and self-pity into which I had fallen. Still in that eternity while the boat slowly came to rest among the water-weeds, and while I leaned over my sculls, my head bowed, I passed round the circles of that inward hell, the hatred, the shame, the embrace of murder. From one after another I extricated myself, mandrake-wise, tearing myself up by the roots from this horror, acknowledging that the betrayal was in me, not in the lovers.

Then, in a flash of insight such as I felt in childhood, one winter morning at Broadstairs, while watching the sunrise from a window in the sanatorium, I saw a new power fall into my possession. It was absolute, unequivocal. It was a presence, almost a person. It must control my life henceforth, so far as I was able to follow it.

I knew, with final conviction, that self-interest must be destroyed, cast out of my world. Unless I did that, my dream of the triumph of poetry, the summing up and the unification of this art, the most exalted of all the arts, would never be fulfilled. "Christ is work, Christ is work," I found myself murmuring silently. And I half-knew what I meant; the weakness of vanity, the folly of seeking applause, the self-mutilation through a concern for fame and one's own appetite.

I knew, in that incandescent moment, that no creative work could be complete, and wholly satisfactory, unless it were sacrificial, a form of prayer, moulded joyfully out of pain as well as pleasure. The artist, too, must be a Franciscan, his poverty his only riches.

The song ended, and Bertie's hand dropped to the gunwale. He turned to look at me, and I saw the happiness in his eyes. He was about to speak, but stopped. The blood mounted to his cheeks, and his eyes clouded with trouble. Silence fell over us all.

In that pause, that break in the continuity of things, my mind flew back to a boyhood scene: Father confronting me with his refusal to let me take up the Art Scholarship. I stared, with renewed horror, at the bread-knife, and at the cruel blade of my anger.

"Richard has stopped rowing," cried Maudie, her speaking voice bubbled with laughter.

I dipped the sculls, and forced the boat again through the weed-clogged water of the canal.

CHAPTER EIGHTEEN

Approaching the Main Road

AFTER THE HOLIDAY, I was faced with the problem of fulfilling my resolution. The dream must be made to come true. I set about the task of rationalising it, and further planning my mode of life to make the discipline a practicable routine. I had not been home for a week before I had a letter from Bertie Bridge announcing his engagement to Maudie. She did not write.

I was now in a state of emotional numbness, going about the motions of living like a skater gliding mechanically, his mind asleep. The ice on which I moved was my own frozen despair.

Jack was observing me. He continued to get me invited frequently 'over the hill', and I saw more of my future sister-in-law, and of her mother, whose prescription of duck-eggs and heavy puddings was redoubled as a medicine for what she called 'the dumps'.

"I never saw such a pair of brothers," she cried. "The two of you, going about like undertakers! Boys of your age ought to be sweethearting!"

I could not explain how that was precisely the trouble.

The news of Bertie's engagement reached London. Jack said little, but pursued his policy of seeking to fill my leisure hours with music. He added to my books, so far as he could afford to, and took me to several concerts and recitals during that autumn and winter. Returning one night from the Bechstein Hall (now called the Wigmore Hall), where we had listened to a Beethoven recital by Frederick Lamond, Jack abruptly asked me why I was not working. I replied that I had been stocktaking, and that this job had somewhat disordered the furniture of my mind. He walked beside me, silent again, his mouth set grimly, the great nose jutting out every time we passed beneath a street lamp.

"You know," he said at last, "you're well out of that entanglement. You'll recognise I'm right, when you've cooled down a bit. One or two of us believe in you already. But you won't go far if you're tied by the leg."

I accepted this unexpected compliment demurely. Praise from Jack was usually followed by a detailed criticism that rattled like grape-shot against the armour of complacence. I waited for it now, but it didn't come. He may have thought that I had taken enough punishment of late. He was also concerned about leaving me to carry on alone at the flat. We had arranged to give up one room, and for me to pay eight shillings a week for the remaining three: the sitting-room, my small bedroom and the kitchen. During those last months before his marriage, while I was sunk in this lethargy of spirit, Jack devoted himself to me with all the old admonitory affection that had enriched the early years.

"Keep yourself free from now on," he said, pressing his argument home. "And another thing: don't turn down the Old Man altogether. I'm beginning to be sorry for him."

He would say no more, and retreated into his habitual shyness over personal matters.

That winter passed, and another Christmas Day was spent at Father's half-recognisable home at Putney Bridge. Again Jack and I lifted that polished brass knocker, and again the elder daughter, even more handsome and statuesque than she was a year earlier, opened the door to us, grimly ushering us in. I studied her face, the moulded chin and full mouth, the heavy brows, and saw a firmer delineation of character there. Here was a person wholly incapable of dissimulation, or even diplomacy. I was certain she would call a spade a spade. So far as Father was concerned, she would be prepared to attack him with it should he attempt any of his sentimental approaches. In the course of the day, Jack and I saw her raise that spade threateningly, as though her patience and good nature were at last being tried beyond endurance. Her training, and perhaps her regard for the two somewhat exotic visitors who were yet not quite visitors, restrained her. Once I thought she was about to appeal to me after a sly and half-sarcastic barb from Father had stung her.

"Thank God," said Jack, when we left. "Another year's respite."

I was not prepared to agree with him in his hostility toward both mother and daughter. I believed Father was trying to manipulate them to suit his own way of life, behaving like a cuckoo in the nest. I appreciated the candour and simplicity of the daughter's character, and respected her courage. I could see that Father was determined to get her out of the home, or at least out of the authoritative position of housekeeper. Several times during the Christmas festivities he had spoken about "a wife's duties in the home". His congenital obstinacy was being prodded. Mother had known how to circumvent it, but now nobody was willing to take that trouble. Life was trying him sorely.

Soon after the New Year, my bundle of poems came back from the publisher, A. C. Fifield. His covering letter told me that W. H. Davies was unique because his little books of verse sold profitably. Mine would be stillborn. He added, however, some encouraging words about the promise I showed as a writer, and that in two or three years' time he would like to see what I might have to offer.

I was not greatly deterred by this lukewarm response to my first effort at publishing a book. Another four years' practice, resulting mainly in trial and error, was to follow before I was successful. The courage of young people is remarkable. Empty-handed they choose a career and set out on it; ignorant, un-trained, naïve. They have no conception of the distance to be travelled, and the complications, pitfalls, *longeurs* that will lead them astray, or bring them to a halt. Yet on they go, armed with regal illusions and *folies de grandeur*, entering where sophisti-cated old professional angels fear to tread. Without that un-justifiable self-confidence, they would never be able to start, and therefore it must be accounted a virtue, as valuable to them as their youthful muscles and physical organs.

One spring day in 1913, a young Excise officer in the

Laboratory, who was studying for an external Arts degree at King's College, suggested that I might profitably come with him one evening to hear a lecture by the Professor of English. He said that Israel Gollancz was a most inspiring guide.

This lad, named Barbour, had come up from his home in Exeter, and lived in lodgings, as did most of these unattached Excise officers during their first years in the Service. Their régime had to be austere, for after the landladies were paid, week by week, very little remained for clothes, meals out, and minor dissipation. Barbour was working hard to take a degree in English, and his health suffered. He was tall, bony, with a lantern face under reddish hair; a quiet, friendly fellow who attached himself to me personally rather than to the group which had become a kind of literary coterie in the Custom House Club.

Barbour had a will of iron. He appeared one day at the Laboratory with the side of his face black with bruised flesh. It was caused by violent neuralgia. He must have suffered acutely; but he had done his four hours' study the night before, cramming away at that monotonous poem, *Beowulf*, and the barbaric tongue, Anglo-Saxon, which for no sane reason is still a compulsory subject in the English Degree course. He died at twenty-one, and I mourned him, for he was an example of integrity and moral courage. I inherited his Anglo-Saxon grammar and copy of *Beowulf*, and I look upon them as I would regard the reliquary hair-shirt of a saint.

As Barbour had proposed smuggling me into the lecture theatre at King's College, I felt no compunction. I went with him once, and heard Israel Gollancz lecture on *The Faerie Queene*, a poem which had been my quarry since I first began to read verse five years earlier. I knew instantly what he was talking about; but I had never before heard such public eloquence over things sacred to me. "This grand cathedral," he cried, raising his arms to the tiers of the amphitheatre crowded with evening students, his pince-nez on the end of his Old Testament nose, his dark eyes glistening with literary unction, his voice thick and ripe. "This vast cathedral . . ."

How could I keep away? And how was I to find out the

legitimate means for attending these wonderful lectures? I had no sense, or even consciousness, of social and official procedure, in the academic or any other world. If I saw a thing, a course of action, a personality that appealed to me as being supreme, I went to it as a moth to a candle-flame. Again and again I accompanied Barbour to King's College, leaving the Laboratory at four o'clock, walking beside my loose-limbed companion through Cannon Street, down Ludgate Hill, up Fleet Street to the Strand, stopping at an A.B.C. for a cup of tea and a bun, and sometimes breaking the journey to spend ten minutes in St. Paul's where evensong was in progress, and the sexless soprano voices of the choir-boys rose, disembodiments of the semi-transparent figures from the paintings of Fra Angelico.

I expounded to Barbour on the way, for he was a silent scholar, and I had much to say, still not having learned to curb my tongue or to take regard of how my words might be received and remembered, for or more probably against me. So I would arrive at King's College, already half-exhausted by the passion of my own oratory, there to be recharged like an electric battery from the main of Israel Gollancz's professional but still perfervid love of literature.

The end of term approached, after a study of Milton's *Paradise Lost*. The Professor set the students a task. He wanted them to write a sonnet in the manner and form of Milton, in which the poet debated in mid-life what path he should take, poetry or politics.

I pondered on this. It was my own problem, writ larger. I had chosen poetry, compromising by being content with a mere bread and a thin scraping of butter job in the Civil Service, assured that I should never need more of this world's goods.

It was impossible, however, for me to submit a sonnet, for I had no right to attend the lectures. Misgivings at last assailed me, and the old fear of the police revived. I told Barbour of this apprehension, but he merely grinned and told me to attack the task nevertheless, just as a bit of practice.

I needed little urging, and during one somnolent afternoon, when the laboratories were warm with the flare of Bunsen burners, I fled along the corridor to the two-compartment water-closet adjoining the wash-house where the Watchers cleaned the apparatus used by the chemists.

These were not like the modern, hygienic water-closets. They had a Georgian mode. The whole back of the compartment was seated with mahogany, and the pan was revealed only by lifting this wide seat. The flush was worked by pulling up a handle from a brass half-sphere let into the woodwork surrounding the pan.

With the mahogany seat down, and thus giving me a sense of ruddy luxury, I sat with my legs up (for verse-composition always affects my stomach, causing a kind of cramp round the diaphragm), I pulled off a piece of lavatory paper, and wrote on the unglazed side, with a blue grease-pencil used for marking on glass beakers, the following sonnet, to be ascribed to Milton:

> "I see, O Lord, my years divided twain,
>   And know not of which course to take, for each
>   Is set with flowers of love austere, that reach
>   With fulfilled blossoms up to heaven's plain.
>   Shall I for Cæsar labour, mine own gain
>   To seek within the Senate, where with speech
>   And counsel long-considered I may teach
>   The many-headed monster to retain
>   Me as its monitor? Or shall I rise
>   To that remoter aim of my first years,
>   Ambition lordlier, but truly mine,
>   To sing of Man expelled from Paradise?
>   Mine eyes refuse; I am beset with fears:
>   So judge Thou, Lord, Thy wisdom is divine!"

I must have spent over a quarter of an hour on this pastiche, for I was summoned back to everyday life by a thundering on the door of the W.C., and the voice of the old chemist from Stratford-on-Avon, who made it his vocation to protect me from my follies. "Algy! You're wanted! There's a sample result we can't find, and Francis is flaming with rage! I knew where to find you!"

I was nicknamed 'Algy' from my habit of drinking a glass of

cold water every morning on arriving at the Laboratory, to restore me after the fatigue of the journey. The abbreviation came from 'Freshwater Algæ'!

The voices of two Watchers, hearty ex-sailors, penetrated through the wall from the wash-house, over the clatter of crockery and glass, and the rush of boiling water from the taps.

Thrusting the sonnet into my waistcoat pocket, I flew along the corridor, my long black soutane streaming out behind me. I enquired demurely if my chief wanted me.

"Want you! You've been missing for twenty minutes. And what have you done, my boy? You've indexed Cadbury's Praline Soft Centres under the Great Northern Railway!"

To my amazement, I found that he was right. My contrition lasted for the rest of the day, and pride of composition was forgotten until the next morning, when furtively, still smarting under disciplinary action, I showed the sonnet to Barbour.

"I'll copy that out," he said solemnly, looking over his gold-rimmed spectacles at me with a curiosity that was a mild antidote to the humiliation of the previous day.

Perhaps because my aptness as a clerk was despaired of, I was put to more practical work. Showing some delicacy of touch with a small scalpel, I had to dissect imported chocolates, cutting them in half and scraping out the soft interiors. Then I weighed each part, the chocolate covering, and the centres, on a Becker's balance, entering the weights in grammes in the note-book of the chemist for whom I was making this preparation for further analysis. All the work in the Laboratory was quantitative, and more or less mechanical. But it had to be accurate, for the small samples represented large consignments of dutiable goods, and the assessment of much revenue depended upon the results of our analysis of ingredients, each having a statutory rate of duty.

The Tea, Cocoa and Coffee Laboratory, where I sat, had doors at both ends. It was thus a corridor between the laboratories and offices (including that dreaded sanctum of the chief) on the south and river side, and the north and Thames Street side of the Custom House. Members of the staff passed through to make a short cut. They sometimes made a short cut also at the rows of chocolates laid out for my dissection. The problem arose, how to stop this pilfering.

Ransacking the packing-room, I found a strip of thick cardboard. On this, in letters of crimson paint, I scribed: "Mene, Mene, Tekel Upharsin!" This admonitory writing on the wall, which appeared at Belshazzar's feast, "Thou hast been weighed in the balance, and found wanting," I fastened over the glass case of my Becker's scales. The complete success of my device was humorously recorded in the Laboratory magazine *Spirits and Whines*, and I added a cubit to my official stature.

As the end of the term at King's College approached, I had thought it prudent not to go there, for fear of a day of reckoning, on which I foresaw myself being handed over to the police, along with forgers, defaulting solicitors, and other enemies of society. One day, however, Barbour said that I really must accompany him, because the occasion would be a public one, with all kinds of academic swells on the dais. Fortunately, I· was wearing a new suit, bespoken at a small haberdasher's on Camberwell Green, made for me at a cost of thirty-two shillings. It was of a stiff and hairy tweed, that stood out like armour from my thin body. The cut was impressionist, for the sleeves were at least four inches too long. I got over this fault by turning up the cuffs and showing the striped lining. This had a cavalier effect; somewhat conspicuous.

Timidly, because of my fear of police intervention, I followed Barbour into the lecture theatre of King's College that afternoon. It was crowded, and we had to sit on a back row at the top. We looked down to the dais as into a well. Dignitaries entered, including the Dean, and I saw them seated as gods, creatures of a different order, their movements slow and stately; their discourse, whispered as they bent gravely to each other, head to learned head, doubtless on an heroic plane.

Amid them beamed little Professor Gollancz, his pince-nez flashing, his benevolence standing around him like an aura. The end-of-term ceremonies began, with speeches, an address from the Dean, and rounds of discreet applause. I began to feel desperately sleepy. The crowded theatre was hot, and my body was showing its usual reaction to lack of air. My mind wandered, faintness sent clouds of obscurity through it.

Suddenly, Barbour prodded me in the back. I woke from my half-sleep, and saw Professor Gollancz rise and step forward. He beamed at the Dean, flashed his pince-nez like two heliographs over the audience, and began to speak. He explained that he had set an end-of-term task, the writing of a sonnet to be ascribed to Milton, and that one of these essays had filled him with astonishment. He would now read it; and after he had read it, would the student come forward and receive a prize!

Then, holding the paper close to his eyes, he began: "I see, O Lord, my years divided twain . . ." The rich, unctuous voice rolled the phrases out like separate little grilled entrecôtes. When he came to the last line, he threw his head back, and remained in that posture of ecstasy for several seconds, while the applause burst out, from audience and the gods on the dais.

"Go on," stage-whispered Barbour, giving me another prod in the back.

A kind of eidolon of myself made its way hesitantly down the broad steps of the theatre, and found itself being grasped warmly by the hand. Professor Gollancz's face, glistening with good-humour, peered into the culprit's. He handed a leather-bound book to the impostor, and said: "Come to my room afterwards."

The impostor, the culprit, the eidolon, ghostly simulations of identity flickering in and out like a defective sign-writing, bowed, turned, and faded up the Parnassian slope of the theatre to the seat at the top, where my real self awaited it.

"Now I'm done for," I said to Barbour, accusingly. "He's told me to see him afterwards. He's found out!"

Barbour and I lingered in the great entrance-hall, until Professor Gollancz appeared, followed by half a dozen women students, whose umbrellas he was carrying like a faggot of sticks on one arm, his books and papers in the other hand. His pince-nez flapped on the shining nose, which was outshone by the brilliant eyes behind it.

We found ourselves being given glasses of sherry, and then Israel Gollancz took me aside.

"Tell me, young man . . ." he began. I believed the accusation was coming, and I interrupted him with a full confession of my fraudulent presence at his lectures.

"Ah," he said. "Is that it!" He studied me more closely. "Then you will want somewhere to read and work. You may use the library here freely. And do keep in touch with me. Come to my lectures, and let me see more of your poems. You will go far, young man, if only you work and are patient."

That was the second intimation, from the world outside my immediate circle of acquaintance, of a belief that my grandiose dreams might have a basis in reality: first, the note in the *Clarion*, by its editor Robert Blatchford, and now, in almost the same words, this recognition by Israel Gollancz.

He followed up this generosity by frequent talks with me during the subsequent year. His gift was a copy of Wordsworth's *Prelude*, edited by Basil Worsfold, a name unknown to me. I've since seen it, at the entrance to chambers in the Middle Temple, and more recently in Frank Swinnerton's second volume of wise literary history of the twentieth century, *Background with Chorus*. This masterly novelist and shrewd critic refers to Basil Worsfold as "a poor wretch who wrote at least two opuscles derived from Aristotle, Longinus and Lessing's *Laocoön*": deadly, but a good example of my friend Swinnerton's rapier-work. Gollancz gave me subsequently a copy of his own modernisation of the medieval elegy 'Poem of the Pearl', the Elizabethan sonnet sequences of Daniel and Drayton, and Chaucer's 'Parliament of Birds'.

That was not to be my last contact with the Gollancz family, for some twelve years later Israel's nephew, a young publisher, started a series of contemporary poetry, in pamphlet form at a shilling each, with a long narrative poem of mine called 'The Portrait of the Abbot', and followed this with several selections of my lyrical verse. Poetry priced at a shilling sells, even among the Philistines.

CHAPTER NINETEEN

The Nuptials

MY BROTHER'S MARRIAGE did not remove him far from me. He went to live 'over the hill', ten minutes' walk away, in an early Victorian house, faced with stucco and standing in a long narrow garden. Jack, his bride and her parents moved into this new home together, the young couple making a flat for themselves on the two top floors. The house had formerly been the home of the Victorian poetess Eliza Cook, whose work and reputation time has obliterated, except for the opening couplet of a verse called 'The Old Arm-chair'.

> "I love it, I love it; and who shall dare
> To chide me for loving that old arm-chair?"

Nobody is chiding her today, and that couplet, surviving here and there in books of quotations, and in a jackdaw memory such as mine, is slowly crumbling, to join the dust of the chair it once celebrated.

The house was a spacious villa, with a warm semi-basement from which steps rose to the garden. The ground floor had an iron balcony at the back, and an iron staircase down to the garden. Up from the basement, or down from the hall, one stepped into a suburban world of a hundred years ago. The garden, confined between high brick walls, was a miniature orchard of apples, pears and plums, bordered by herbaceous beds under the walls. One of the borders, on the sunless side, had been invaded by lilies of the valley, deep-toned green foliage, out of which in Maytime the waxen little cups spilled their perfume, a funereal reminder of things vanished, music long silenced, Villon's *'neiges d'antan'*.

Across the bottom of the garden, hidden by the fruit trees except for an occasional glitter of glass, stood a greenhouse, overshadowed by a row of tall black poplars. Little could be seen from the back windows of the villa but green; the deep, melancholy green of London gardens, where luxuriance and decay contrive to exhibit together; sooty lilac, dusty roses, William pears tainted with urban lacklustre.

The garden was a quiet retreat, shadowy under its trees. On a small clearing half-way down, where the grass lay in sunlight, my brother set a dial on a stone pedestal, a monument to mark the shining hours, days, years that he intended to devote to married love, and his too miscellaneous cultivation of enthusiasms: the music, the painting, the cabinet-making, the designing and building of gramophones, and, above all, the remote meditation behind those cavernous eyes, where nobody dared intrude.

Though I was offered the freedom of this garden, and the ever generous hospitality of the house, I knew that Jack's withdrawal 'over the hill' closed another chapter of my life. All that had lingered from the deep, passionate relationships of the small family circle of my childhood now quietly came to an end.

After the wedding party under those apple trees, whose hard green fruit thumped on the hats of the guests, startling them amid their chatter, I returned to my rooms, and to a solitude that stared at me. I had been best man, and had done my duty in a half-bemused way, as I performed always in public, never wholly convinced that this activity was real, while I feared that I was losing time and opportunity for achievement in some other world, whose emissaries clamoured invisibly about me, luring me on with hopes, visions, illusions; chimeras touched with vain madness.

Father and his wife came to the wedding, but I did not say much to them, for I was deeply embarrassed by an incident which occurred when Jack and I arrived at the church. Standing in the porch was our step-sister, handsomely dressed, and obviously nervous. She was alone. "I hope you don't mind," she said, addressing us both. "I know I wasn't invited, but I did want to wish you every happiness."

Tears were in her eyes, and she tapped her foot on the tiles of the porch, as she had tapped it when Jack and I first met her two years earlier, on the threshold of her invaded home.

Jack studied her gravely, his mouth twitching. Then he thanked her, and walked on into the church. I was at a loss what to do. I could say nothing. I took the girl's hand, shook it warmly, smiled at her, and had to hurry after Jack, now on his way to the altar.

For the rest of the day I was haunted by that figure who had not been invited to the wedding. She must have sat at the back of the church during the ceremony, and gone home alone after it, a latter-day Cinderella who had put on her best clothes and travelled from Putney Bridge to Camberwell and back, solely to offer her compliments to the bridal pair. My mind and emotions hovered round the problem of what must lie beneath that generous impulse. Was she merely curious to see the ceremony, or was she deeply hurt, and acting thus in order to register the slight?

During the wedding feast I spoke to Bertie Bridge about it, in the garden. His parents and brother were there too, the mother only faintly anxious, and the 'cellist studying the apples on the trees, his brow puckered as though he were puzzling over the question whether or not the fruit was real or artificial, part of the wedding décor. Both young musicians were beset by the ladies of the party.

"Don't you worry about it, old man," said Bertie. "She's a sensible person, I'm sure. She looks it. Your dad introduced me, for we arrived together, and I put her into a pew."

But I did worry about it, and now that I was alone for the first time that day, relapsing from the tense excitement of the events and my efforts fully to realise their significance, I found myself haunted by that handsome young woman, her smart clothes, her open and friendly candour.

It suddenly occurred to me that she was appealing for help. Why, otherwise, should she have been so emotional? I thought, with suspicion, of my father, who had been exuberant at the party, leaving his wife to look after herself amid a crowd of strangers. I had filled her glass, as she sat on an iron seat under the trees, and she had almost tearfully invited me to Sunday dinner for the following day, explaining apologetically that she thought I might be lonely in my rooms on the day after Jack's departure.

I now recalled this invitation. Had I accepted or not? I could not remember. The Bridges had also invited me, but for the usual musical evening, and I was not prepared to miss that. Since the moment of bitter self-exploration during the boating picnic on the Hythe Canal, I had found much to contemplate in this conflict of love and friendship. I was learning the lesson of the value of renunciation, the wisdom of travelling light.

That evening I was alone in the house. My landlord and landlady, who had come to the wedding, went on to a theatre. I sat in the denuded room, whose floor was no longer sagging under the threat of the Erard and the little pipe-organ. My few books looked like last autumnal leaves on the shelves which Jack had put up. I thought I saw my future stretching before me, from now to old age, a hermit life, wholly dedicated, strictly disciplined. Poetry and religious consolation would bring me more serenity and understanding than I could win by any other pursuit: a worldly career, love and marriage, action and adventure.

The evening sunlight flickered in through the bay window, bringing the London scent of flowering privet. I heard the distant voices of children who played in the street. Without a piano, the room was a prison cell. I ought to have accepted the invitation from the folk downstairs to go with them to the theatre. But I had refused. Why had I refused? I had to sort things out. I had to shift a burden from my back.

I could not endure it indoors. Still wearing my morning-coat with the 1890 lapels, and the silk topper which Jack had bought for me, I walked out, over Champion Hill and through Dulwich Village, past my old school, to the picture gallery. The gallery was closed, but the garden was open, and I walked round it several times, while the shadow of the mitre-shaped steeple of the Old College lengthened along the lawn, darkening the great mulberry tree, and muting the sunflowers that had been shouting toward the west.

I thought of my brother and his grave young wife, on their way to the Norfolk coast. Was he satisfied now, I wondered? And should I see some powerful metamorphosis when they returned in three weeks' time? Was marriage like the other sacraments, birth and death, but with spiritual and mental changes instead of physical?

The sun sank lower, but the evening remained hot, the air heavy with the aftermath of a dusty summer day. I sat on a seat at the further end of the lawn, looking back to the colonnade where the carved leaden tank stood, and to the back of the College behind the pillars.

I stood my top-hat, like a flower-pot, on the seat beside me, and stared into it, reading the name of the maker, 'Atkinson', again and again, my mind a blank, a vacuum.

Time passed. The sun had sunk, twilight had given place to a luminous darkness. The moon rose behind me, over Lovers' Walk, throwing its tallowy light along the lawns, with a new set of shadows cast in the opposite direction to those of an hour, or an eternity, ago.

So tense, so strenuous was my inaction that the sweat gathered in my hair and trickled down my temples. What was happening inside that emptied mind, that stilled heart? I grew more aware that I was looking on at myself. I could see the figure sitting there, with his top-hat beside him, both formal and upright, the gleaming silk, the forlorn flesh.

A bat flickered around the garden, and yet another, creaking and swerving as they closed near this breathing statue.

CHAPTER TWENTY

Voyaging Alone

THE YEAR that followed Jack's marriage passed monotonously, without much incident. I went 'over the hill' every week, to enjoy the music, to share in the happiness of the married pair upstairs, and the sagacity—and duck-eggs—downstairs. Jack had sold the Erard concert grand and bought an overstrung Kemmler upright, a pleasant instrument, Bechstein-like in tone, but somewhat less affirmative. It suited his increasing quietism. The happier he grew in private life, the more elegiac his music, and the more fragile his physique. His brooding personality drew its hood closer over the heavily pronounced features. One had the illusion of needing to stoop and peer under the cowl to see his face. My love and reverence deepened, and often I walked back to my rooms, late at night, with my heart full of those misgivings which are the outriders of a strong affection, as though we fear to hold such treasure, and must protect it by hedging it with doubts.

My way home lay past a small local brewery beside the railway line, and the association of the tang of the barley-mash with the lyrical lingerings of the modern French and Russian composers, Rachmaninov, Glazunov, Liadov, Scriabine, Debussy, Ravel, in whom Jack delighted, became a fixture in my memory, just as in childhood I had paired Mark Twain's *Joan of Arc* with Stephen Heller's pianoforte studies. The chemistry of the human mind has a complicated valency.

A period of life that is outwardly monotonous, however, may be revolutionary within. I was never aware of nothing happening, as I repeated day by day, month by month, the tram journey to work, the seven hours in the Laboratory, the return to my rooms, the meal in solitude in that kitchen under the rabid scrutiny of the demon which I had painted on the wardrobe door, the long evening session with Gibbon, Ruskin, John Addington Symonds (for the magic of Italy had touched my wits); with much ephemeral reading in science and novels, and the closer attention given to the English poets, from Chaucer to Masefield. John Masefield, a masterly story-teller and an impassioned poet, was at the height of his popularity in 1913. But at that time I knew nothing about popularity. My world was sparsely inhabited, and everything in it was being newly discovered by me. Each day brought revelations that made me catch my breath. I broke virgin soil, and my appreciations were absolute, never comparative.

One evening, a lecturer named Mary Sturgeon gave a talk on contemporary poets at a local evening school. I heard about the Georgians, and the newly founded Poetry Bookshop, run by the poet Harold Munro, in Bloomsbury. I was condescendingly interested, having come down the slopes of Parnassus to give some attention to what was going on in the twentieth century. I was led by that talk to read the poetry of Walter de la Mare, Lascelles Abercrombie, Gordon Bottomley, John Drinkwater, never imagining that I was later to be given the friendship of de la Mare and Abercrombie, about whom, as remarkable men and poets, I should like to pause and write in appreciative analysis.

Gordon Bottomley I have since worked with, over many years, but I respected his work more than the man, for he was vain and self-concerned, a character in contrast to that of Laurence Binyon, with whom I worked in the same conjunction. Binyon was a gentle, considerate person, moving through life with an air of sad nobility.

At this talk by Mary Sturgeon, which introduced me to these near-contemporaries, I sat beside two young men who invited me to their flat in one of the period houses at the top of Camberwell Grove. They were medical students and Oxford graduates. Their gracious manners and careful speech both intimidated and pleased me. I had known a rougher, more brusque society, that of the lower middle class at the turn of the century. I fancied I should prefer that to which I was being introduced, though I trod warily. I believed I detected a lack of vigour, and perhaps of sincerity.

One evening, acting upon a general invitation, I called again at the flat, hoping for some lively conversation upon this new aspect of letters, the writers of our own time. Only one of the students was at home. He asked me in rather sheepishly. As I entered, I glimpsed through the open door of a bedroom a young woman with her clothes hastily bundled up in her arms. She had not been entirely successful, however, for one stocking lay on the sitting-room floor. The medical student pushed it under a chair with his foot. From all this evidence I surmised that he had been putting in some extra work at anatomy. I was much disturbed, for and against, and decided that I must retreat as quickly as possible. After drinking a glass of sherry, I fled, and never found the courage to intrude there again. I was not yet prepared to bring literature so close to life.

I went occasionally to Clapham, to the Sunday evenings of chamber music, and Bertie continued to smuggle me in to rehearsals at Covent Garden. He gave me a ticket for the first performance in England of Debussy's *Pelléas et Mélisande*. I sat through the opera, convinced that I was immersed in a glaucous, underwater world, where all motion was slow and tidal, and all colour but gradations of green.

I valued Bertie's friendship too deeply to allow my recent sacrifice to diminish it. Indeed, it became only the richer for being augmented by my devotion to the mezzo-soprano, who now treated me with a charming, half-humorous deference, probably under instruction from Bertie, who had a naïve respect for my not infrequent discourses on the theory of the arts, and their relationship. I had recently discovered Lessing's *Laocoön* and Schopenhauer's *The Art of Literature*, and thus had strong views about the inter-relationship between the arts and where the frontiers between them should stand. As I consider what has happened in music, painting, sculpture, and letters since Mallarmé and his followers broke down those fences, I think it may be fortunate that I fixed my prejudices, as a practitioner, thus early in life, upon the resolution never to force words to forsake meaning, in the effort to imitate the possibilities of music or paint.

When I met Bertie and the mezzo-soprano in London (for she visited the Clapham home frequently before their marriage), I found myself nervously loquacious, disguising my bewildered emotions behind this swordplay of mental conceit. But they listened to me, for any background noises would serve to set off the isolated rapture of their love.

After these sessions, however, I suffered a reaction. I crept home to my rooms like a cripple, a hunchback of self-pity, dramatising my despair. But I turned it to account, for now I had my armoury always at hand, the flashing blade of poetry. Misery, loneliness, worship, curiosity, wonder, and even physical moods and contacts (stomach-aches, the touch of fabrics, the play of light and shadow) were arrested into verse. Poem after poem was poured out, almost in a delirium of living, and I moved about in my small but ever-expanding universe like a fiery star, self-consuming yet self-generating, a vivid contradiction, always on the edge of exhaustion, always exploding with outbursts of renewed energy.

My essays in verse, usually written in set form because I was still labouring in the elementary stages of technical practice, were shown to those people in the Laboratory who were interested. Some found their way downstairs to the Secretariat and the Collector's Office, where men of First Division rank (and therefore of university graduation) worked. I accepted the praise and moodily noted the adverse criticism, privately observing that where one critic commended a verse, another condemned it. This cancelling-out of readers' reactions has been usual in my later experience, and I have learned to balance the positive critics, trying not to be elated or deflated accordingly. Such a neutral stance is not easy to attain, for the creative impulse in all human beings must feed on praise. Vanity is a protective garment, and the more we are heated by the larger and sustained creative effort, the more we feel the cold afterwards.

This circulation of my verses in the Custom House was valuable because it increased my circle of acquaintance. I met men whose interests were as various as those of Fellows and students in a university, and probably I learned as much, even in formal knowledge, as I would have done had I been at Oxford or Cambridge.

Further, the almost military discipline of the Civil Service prevented me from acquiring a manner of condescension, a loftiness, which is sometimes affected by the university graduate, to harden into a habit that can isolate him from the rest of the community. But I believe that this personal stylisation, most marked in Balliol men from Oxford and King's men from Cambridge, is much preferable to the formless and ugly cult of equalitarian ill-manners so fashionable in Left-wing society. Ceremony is a lubricant, and the working parts of our human relationships are apt to over-heat, and finally to seize up, without it.

Perhaps one of the most valuable experiences during my nine years at the Laboratory was that of being forced, by the discipline of work, into daily contact with certain men who actively disapproved of me and my pretensions. One such character was a thick-set man, with a head that sloped backwards. He was a Christadelphian, and believed himself to be of the Elect. This faith was obviously in direct opposition to my belief in my individual election to the pantheon of arts. My adverse critic, who came out of Lancashire, was also a Fundamentalist, and he refused to accept the theory that the earth was a sphere.

Every time I encountered him, the hair at the back of my head rose like the ruff of a dog. His covert sneer, his contemptuous dismissal of the arts and all æsthetic values, roused me to a murderous fury. But I could do little about it, for he was my superior officer, and had I rebelled, I should have been hauled up by him for insubordination.

For a short time I had to work directly under this Fundamentalist, and he made my life a hell, merely by sticking to the regulations. At periods when there was no work to do, I used to study or write. While in his room, I was writing an epic drama in verse, called *The Flood*, based on the Rosicrucian mythology, the structure of this spacious work being maintained by repetitive phrases, in the manner of the 'song-motifs' in Wagner's *Ring*.

The writing of this poem held me for a year, concentrated in mind and emotion, oblivious of the world around me. Every moment of spare time went to the work. Then came this philistine, who accused me of dishonesty in following private interests during official hours. He was quite right, but that only made his obtuse attitude the more repulsive to me. There came a deadlock, a final accusation, and I retorted by telling him that he was blaspheming against the high god Apollo, the earlier incarnation of Christ, the symbol of the Light of the Divine Mind, and therefore of the Word which was in the Beginning, and was now openly apparent in my poetry.

A round of applause greeted my outburst, the half dozen chemists and Excise officers in the room cheering and tapping on flasks with glass rods to make a music of assent.

The Flat-earth Isolationist glared at me in horror, and left the room. He returned ten minutes later, and ordered me to report to the Superintending Analyst. This was equivalent to being led to the scaffold, for the Chief was an enthroned Terror. He sat in his little room, a bulky figure in black morning-coat, his large head aureoled by a light shimmer of red hair, the flames round Jupiter's brow. His angry eyes were also tinged with Celtic redness, and they smouldered behind large lenses that magnified the pupils. There he sat, contemplating whom he might devour; a martinet who normally made no allowance for personal problems or idiosyncrasy among his quaking staff.

I knocked at the awful door, and entered. He never answered to a knock. One had to knock, wait a second, then creep in. A dark, short passage, past an ante-cupboard, had to be trod. It was like crossing the Sahara. Then the victim was in the Presence, standing before the desk, and staring hypnotised at a ball of tiny snakes preserved in alcohol in a bell-jar on the Georgian mantelpiece.

The Chief did not look up when I entered. This was his habitual gambit; a very successful means of starting in the ascendancy. One minute, two minutes passed, while I studied the huge cranium burning unconsumed in its halo of flames. Then he suddenly threw down his pen, and glared at me.

"Well, what have you to say for yourself?"

I looked demure, like a virgin brought to the sacrifice, faintly praying for reprieve, and prepared to offer her charms as the price of it.

"Are you aware, young man, that you have been reported for insubordination?"

I remained contrite. There followed several moments of silence, and I heard the distant traffic of the river; knocks, moaning of cranes, puffing of tug-boats. It had a dying fall.

"Do you realise that this is the worst crime in the calendar? The Service never overlooks it. Once guilty, and your career is ruined. Are you conscious of this, young man? Your superior officer reports to me that you were both insolent and obscene when he corrected you for unofficial behaviour! What have you to say?"

I was still in a state of exaltation, the spill-over of my revolt against the Fundamentalist. He was there in my mind's eye, with his habit of furtively wiping chocolates and other sweet-meats into his mouth by a gesture of concealment, the back of his podgy hand uppermost.

"Sir," I began, "Schopenhauer says in *The World as Will and Idea* that sympathy and not tyranny is the key to right understanding and behaviour, and I have not found it in . . ."

"Neither Schopenhauer nor Keats is an authority on the Customs Codes!" thundered the Chief, thumping the desk with his fist.

"Keats?" I echoed.

"Only the other day you quoted Keats on a point of grammar. And now you bring Schopenhauer, a German, as a defence for your breach of the unwritten laws of the British Civil Service! I have a good mind to return you to the Commission. They might give you a second chance in some lower branch of the Service. They would more probably dismiss you."

"But I have been so happy here," I protested. "I have learned so much. It has been a university to me."

"And have you learned obedience and humility? These are

the stoical virtues we want you to cultivate in the Service, young man."

At that moment, the door opened, and the feline Deputy Superintending Analyst darted in.

"Ah!" he said. "Later! Later!" and was about to dart out again, when the Chief stopped him.

"Stay! Tell me what we are to do with this young man. You have heard?"

The dark figure stood between me and the snakes, frowning, biting his lips, applying imaginary thumb-screws to himself, cracking and pulling the joints of his fingers, one hairy but shapely hand wrestling with the other.

"Death!" he exclaimed. "Extinction!"

Then, after some more ejaculations and miming of the minor tortures, he suddenly changed his mood, studied me sadly, and spoke.

"There may be some faint shadow of a doubt, the slightest extenuating circumstance. Unwise provocation, perhaps? The intrusion of religious ideas into official matters?"

He was a Rationalist, and despised the Christadelphian, who looked upon him as a damned soul already smelling of brimstone.

I watched the nostrils of the short and rather brutal nose in the Chief's fiery face. They twitched! Jupiter was amused. Then he glared at me again.

"You may go! We will overlook this offence. But remember: between the hours of nine and four, so far as you are concerned at present, *the Earth is flat*!"

The Deputy muttered, frowned, darted yet again to the door, and held it open for me. As I backed away from the Presence, the dark attendant angel whispered, or rather hissed: "Imbecile! Remember Jean Paul's dictum: to disguise your message in the presence of fools!"

Sadly shaken, and puzzled by this last oracular remark, I returned to the Laboratory presided over by the Fundamentalist with the flat head. Silence reigned. Nobody looked round, all were at work, including the Elected one.

I sat down at my table and opened the large folio register.

Inside it were several loose sheets of manuscript of my epic drama on the Biblical Deluge. I stared at a descriptive passage written in hexameters (imitating Chapman's translation of the *Iliad*). Then, belatedly, I realised that during the grilling nothing had been said about my writing poetry during office hours.

While I sat amid the silence, pondering on this discovery, one of the chemists left his bench and came to consult the register. He was a tall, laconic Yorkshireman, shrewd and somewhat formidable (later in life to become managing director of a large manufacturing chemists' concern). He put a hand on my shoulder, and squeezed it. Then, turning his head as he retreated to his bench, he gave me a slow-motion wink.

A week later, I was moved back to the Tea Laboratory, and more congenial authority, where the only tyranny was that of an excess of goodwill.

CHAPTER TWENTY-ONE

A Crack in the Universe

THE LIFE of a hermit tends to encourage his oddities. Self-criticism, no matter how austere and ascetic, is more indulgent and ingenious in excuse than that of one's fellow-creatures. Even saints develop disproportionate habits if they live alone. Delusions of grandeur come all too easily.

For the next twelve months I moved between two extremes. During official hours, for six days a week, I was a junior member of a strictly disciplined community, working under the traditions of the Civil Service, at that time a Stoic organisation in which the individual's private life counted for nothing. The smallest official misdemeanour was recorded in his personal file, to be weighed against him years later if he were being considered for promotion, or in connection with some further fault.

Idiosyncrasy and originality were frowned upon. All went by precedence, even the phraseology of minutes and letters, as the public well knows. I hated this tradition. It was not for me, and as time passed and I had continually to submit to so uncongenial a regimen, I began to grow uneasily aware that I was paying too big a price for safety. My being in the Service was the result of a conspiracy between my Father's coercion and my childish dread of the unknown.

But now I was beginning to look around more largely, and coming into contact with men of a wider intellectual force and training than my own.

One of the chemists, for example, was a doctor of philosophy from Heidelberg. He spoke German fluently and introduced me to the influence of Goethe. He gave me a Classical Dictionary which is still in use on my work-table, forty-five years later. He had the European outlook, which I instantly detected and took advantage of, walking into a friendship with him as into a wide landscape, exhilarated and joyous.

I found other men who practised the arts: writers, painters, musicians, and one young Exciseman, distinguished by a close-cropped head of hair (most unusual in 1914) who gave himself to a study of the more mystical philosophers, Plotinus, St. John of the Cross, St. Teresa; hovering in his beliefs between Eleusis and Calvary.

Each personality stood up before me like a tree in blossom, and I fed from one to the other, loading the panniers of my mind with this golden pollen of every human variety, carrying it home to my solitude, and there digesting it.

That solitude was the major factor in my life. It was a familiar one, for I had known it in childhood, during long spells of sickness alone in the house at Battersea, and I had learned to value it. Like a presence, an angel, it towered over me with folded wings, engaging me always in a wordless debate that kept my mind alert, and my nerves tuned to serenity and that quiet mood of acceptance, the perspective—a line of judgment —over and under which all disturbances caused by the passion of circumstance fluctuate, until they are induced to settle.

Week-long, I spent my evenings alone in my rooms, reading or writing. The reading nourished me; the writing exasperated me. I was like a novice learning to play the piano; hour after hour at scales and exercises, while in his heart the concertos of Mozart and Brahms are under his translation. But I was beginning to use English with an elementary sense of selective-ness, my grasp of this elusive medium growing more firm as the muscles of my mind developed and matured.

The art of writing may usefully be compared with that of playing an instrument, such as the pianoforte or the violin. It needs just as regular and constant a practice. To keep a diary is therefore valuable to a person who intends to become a word-master. To record facts accurately and briefly is one of the most difficult and humiliating undertakings. When I read the newspaper, I am often touched to envious admiration of the technical skill of the average journalist and his sub-editor.

As time passed, I began to suspect that the legalistic restrictions of the Civil Service discipline, and their articulation in minutes and correspondence, were likely to engulf me in the bog of circumlocution, and I longed to escape. Why should I not? I found that the majority of people lived from hand to mouth, with no economic guarantee, and contrived to be far happier than Civil Servants, who, having begun by playing for safety, have during the rest of their lives to work for it!

As confidence and experience in literary skill increased, I grew restive in the Laboratory, and began to speculate on the possibility of forsaking the Service (and the pension at sixty) to seek work on a newspaper. But I was foolish enough to discuss the project with some of my official elders, who attacked me in solid formation. My health would never stand the strain, they said; I was too innocent and naïve a character, and far too oblivious of what was happening in the world around me.

"I don't believe you'll ever know the difference between two bob and half-a-crown," said the kindly cynic from Stratford-on-Avon. "And you'd get your feet wet and be dead in a month!"

This did not deter me. I began to send out poems and articles to the journals, weeklies and monthlies, of which at that time there were more with a literary interest than there are now. But as the poems were in the manner of Keats, and the articles roared with the rhythm of *The Areopagitica*, I had little success. Some of the verse was taken, here and there, but none of the prose.

This double discouragement, together with my own timidity in the minor, practical problems of everyday life (such as entering shops, banks, and post offices, buying railway tickets, catching trains, carrying parcels, guarding my pockets from Artful Dodgers, conjuring up small-talk), prevented me from taking reckless action.

In the meantime, the fourth of August, 1914, brought war. It was Bank Holiday, and everybody in my world was away. Father had suggested that I should go with him for a ride on his motor-bicycle, down to Hampshire.

"We'll strap a cushion on the luggage-carrier," he said. "Quite simple, my boy. Lochinvar!"

He frequently astonished me with these out-of-the-way allusions, and that made them memorable.

"Do that tummy good, too. Brace it up!" he added, as a critical reference to my sedentary habits, of which he strongly disapproved.

My attitude toward him at that time, however, was less sympathetic than it had ever been. Whenever I visited his home, I observed the domestic tension, the atmosphere of nagging and his increasing obstinacy and slyness. It was obvious that the marriage was being repented of at leisure, by both partners. Between the two, thus at loggerheads, the daughter-housekeeper was suffering badly. Her genial temper was becoming frayed. It was impossible not to support her. She was alone, and my father intended to drive her out of the home. During a fracas, at which I was present, the week before that fatal Bank Holiday, he had plainly spoken of his intention.

My reaction to that ugly scene was to refuse his invitation, and to suggest to my step-sister that she might like to visit Dulwich Picture Gallery with me on the coming Bank Holiday.

The summer day was heavy, oppressive. We walked through the Village in the early afternoon and I listened to the firm click-click of my companion's heels on the old pavements; the only sound in that rural world. Humanity had vanished during the dog-days of August.

I introduced this shy stranger to the Gallery garden, to the mulberry tree and to the leaden tank under the arcade. She appeared to be interested, but remained reticent, looking at me from time to time with a puzzled and enquiring glance. I admired her smart suit and hat, and my remark made her blush. "All sewn on the premises," she said bitterly.

I took this as a hint that she wanted no personal comment, and that she was hostile, not only to my father, but also to his sons. Pondering on this reduced us both to silence, and I led the way to the Gallery.

At first my companion passed from one picture to another without interest. She merely stopped in front of each, tapped her foot on the parquet or the iron grille over the heating-pipes, and allowed emphatic expressions to fleet across her face.

Something was brewing, and I was much disconcerted, because I was so warmly sympathetic. I knew what her distress was about.

We stopped before the portrait of Richard Burbage, Shakespeare's and Alleyn's contemporary, the first actor to interpret the character of Hamlet. Making a circuitous effort to break the tension, and perhaps to induce her to confide in me, I told her about the Elizabethan actor and the theatres of the period, how both Shakespeare and Alleyn had made their fortunes on the south bank of the Thames; Alleyn first as boy-actor taking women's parts, and later as co-manager with his father-in-law, Philip Henslowe. I described the Globe Theatre, and the apron stage, and the character of the Tudor audiences. All this I had learned as a boy at Dulwich Hamlet School, "my most kindly nurse". That puerile knowledge had since been augmented by reading, though I felt that all matters connected with poetry and the manipulation of words were part of my own personal life, an atmosphere which I inhaled unconsciously.

Warming to my theme, I broke through the restraint with which I had entertained my step-sister—still really a stranger—since we set out from Victoria, where I had gone to meet her half-way. My imagination began to work, like the rumbling machinery switched on in a sleeping power-house. It had the usual physical effect upon my person; I felt the warmth flooding my veins, the tensing of nerve and muscle up my limbs, the burning sensation in my stomach, as though I had swallowed a glass of brandy. My mind and vision cleared. I saw everything luridly illuminated, the very walls and floors taking on a significance, an associative symbolism. I could have reached out a hand and grasped anything near-by, to illustrate my passion.

Thus armed, I told her of the world in which I lived, and where I was beginning to claim authority.

It must have bewildered her, as she contemplated the youth who poured out this oration, with its fantastic claims. She saw me, no doubt, as the obstinate and conceited cub of a man who had invaded her home, bringing dissension and alien ideas into it.

Suddenly, though I was in full flight, I saw her full lips tremble. She was weeping! Half turning away, she fumbled in her handbag for a handkerchief, snatching off a washleather glove to do so. I saw that one finger was bandaged.

I dropped to earth. The fires went out. Instantly, I was a boy again, seeking to comfort my mother after one of her paroxysms of asthma. I touched the girl's bent elbow, and whispered urgently, pleading with her to tell me what was wrong, assuring her that I knew it, that all my sympathy was with her, none with my father.

It was fortunate that the Gallery was empty, except for the custodian. That was the condition of most picture galleries and museums during the period before the radio came as midwife to the renaissance of the arts amongst the British people. Round and round the Gallery we walked, as I half supported the unhappy young woman, while she unburdened herself of the load of misery and anger which had been accumulating since my father came into her life. I heard about her own father, his character, his death from cancer, his heroic suffering. Here was an intimacy, and an invitation to intimacy, which I was expert to use. I was more at home in such a relationship than in mere politeness and small-talk.

"You've cut your finger," I said, agonised for all womanhood. "How did you do that?" And I took the injured hand in mine.

When we came out of the Gallery, I suggested that we must have tea before she went home to Putney Bridge.

"Are we far from your rooms?" she asked. "I'd like to see where you live."

It was a simple statement, and I followed it up by saying that we would have tea there, and that afterwards I would escort her as far as Charing Cross, where she could catch a bus westward.

The Village still slumbered under the August afternoon. The giant elm trees were silent; not a bird-note, except for the lazy twitter of a sparrow. I pointed out the shawl of creeper over Beech House, and the wrought-iron gates of the Huguenot cemetery where the mouldering graves were half-hidden by stockades of dried grass-heads and brittle cowparsley.

I showed her, with pride, the village school where I had been so happy, and where I had discovered the intoxicating use of the dictionary, the study of English and French grammar, and perspective drawing. I pointed across the meadow in front of Beech House to the large willow tree in the school playground, and described how I had looked out at it from the schoolroom window, where I sat one June day reading *The Tempest*, and had suddenly woken up to the glory of Shakespeare's poetry, simultaneously with recognising the fire of the sun resting in the bosom of that tree, in a tremendous sensuality of kindling light.

"You understand?" I urged. "You understand?"

The fire was kindling again within me, and I craved to share the richness, the intensity.

The Galatea beside me moved, responded, and we walked on, the understanding accepted, a dangerous compact.

We reached my rooms, and I led the way upstairs. To my dismay, I found my landlord and landlady, covered in distemper, at work on trestles in my bedroom, and the furniture from it removed into the study.

They were momentarily disconcerted, and the landlady explained that they had intended to surprise me, so that I should come home that night to find my room re-decorated.

I introduced my step-sister, and we were at once invited to tea downstairs. She thereupon offered to make the tea and to be generally helpful over this embarrassing situation.

"That's more my department," she said, and laughed, on G sharp.

I looked round guiltily, but of course Jack was not there.

Later that afternoon, we took a bus from Camberwell Green to Charing Cross. The day was still hot and oppressive, and we sat on the front seat of the open-top bus, looking down on the stale streets. Dulwich Village was far away; perhaps in fairyland.

We reached Westminster Bridge, and my step-sister remarked on the number of people walking over it, hurrying towards Big Ben and the Houses of Parliament.

"What is happening?" she asked.

Before I could reply, the bus was halted at the entrance to

Parliament Square, before a dense block of humanity. It filled the Square, and spread up Whitehall. Then a ripple appeared in it, and cheering began.

"Look! Look!" I said. "Stand on the seat. I'll hold you."

I put my arm round her legs to steady her there, and could feel her half-leaping with excitement. Mr. Churchill, wearing a grey topper and carrying a walking-stick in the air, was walking, accompanied by another member of the Cabinet, from Downing Street to the House, guarded by policemen who paddled him along through the crowd. Hats and handkerchiefs were waving, a roar of mob emotion filled the Square. Mr. Churchill took off his hat and carried it in his hand, while a beatific smile spread over his rubicund face. He was in his element. Britain was at war with Germany.

CHAPTER TWENTY-TWO

Sloughing a Skin

I EXPECTED the war to blow my private life sky-high. The expectation was not unwelcome, for the first effect of the national excitement was to make me realise that for a long time I had been growing discontented in my hermit's cave. I had turned twenty-one, to discover the waking of new interests, and a much greater sense of obligation towards other people.

My hermit life was congenial, but it was also theoretical. I wanted to put my knowledge into practice. How wonderful, I thought, if I could have followed medicine. But I had no means to do that, though I had the example of an Irish colleague in the Laboratory, who boldly took the step of throwing up his safe job as a Government Analyst.

We became friends because he was a man of vigorous mind, interested in the arts as well as in surgery. I often stole into the small laboratory, where he worked alone, testing imported boxes of matches in order to reject the consignments if the match-heads contained white phosphorus. He might also be dissecting a rabbit, as an aid to his medical studies. I would watch his skilful hands at work, and would appreciate, through the pores of my skin, the intensity of his concentration on the task, though I might be chattering away nineteen to the dozen.

I was to maintain this valuable friendship, though we went by different ways toward the fulfilment of our hopes, he to become a distinguished orthopædic surgeon and teacher, I a professional writer who has never wholly emerged into the world of actualities and human affairs.

Many years later, when I needed to describe an operation, in the process of writing a novel, I went to a famous hospital in central London and watched those same hands remove a woman's cancerous breast. My imagination, terrified by this spectacle, fled back over thirty years to that laboratory and the dissected rabbit. I had to recall myself, with a military discipline, to the work in hand and the purpose of my intrusion into the operating theatre.

At twenty-one I was already aware of my deficiency in experience of life, and I welcomed the disturbance likely to be caused by the war. I had read enough history to know what was likely to come, and even at that callow age I believed that Britain had given mankind something worth fighting for— English Common Law administered within a constitutional monarchy, a form of government least likely to become a Moloch because it is controlled by a passionless, undoctrinaire code of detached justice that may not be swayed by political interest or the hysterical bestiality of mob emotion.

The day after war was declared I cleaned and polished my noble new Hudson all-black bicycle, and changed the oil in the gear-case. In spite of my slight build (I weighed eight stone) I was an indefatigable cyclist, so long as I had frequent rests and snacks. My wind was good, for I had made deep-breathing into a mystique, part of the technique by which I absorbed more oxygen than most earthbound people; oxygen, the life-giver, the death-repeller, which I had administered to my mother, to hear it rushing from the cylinder under my hand into her wasted frame, rekindling the dying fire again and again.

The next week-end, I cycled over to Putney Bridge, and told my step-sister of my project. I rode from the house to the head-quarters of the Army Cyclists' Corps, with the intention of offering myself as a scout. I said that I hoped to come back to tea in uniform.

I rode up to the depot and past the guard at the front gate. Leaning my bicycle against the wall by a door marked 'Guard-room', I went in. An old soldier, bedraggled and depressed, sat reading the *Star* and sucking a cup of tea through a drooping moustache. I explained my purpose. "This is Saturday ar'ternoon," he said. "D'you expect anybody to be 'ere on a Saturday ar'ternoon?"

Then he looked me up and down.

"You one o' these college blokes?" he asked, deprecatingly. No, I said, I wasn't; but I was a life-long and expert cyclist, having ridden tandem from the age of seven and solo since I was twelve.

"You'll have to undergo a medical," he said, in a tone that abandoned all hope, though he was more cordial after discovering that I wasn't a college bloke. "You'd better come back a week-day, when the M.O. is on duty; any evening, during the recruiting campaign."

I returned on the Monday, having cycled to the Custom House from my rooms that morning and ridden along Thames Street in the afternoon, keeping to the river all the way to Putney Bridge, along the several embankments, with a detour round the Houses of Parliament. My bicycle was in good fettle, tuned and oiled as a result of my passion for well-working machinery. I was joyous, expectant. Something new had come into my life, larger than that life. I was not quite sure what it could be, but I sensed an opportunity for larger decisions, for taking on responsibility again. 'Good heavens,' I thought, as I pushed along on top gear, avoiding the tram-lines, the chain humming like a dynamo inside the gear-case, 'I've been hibernating since Mother died. I failed with the mezzo-soprano, and I've tied myself to a life of poverty in the lower reaches of the Civil Service. I begin to feel like Gulliver in the land of Lilliput. I want to meet some of the bigger people, the master minds comparable to those whom I have consorted with in books. I want freedom.'

My step-sister was at the front gate, expecting me. She looked happier, and that mood pronounced the handsome quality of her features; the clear brow and steady gaze, the statuesque carriage. Perhaps the war had wakened her, as it had wakened me, to new resolution and a desire for adventure in the world of action.

I stayed to tea, and as Father was not there, the household remained at peace, though curiously alien to me. The conversation was solely about neighbours, friends, chapel personalities; never about ideas, or the war. No question was asked about my appearing again on Monday, after having been there on the Saturday. I had asked my step-sister to say nothing about my purpose.

The Cyclists' Corps headquarters was packed and I had to wait in a queue. My interview with the doctor was summary.

"Troubled with a cough ever?" he asked, his stethoscope flopping back against his waistcoat. "No," I said, annoyed by such irrelevance. "Humph! Well, you're too short-sighted, in any case. Try a sedentary job."

I was dismissed.

So angry and chagrined was I by this that I did not return to my father's house, but rode straight back to Denmark Hill. I could do no work that evening, and at last I gave up the effort, and walked over the hill to Jack's home, where I was welcomed in the usual way with a glint of affectionate amusement, half conspiratorial, half ironic. I told the happy couple what had happened, and at that moment the mother-in-law came upstairs with the evening newspaper, which contained the announcement that school-teachers and Civil Servants would be allowed to desert their posts only if they were already in the Territorial Army or Naval Volunteers.

The responsibility thus being lifted from my shoulders temporarily, I accepted Jack's suggestion that we should solace ourselves with some duets.

As the dreadful months passed, however, with news of slaughter and defeat, I found myself becoming more and more divided. The stalemate on the Artois front all through the spring and summer of 1915 led to the terrible loss of sixty thousand men in a few days, during September and October. Private life went underground. I carried on as before, with my days at the laboratory and my early mornings and long evenings with my books, making up a nineteen-hour day. I wrote doggedly and fiercely, knowing still, and indeed with more conviction than ever, that poetry and all that it implied of religious faith, philosophic method, and verbal artistry was my whole life.

But behind it all was the thunder of the war, and the sense of guilt in being an onlooker. I felt belittled, smirched. The strength of solitude was undermined, and, as a substitute for taking a responsible share in things, I went more frequently to the house by Putney Bridge, to encourage my step-sister and to get from her that familiar feminine response on which my vitality depended. I had been starved of it for five years, not realising the cause of this emotional and spiritual malnutrition.

Then came conscription, and the opportunity for Civil Servants to enlist. I went the round of various recruiting stations, and at the last, Chelsea Barracks, I spent a whole day waiting to be examined. By this time, I was prepared for the long wait, and I took with me William Morris's *The Earthly Paradise* to read while I stood in the queue. I was habituated to reading while standing up, for I practised this method when overcome by sleepiness in my rooms, toward midnight. I had found that by standing with shoulders pressed against the wall, and the book held up so that my head was well back as I read, I could overcome the sensation of a brass circlet closing round my skull and my vision floating into kaleidoscopic confusion. If this did not work, I banged my hand or knee against the wall, to provide a counter-irritating minor torture, or shock.

Chelsea Barracks was a big recruiting centre, and conscription had brought there men of every kind, including the dregs of our urban civilisation. I stood in my place amongst them, loathing the stench of unwashed bodies and filthy clothes. I read one narrative after another in Morris's too-fluid verse, overlaying the present scene with this pre-Raphaelite tapestry. But the smell came through the arras.

At last, overcome by physical disgust and the strain of standing for so long, I began to feel the ominous signs of faintness, as at that moment on London Bridge when the giant Welshman picked me up and carried my unconscious body to the 'Elephant and Castle'. Another Samaritan now came past. He was the sergeant in charge of the queue of miscellaneous humanity, a smart regular, with waxed moustache, and a stick under his arm.

"Here, sir," I heard him say, as from a vast distance. "Take a chair."

He had brought out a cane-bottomed chair from the guard-room. I vaguely thanked him, and the men around me who shuffled me on to it. I noted, with the puzzlement of a person who is embarrassed by suddenly being singled out from an accepted background, that the sergeant had called me 'sir'. He must have thought that I was "a college bloke" because I was reading a book.

Possibly the faintness was due to anxiety, for I believed that this time I must not fail to be accepted for military service. The reason was that I had seen a way out of the unhappy situation caused by the antagonism between my father and his step-daughter. I had put the scheme to her and she had been wholly agreeable. It was that we should marry, and that I should go off to the war.

I had learned that a Civil Servant retained his salary if he enlisted, the only deduction from it being the pay of a private in the Army. Thus, by getting myself promoted as quickly as possible to the rank of sergeant, I should be able to save quite a capital sum, while my step-sister, as my wife, could set up a home for herself and await my return, by which time we should have enough reserves for me to look around the field of literary journalism, with a view to stepping out from the enervating safety of the Civil Service and its dangerous insistence on the use of jargon.

Now that this project was under way—my first plunge into financial interests—I was obliged to fulfil it, so far as the partner was concerned.

This time, the medical examination was more thorough. I passed from one doctor to another, seeing four altogether. Finally, after another wait, I was summoned into a small room where a doctor sat at a table, with the reports before him.

"You won't do, my boy," he said, kindly. He had an old-fashioned manner and appearance, as of a horse-and-buggy country practitioner. "And I tell you what, I'll give you a certificate for extra butter rations. And if you take my tip, you'll go and live in the country."

I rode back thoughtfully to Putney Bridge, a demon of recklessness whispering at my ear. What I had begun could not be stopped. I had lived through five monastic years, and that was but half-living. I had by now sufficient quiet confidence in myself as a writer, to be assured that whatever experiences might come, they would be drawn into this indestructible unity, my creative consciousness.

CHAPTER TWENTY-THREE

"And Pastures New"

ONCE RESOLVED, I acted quickly, and was astonished by the way obstacles vanished, and antagonism was dropped. Even my brother accepted the *fait accompli*, and offered to help in the practical jobs, such as putting up book-shelves. I also found that the people at the Laboratory approved, the old Stratford cynic remarking that now I should get some hot meals and a warm bed. He even invited us to stay with him until we found a home in the country. Wedding presents, given collectively and individually, appeared on my desk, from colleagues in the Laboratory and officers in the Custom House who knew me through the dissemination of my verse.

Nor was that the limit of this generous interest. Women were replacing some of the men who had gone into the forces, and the dreaded Chief asked me if my wife contemplated "doing her bit", and if so, had she any knowledge of analytical chemistry? I said that she was a good cook, and that this form of synthetic chemistry was merely analysis in reverse. Thereupon, she found herself on the temporary chemical staff of the Laboratory, earning more than I. My salary was then £65 a year.

Meanwhile, the head of the Tea Laboratory, my immediate chief who was always so urgent that I should sit for an examination to become an Excise officer or a Second Division clerk, told me one morning that he had found us rooms in the country. Every Saturday morning he came to the Custom House in a grey-green uniform, as an officer in the new militia. He studied little square-shaped books on strategy, tactics, trench-digging, and the structure and use of mortars and machine-guns. His Sam Browne belt and buckles were polished by the Watcher attendant upon our room, until they shone like the accoutrements of a field-marshal.

This masquerade was connected with the analyst's week-end activities. He went off to the Surrey Downs with his platoon, and dug trenches in the chalk slopes, thus committing no nuisance upon the farmers. In the nearest village of Limpsfield he had made enquiries, and found us rooms in a rose-red cottage occupied by a young widow and her two children. Her husband had been killed, along with most of the men of the village serving in the East Surrey Regiment, at the battle of Loos a year earlier.

The parting from my landlord and landlady on Denmark Hill, with whom I had lived for nearly five years, was a sad ordeal. I had taken shelter with them, a grief-stricken, bewildered youth, vaguely grasping at a sense of destiny. I left them as a young man convinced, perhaps insanely, of my vocation, armed with the fruits of five years of close study of language and letters, and the discipline of my days in the Service, married to a young woman of sound health and practical outlook, firm moral nature and a handsome person. The success of my rash step into matrimony, as it seemed then, had given me more authority over my own nature, and a point to my purposes. I *must* not fail now. Pegasus had to be harnessed.

With Europe tumbling to pieces round us, we followed our furniture and the many gifts of tea sets, dinner sets, cutlery, spoons, kitchenware and books, from London to Limpsfield, on the Saturday of September the fifteenth, 1916. It was also memorable because tanks were first used in warfare that day.

I was sent down in advance, to receive the vanload, and sat awaiting it, on Limpsfield Common, by the roadside, with my head in my hands, trying to take stock of the rush of events into which I had been plunged of late. New emotions, more complicated circumstances, fiercer contrasts of character, relentless need for decisions, all were clamouring at my brain, demanding my comprehension and a right ordering.

As I waited, dismayed by my inability to sort out this new wealth of experience, I felt a vibration through my limbs. It came from the ground. I looked around, but the Common was empty. Gentle sunshine gilded the bushes of gorse and the turf. To the north, the high downs lay draped in a warm autumnal glow, half mist, half lustre. No traffic, no human being, moved within sight.

The vibration faded, then rose again, more clear, more insistent. Suddenly I knew what it was, informed not by intelligence, but by a folk-sense, an age-old instinct of fear. I lay back on the turf and put my ear to the ground. Instantly the vibration swelled to a deep throbbing that shook the foundations of the earth. It was the beat of the gunfire from Flanders, transmitted beneath the Channel, passing through the subsoil of Europe, undermining the basis of our Western society which held the superstructures of Christianity, feudalism and democracy.

"What am I doing?" I asked my demon. "What am I doing? Is it not too late? Is not the individual doomed; the responsible soul, the civil career, the free vocation as artist, as master in his own right?"

My fear was premature, and short-lived. The genius of place, concentrated in Limpsfield, one of the most beautiful villages in south-east England, instantly began to influence me. On our first night there, after the furniture had arrived and we had disposed it about our two rooms, I went out into the cottage garden and looked around me into the darkness.

The night was calm and silent; utterly silent. The gunfire in Flanders must have ceased temporarily, and old mother Earth withheld her breath, preparing a sigh of gratitude. The scent of burning pinewood hovered above the village; a holy, ancient smell. I breathed it into my lungs, and stood, leaning backward with my face uplifted, to stare vertically into the meridian of the night sky at the procession of the stars. I saw the Milky Way smeared across the dome, and the dusty light falling from it. I located the Hay-wain and the North Star, lying above Titsey Woods. Hardly had I done so, when a meteor, followed by another, slid along the ridge of the downs, like gestures of right hand and left hand, silent, divine, re-assuring but terrible.

I accepted this sign, my mind knowing the natural occurrence for what it was; my imagination, that probing instrument of truth, seizing upon the promise. I lifted up my arms in a gesture of passion toward everything around and above me: the stars, which for a second stood back into perspective, constellation behind constellation, above my thrown-back head and aching neck; the blessing of that holy perfume of wood-smoke; the deeper, older smell of the woods, the soil, the autumn vegetation.

All this was new to my town-bred senses. I took it as a personal approach, and as a pledge. Such a direct revelation must be accepted, no matter how heavy the obligation to express it in poetry as simple and as deep-rooted as these demonstrations during my first night in the countryside.

The influence of that communion was never lost, though the war dragged on for two more years, and the problems of marriage, daily work, and the gradual approach of the spiritual squalors of middle life, common to everyone, played in their inevitable malice upon my faith and certainty of vocation.

I had sold my Collard pianoforte, in order to pay for the removal of the rest of the furniture from London to Limpsfield, but here Jack and his wife came to my aid by giving me a small gramophone, which Jack had bought second-hand and reconstructed so that it gave out double the volume and particularity of sound. Even so, gramophones in 1916 were poor, ghostly instruments, the music emerging from them being but two-dimensional, like flowers pressed between the pages of a musty book, faded and flat.

Our quarters would have been irksomely confining, had we not assumed that the whole countryside around us was also ours. Further, for six days a week we got up at five o'clock in the morning, to sponge down in the back kitchen before the widow and her two children awoke. Then we had breakfast in our room, looking along the lane where, an hour later, we should walk together on our way to Oxted Station.

This morning walk filled me with rapture. The lane was an avenue of bird-song, intricate displays of frost, snow, dew, rain-drops and medallions of sunlight, among the details of the set-piece of hedgerow, garden and trees. Everything was new to our urban eyes, and I reached the railway station so glutted with these infinite riches that I sat in the train, lost in moods of joyous despair, a kind of hopeless worship, that put me into a fever of creative energy.

Even the humiliation of the slave-trudge across London Bridge, that unshielded phalanx, could not reduce me to a sense of normal human values. I spent the day in the Laboratory counting over my treasury, and changing some of it into the currency of verse. My efforts were comparable to the half-articulate prayers of a primitive mortal newly conscious of the mystery of the world around him. I was a cave-dwelling huntsman, standing at the entrance, blinded by light, but my crude weapon firmly grasped in my hands.

The routine in the Laboratory was considerably lightened by the presence of several women on the staff. One of them, a society beauty engaged to an officer in the Coldstream Guards, arrived late every morning, and endeared herself to everybody by her charm and seeming frivolity. She borrowed, and broke, apparatus from her neighbours at the bench, and if called into the sanctum on a matter needing disciplinary action, would perch herself on a corner of the magisterial table and ogle the person of Jupiter with devastating unself-consciousness.

One or two of the puritans in the department looked on this as the beginning of the break-up of civilisation. The Christadelphian, when he saw this Cytherean approaching him in the corridor, dodged into a doorway, and was never known to address himself to her, even in the course of duty. One young Excise officer, susceptible to her person and the exquisite scent that proclaimed it, fell in love with her, and was forced by the violence of his feelings to tell her so. By a miracle of good manners, brought from a world at that time outside our social ken, she contrived to freeze without offending him.

She frequently brought additions to the Laboratory luncheons: cold chickens, pasties, pots of cream, either from her home in the counties or from Fortnum and Mason. She insisted on me and my wife sharing these feasts, for she professed to a humble regard for poetry, and flattered me to my heart's, but not to my critical mind's, content. I appreciated her generosity more than her judgment, for I could not then, as I cannot still, accept praise without being embarrassed by a sense of shame and of shortcoming between the will and the deed. I had already memorised Chaucer's admonitory lines:

> "The lyf so short, the craft so long to lerne,
> Th'essay so hard, so sharp the conquering."

These words had fastened themselves as the writing on the wall of my palace of art, because they confirmed the attitude which my brother had always taken toward me and my pretensions from childhood. Until his death, he never relaxed that tonic stance; but also he never lost faith in me, though shaken by my marriage, my fruitless years, and the ill-health that dogged both him and me.

For he too had been rejected by the army doctors, though throughout boyhood and youth he drove on through school and college without a day's absence. His present work, teaching in a slum school in Peckham under conditions similar to those which had killed our mother, were beginning to tell upon him, with further aggravations from the stress of war, both mental and physical.

In spite of his extreme reserve about the step I had taken, he came down at once to our rooms in Limpsfield and adapted my bookcases to the little living-room, fitting them with a cabinet-maker's precision round the north and west windows on two walls, and the fire-place on the inner wall.

Nor could my father maintain his pique and disapproval. The nest in Limpsfield village had hardly been lined, before we heard one day a repeated three hoots (the old family whistle) from a motor-cycle horn. Our momentary embarrassment was swept away by his breezy enthusiasm.

"Best thing you ever did, my boy," he cried, as he glanced round the room, averting his eyes from my book-shelves and making an operatic gesture towards the distant downs. "Stride out, both of you! No good without a healthy frame! Come for a ride now. We'll jaunt down to Canterbury, and home by bed-time."

But his step-daughter had a sober memory, and was not to be bamboozled. She was now independent of him, and though this freedom had calmed her temper, it had not diminished her distrust. Her refusal was abrupt, instinctive. She was to maintain this uncompromising attitude so long as my father lived with her mother. That marriage, however, could not last, and two years later man and wife separated, my father going off to lodge in another suburb. Oddly enough, from that time his step-daughter's temper relented, and she treated him with a dutiful civility, as toward her father-in-law. But there was never a marked cordiality between the two.

I, too, found difficulty in approaching him, though I appreciated his loneliness and his sentimental fondness for his sons. But his hostility to my work was, from my point of view, a hostility to my whole life and the right structure of human society, a fabric in which the poet marked the warp, and the statesman the woof, of the pattern.

"How's the writing, my boy?" he enquired, every time we met. "Making a *do* of it? Don't neglect the Service, though!"

He was deeply hurt when, years later, I resigned from the Civil Service and lived by my pen. He regarded this step as an insult to the regiment, and an act of economic insanity. In spite of his profession of socialism, he was instinctively conservative in an old-fashioned, aristocratic way, with a contempt for 'cleverness', and 'scribbling'. He once told me that he found my novels 'too sexy', and urged me to write more about the open road, like "that fellow Jeffery Farnol". This was the only indication that he had ever looked inside any of my books, dutifully presented to him on publication day, no matter what the degree of family embarrassment might be at the time. And that was not infrequent, for as he grew older he developed an ingenious faculty for upsetting his 'women-folk', as he called them. And they increased in number too, for he had a long span of life still before him.

During those ensuing years he graduated from bicycles to motor-bicycles, and finally to cars, spending as many of his waking hours as possible out on the roads of Britain, storing up their contours and detailed features in his astonishing geographical memory. When he was eighty-two, he proposed to me that he thought of "investing in one of those trailer caravans" and making another journey to the hills of North Wales, "before I take the last, long road, my boy." And he meant it, though as usual he was watching the effect of his words, and winging them with just a slight pressure of critical malice.

CHAPTER TWENTY-FOUR

The Sprouting Corn

CONDEMNED to carry on at the Laboratory, I found my life too full for me to be sulky about the confinement, or ashamed that I was taking no part in the war. Inevitably, I read less than during my monastic régime before marriage, but I now began to write even more verse, as a means of expressing my ever-increasing wonder and worship. The beauty of the Surrey and Kentish countryside kept me in a condition of mental fever.

The rigid discipline at the Laboratory had been so broken down by war-time innovations that my wife and I were allowed to leave at five minutes to four every afternoon, to catch a train from London Bridge Station at ten minutes past the hour. The official concession was that, on medical grounds, I must spend as long as possible in the country air, in order to put on weight. But instead I put on vast quantities of verse, some of which I continued to send out to the weekly and monthly magazines. Here and there, poems were accepted, especially by *The Spectator* and *The Nation*, then edited by St. Loe Strachey and H. W. Massingham respectively.

In 1917, that desperate year after a cruel winter, when the war had the prospect of lasting until Europe should crumble away like a sand-castle, I was especially active and burning with hope. I read Birkbeck Hill's vast edition of Boswell's *Johnson*, Sterne's *Tristram Shandy*, Cowper's poems and letters, and Pope's *Essay on Man*.

That summer was my first at Limpsfield, and the fecundity of the woods, the fields, the commons, drove me nearly mad with an insatiable desire. I could not rest at night, and frequently got up in the small hours, leaving my dormant companion, creeping downstairs, pulling on some clothes in the living-room, by candle-light, and venturing out into the scented summer night, to wade through dawn-mist and to stain my garments with dew-soaked pollen from umbel and petal-cup, seeking I knew not what, every sense inflamed, but at the root of all the personal agitation a deep, penetrating recognition of the source of this relentless life, in all its unity and simple force. Every bush was a burning bush, and I must seek to understand, and to represent in my verse, the dictum of that inescapable authority.

During that summer of 1917, one of the senior officers in the Collector's Office, down in the Long Room of the Custom House, suggested that the time had come for me to collect a number of my poems into book form. He said that he would pay the cost of publication.

I thought the matter over, and accepted. For the second time a parcel went to A. C. Fifield in Clifford's Inn, and on September 15th, exactly a year after I went to live in Limpsfield, an edition of two hundred and fifty copies of my first book appeared. It was well reviewed, and the edition sold out in a few weeks, for the war-time boom in poetry had begun. Several other poets appeared at that time, notably Robert Graves and Edmund Blunden, the latter to become, in after years, a well-loved friend. I believe still that his poetry, and that of Mr. Graves, are likely to survive the set of fashion, and to take permanent places in our literature. There are others, such as Rupert Brooke, Wilfrid Owen, and Edward Thomas, who will keep company with them.

It is dangerous, however, for one practising artist to appraise the work of others, because he is likely to be biased by his own creative predilections. For example, I have never been able to appreciate the elaborate poetry of Gerard Manley Hopkins, though it was much worn in the nineteen-twenties. I found it verbally foppish, with a few exceptions, and I thought his play with what he called 'sprung rhythm' nothing but much ado about an old device used by the pre-Elizabeth playwrights. Again, I found Mr. Eliot's poetry too dialectical and loaded with learning. The fact that I have said so, in the press, from time to time during the past thirty-five years, has done me no good amongst the fashionable younger critics. It is a mark of Mr. Eliot's quality that my reservations about his work have never diminished his personal friendship with me, or prevented him from publishing one of my books of verse, a set of experiments in *vers libre*. The fact that I was one of a small minority may have been an emollient to his bruised pride—*if* it was bruised.

I was not, however, to meet him until the beginning of 1921, and the third decade of the century, a period outside the frame of my present picture. In the December of 1920 I was to be snatched out of the official cul-de-sac at the Laboratory and to be attached to the Intelligence Department of the most active body in the Civil Service: the Ministry of Labour. This was done by a Deputy Secretary there, named Humbert Wolfe, a brilliant Civil Servant and a dexterous poet of audacious wit and theatrical sentiments. He had seen my verse in the magazines, and learned that I was too comfortably hidden in a backwater where I was likely to rot away and sink like a derelict boat. The result was that I began the third decade in a new environment, which brought me into contact with several colleagues already active in the world of letters, F. S. Flint, Herbert Read, C. K. Munro, and C. E. M. Joad. I thus met Mr. Eliot, and was one of the little group who first contributed to the *Criterion*, under his editorship.

All that, and the professional expansion consequent upon it, still lay in the future. The immediate effect of my book of verse published in 1917 was that Mr. Fifield showed it to W. H. Davies, whose poetry, as simple as folksong and as artful as the verse of the Elizabethan lyrists, had been introduced to me by my landlord on Denmark Hill five years earlier.

One day I received a postcard bearing a tiny, rounded handwriting that had the quality of blackthorn buds just about to burst into bloom. It invited me to call on Mr. Davies, at 14 Great Russell Street, and warned me that as the bell on the front door was broken, I must go up the staircase beside the grocer's shop looking up towards Bedford Square, and then knock at the door on the first landing, before which I would see a saucer of bread and milk.

So, a few days later, I met W. H. Davies, the first poet of repute whom I was to encounter, and a man whose quiet, generous friendship enriched my life until his death in 1940. Amongst the many writers whom I have since known, he stands unique as being an integral part of his own work. He might have stepped out, a flesh-and-blood version of one of his lucid lyrics, sun-tanned and earth-stained, from any of his books.

The staircase was filthy, and smelled of stale air, London grime, and the overtone of groceries from the shop below. I groped in the semi-darkness, and saw the saucer of bread and milk. Before I could knock, the door opened, and a short figure hopped back a couple of paces, on a stiff leg.

"Just a moment," it said. "I'll light the gas."

He stumped across the room, which I had now entered, shutting the door behind me. He took a spill of newspaper from the mantelpiece, lit it from the coal-fire, and reached up to kindle the gas-mantle. A greenish light revealed the room, a subfusc apartment whose two windows looked up the turning leading to Bedford Square. An early Victorian, high basket-fire burned merrily, fed from time to time by the poet with single nuggets of coal which he took up in his tiny, shapely and grubby hand. Each time, this process was followed by both hands being rubbed together and whimsically contemplated, while the poet interrupted our conversation to explain that "You know, some people would think my hands are dirty. But it's not that; it's the kind of life I've had in the past, when I was on the road."

The interview began nervously, with the poet standing on one side of a large table in the middle of the room, and I on the other. He rested, at a slight angle, on one leg, and this stance, together with the way he carried his head aslant towards one shoulder, gave him the appearance of a resting sparrow or robin, his own "little hunchback in the snow".

While our conversation opened, I covertly studied other details of his appearance; the gypsy-like features, the tuft of hair brushed up and back; the long, loose belted coat; the knotted kerchief in place of a collar, the strong mobile mouth, whose lips met like two over-ripe blackberries about to burst and spill their juice; and, most compelling of all, the huge eloquent brown eyes, restless with apprehension, that suffused with warmth, cunning, pathos, laughter, simultaneously with and often even a little in advance of the words uttered in a nutty South Wales accent from those lips.

He told me that my book was one of the most promising first efforts he had seen, and that if I retained both enthusiasm and health, and kept myself out of the clutches "of educated ladies", I would go far.

I found this qualification most intriguing. My heart warmed to my host, and banished all shyness. He explained further, and I observed the oily gleam of a most engaging assumption of vanity, a refinement upon self-consciousness, in those tell-tale eyes, that since he had become the most famous poet in England *and Wales* "society ladies" had taken him up, inviting him to their dinner parties in order to vie with each other in entertaining the immortals. That was the reason, he said, touching the low hem of his Norfolk jacket, why he had bought this coat, not an ordinary lounge jacket, but something which could be worn for day or evening use, dinner jackets or tails being both inappropriate for a poet of his reputation, and also too costly, as he had only his poetry, and a Civil List pension of £100 a year, to live on.

I observed a Sickert painting on the wall above the fire-place, of an elderly couple in a room as grubby as the one in which the picture hung. On the book-shelves that lined two walls to table-height stood a bust of the poet by Epstein. Augustus John's pencil portrait, a study for the now famous painting, hung between the windows (thus being difficult to see). Another portrait, in oils, by Harold Knight (the most photographic of any) hung near the door.

He saw me studying these, though I had hoped that my wandering gaze was hidden, and he explained that it was helpful to one's work to be portrayed by great artists, as it impressed the public and increased sales of the books. He retreated into the interior of the double room, which lay in darkness beyond the half-open folding door, and returned with a portfolio of unframed drawings and water-colours given to him by some of those 'great artists'. He insisted on presenting me with a charming woodcut by James Guthrie, to start my collection, which would be an essential support to my career, destined (he repeated with increased significance) to be successful provided only that I kept my health and enthusiasm.

When he saw me out, he glanced comically at the saucer of bread and milk, and dust, at the threshold of his room. The oily, cunning humour returned to those eyes.

"That's for the rats," he said. "You see, while I was on the road in America, I learned to be afraid of rats. I've seen them eat a human corpse. So I put my offering down every night before I go to bed, as a propitiation."

We shook hands, and I noticed the smallness and hardness of his fist. It was like a walnut. I was invited to come again, and to be sure to take care of my health.

That was the beginning of a friendship which became intimate. We soon established a practice by which I went once a week to tea with him, reaching there at 4.30. He was always ready, standing by the table, his outdoor face beaming like well-handled mahogany. On the table lay the tea-things, with the two cups turned upside-down in the saucers. He explained that he was a very particular man about dirt, owing to his past experiences on the road and in doss-houses. Therefore the cups had to be turned down to prevent dust from entering them.

Then, from the mysterious inner fastness where only his one foot ever trod, he brought the tea-pot and a loaf of bread. This was followed by an egg for me, because, he said, I needed the nourishment. And he added that he always bought his eggs from Lord Rayleigh's dairies, to ensure their being fresh. An English lord could not afford to risk his social reputation by selling stale eggs, even though, of course, he kept these dairies only by way of a hobby, as 'educated ladies' wrote books.

He said that he was fortunate in having a most considerate charwoman, who came in every midday when he was out at lunch. That loaf, for instance! Now his woman knew he disliked stale bread. Every day she brought him in a new loaf, from which he cut one slice for his tea, and one for next morning's breakfast. The rest of the loaf she took away, so that he had no bother with stale bread. The new loaf was always in its place.

After our tea, and an hour's chat, he would take his crook-stick, and off we went to a pub for a glass of ale. Then he saw me on to a bus for Victoria, standing and smiling, pipe in mouth and stick in hand, until the bus moved off.

One evening in the late summer of 1918, that routine was broken. The hour came for us to set off. Davies had already been out to lunch that day, with Edward Garnett and others of that constellation. On his way home he had met Robert Nichols, another poet who rose on the horizon in 1917, a gifted and versatile writer. But Davies was convinced that he was mad.

"You see," he told me, earnestly, "there is this shortage of matches and, for a heavy smoker, it is a serious matter. Now what d'you think? When I met Nichols today, he was carrying, *openly*, a packet of a dozen of matches! Anybody might have snatched it. And what's more, *he gave me a box!*"

I listened to this story with impatience, for Davies still made no move toward his tweed hat and the rustic walking-stick without which he was never seen abroad. Time was slipping away, and I began to worry about catching my train. Travel, even an habitual daily journey, always makes me apprehensive. I suspect that time-tables may be altered overnight, or that the effort to get to the station will be frustrated by a breakdown of the bus, or in the Underground. Allowance has to be made for losing the ticket, and even for groping in a pocket for coins (this last process being a major problem in winter). Thus I usually reach the station with half an hour to wait. I have read many books, standing at platform barriers, in the course of my life.

Finally, I jogged the poet back to reality, and said we must be off. Once again, that cunning peasant-gleam appeared in his eyes, and he put one walnut hand to his lips, to indicate secrecy. "No," he said, "I'm not going out again."

"Why, aren't you well? The leg hurting?"

From time to time, his wooden leg, that always creaked like a sailing ship as he walked, gave him trouble.

"It's not that. You see, *they* are going to increase my pension from £100 to £150. But now I'm so well-known on account of my poetry, the gossip has got to the ears of the Government that I like a drop of drink. And what d'you think?"

He paused, for dramatic effect, and I responded correctly.

"Well, as I went out this morning, who d'you think I saw outside my front door? Mrs. Asquith!"

At such moments of intensity, the South Wales dialect was accentuated.

"You see! They put her there to see if I come home drunk! So I'm not risking anything until the pension's through."

With that, I fled, pondering incredulously on these symptoms of persecution mania, which took such picturesque forms in Davies's character and conduct. I believed too that I should miss my train, and this fear put me into an agitation that heated my blood. I began to sweat, and finally could no longer walk toward the bus stop. Once again I drew a deep breath and rose from the pavement of Great Russell Street, thus avoiding the maddening obstacle of the crowded street. So I reached Victoria with a quarter of an hour to spare, exhausted and still sweating.

As the following years gathered speed, I saw more and more of Davies. In 1919 he introduced me to Roger Ingpen, the authority on Shelley and editor of the ten-volume Julian Edition. Ingpen was also at that time a publisher, under the name of Selwyn and Blount, and this imprint stands on the title-page of Edward Thomas's poems.

It also sponsored my second book of verse. I did not learn until a year or two later that Davies had offered to pay the cost of this book out of his tiny income. Ingpen, when confiding this news to me, assured me that the sacrifice had not been necessary. He had shown my manuscripts to his brother-in-law, Walter de la Mare (they married each other's sisters), and had been advised to take the risk himself. This venture led toward another valuable friendship, with de la Mare, that wonderful noctambulist in the moonscapes of the human spirit. But that connection did not follow immediately.

Some time later, Fifield retired and sold his publishing business to Jonathan Cape, who with Edward Garnett as his literary adviser made his imprint one of the most distinguished of our time. Davies's fortune expanded accordingly. He married and, after one or two moves, bought a new cottage near me at Limpsfield.

Meanwhile, I had rented a tiny Georgian house on the village street, next door to the grocer's shop about which I was to write my first novel some ten years later. The house, like a doll's house, had a front door with a window each side, and two above. The staircase went up the middle of the building, from a mat's width inside the front door. The rooms to right and left were about ten feet square, and passers on the narrow pavement could look in at the windows, while their footsteps vibrated through the foundations of the house. When a wholesaler's delivery van drew up outside the shop, our dining-room was plunged into darkness. Fragmentary wafts of village gossip floated in at the windows.

I did not mind these foreground noises, however, for I had accustomed myself to isolating my mind wherever I might be, reading in trams, trains, or public places; writing under the subterfuge of official blotting-pads, in picture galleries, and even in public lavatories. Like Gibbon, I was addicted to 'scribble, scribble, scribble', teaching myself to be concise, to allot myself so many words in prose or lines in verse to say what I had to say, so that there should be space available if suddenly the gods should decide to bring a capricious hand to aid the process, and make it incandescent.

I was to meet another poet, almost immediately after my introduction to W. H. Davies. I had contributed to a monthly magazine called *Today*, owned and edited by Holbrook Jackson, a scholar and bibliophile. Another contributor, Clifford Bax, wrote to me, and a week or two later I was invited to his studio in Edwardes Square, Kensington; a large, lofty room which reminded me immediately of the studio in Tite Street, Chelsea, where my brother and I had gone to receive the gift of an aquarium on the first day of the century.

The vast height and the spaciousness of this studio raised my spirits and dispelled all shyness. I found a most gracious person, whose interest in my work was like manna in the desert. Of late, I had been subject to despondency and periods of unaccountable fatigue. The war was petering out, toward that dreary November day in 1918 when the firing ceased, and Europe turned to lick its festering wounds and to stare at its ruined habitation.

Nobody could escape the infection of that racial *accidie*. I had found myself, to my shame, moving about for days on end in a mood of utter unresponsiveness, either to life or books, or to companionship. I had put myself to reading Pascal, the *Pensées* and the *Provinciales*, but the mathematical precision of his mind, and the disastrous self-sacrifice he made, only added to my sense of frustration.

Thus I met Clifford Bax at a time when I was deep in one of those nadirs of the human spirit from which the most assured philosophic system and the most firm faith cannot effectually remove us. Something deeper than any conscious machinery of mind and will has to come into operation to complete the rescue. I have learned to know what it is, though not how to define it. But the conditions in which it acts are patent enough: a humility, a patience, a surrender, a recognition that the final distillation from pain is that *aqua vitæ*, joy.

I found, in Clifford Bax, a man who knew the devastations of these states of moral and physical inertia. We sat, in his silent studio, talking quietly together, and I watched, through the north-west corner of the huge window and skylight, the sun going down.

Shortly after that visit, I received from him a set of Plato's works, in the Bohn Library, and was thus led to extend my knowledge beyond the *Republic* and the *Banquet*. That gift was but the first of many generous gestures made by this gentle, philosophic poet and dramatist, in the course of our continued friendship.

Not long after that first visit to the studio, I was invited to bring my wife. This occasion, however, ended in disaster, for I was seized by a violent attack of those pains and the sickness which had haunted my childhood. That embarrassment and inconvenience only deepened the consideration which this friend has always shown. My physical distress that evening was caused, I suspect, by the excitement with which I responded to our host's reading of the opening canto of his long poem 'The Traveller's Tale', a remarkable, sustained embodiment in skilful verse of the doctrine of reincarnation and the Buddhist faith. The Shelley-like speed and fervour of the verse, contrasted with the clear reflective surface of the spiritual pool over which it flew, so moved me that I felt the symptoms of physical revolt as I listened.

This attack coincided with the world-wide outbreak of influenza which swept, like the Black Death, over Europe early in 1919. The local doctor suggested that I should be inoculated, and accordingly I accepted this new treatment. The result was that I went to bed for three months.

Fortunately, we had previously invited a young Excise officer and his new wife to stay for a few weeks while they looked for a cottage. Both were country folk from Wiltshire, children of village schoolmasters. But the young bride was languishing in. London lodgings. They arrived during the first week that I was in bed. The girl, whom I had met only once before, immediately made herself my sick-nurse, so that her husband and my wife could go off to the Custom House every day.

The bride had brought down a Pleyel upright piano with her, a sympathetic instrument, not confused in tone although overstrung, and she played and sang with amateur charm, specialising in the songs of Schumann and Hugo Wolff. Every morning, after the worker bees had departed for London, she opened my bedroom door and the door downstairs, and gave me an hour's delight.

In 1952 I was vividly reminded of that happy period of idleness and freedom from official routine. I was lying ill in the British Embassy in Copenhagen for a week, interrupting a round of lectures which I was giving in Denmark and Sweden. While I was in bed, in that Hans Andersen little palace of white and gold, Harriet Cohen called on the Ambassador, on her way home from a recital tour in Norway. My bedroom door was again opened, and I listened to this austere musician playing Debussy's *Suite Bergamasque*, as I had listened to the Wiltshire bride over thirty years earlier; the same music, more authoritative and in an enlarged setting, but, and there's the mystery, the same auditor.

The long spell of immobility and isolation gave me other stimulus, and was a disguised blessing. The returned workers, each evening, brought sufficient news from the outside world. I enjoyed talking with my colleague, a rugged and tender-handed countryman with a passion for bee-keeping, exceeded only by his passionate devotion to his young wife. He filled my garden with beehives, for the stay of a few weeks extended to over two years, so difficult was the search for a cottage, and so harmonious was the friendship between the two married couples.

At bee-harvest time, in midsummer, the whirr of the centrifugal separator was heard in the kitchen, and delicious Limpsfield honey, compounded of lime, almond blossom, and pine-sap, was stored all over the house. It even stuck to the door-knobs. Further, my garden adjoining that of our neighbours, the grocer and his wife, was stimulated by the green thumb of my Wiltshire friend, a Richard Jefferies character, into a paradise of flowers and a cornucopia of vegetables.

After each morning recital I applied myself to the writing of my first long poem which was later to be printed. It was a soliloquy in blank verse by the disciple to whom Christ said: "Or else believe me for the very work's sake, Philip." I pictured him late in life, sitting in a room in Antioch, gazing out across the Mediterranean, and talking to a young follower. I showed him, so many years after the event, still trying to reconcile his Platonism, a personal bias, with the happenings and significances of the Last Supper.

The task demanded much imaginative expense, and also I wrote with the music of the verse half-drugging me, a danger toward which I had to be alert, moment by moment. A session until lunch-time was as much as I could endure. For the rest of the day I read *Don Quixote*, comparing the Motteux with the Shelton translation, and making a summary of the string of adventures, so that later I should be able to select, from any point along this road of picaresque events, references to endorse, and mitigate, my own follies.

The poem was printed in 1920 in a magazine called *Voices*, owned and edited by Thomas Moult, who has since combined his profession as a sporting journalist with a lifelong devotion to literature (which is journalism's shy brother). Mr. Moult made a double summer number of *Voices*, of which my poem filled the latter half. It attracted the attention of John Galsworthy and St. John Ervine, both dramatists being particularly devoted to problems of ethical and religious moment, and the inter-play of the two influences.

Three years later, the poem appeared in book form, under the imprint of the bookseller-publisher Basil Blackwell of Oxford, and it was finally included in the *Collected Poems* which Dent published in 1948.

As the first consequence of this encouragement, and of the end of the war, as well as of my return to health, I proposed that my wife should give up her work in the Laboratory. To feel the vital blood coursing once again in my veins was sufficient guarantee and insurance. I was ready to conquer Troy.

Thus a new and fuller domestic régime began, which I hoped to enlarge as I went on, uninterrupted by further setbacks of health or from personal shortcomings, toward a professional life as a writer that should finally enable me to give up my half-hearted career in the Civil Service, where I had been, at my very best, but an octagonal peg in a round hole.

In 1922, St. Loe Strachey engaged me as a reviewer on *The Spectator*, where I wrote every week for the next twelve years, meanwhile beginning to work for other journals.

But such shop-talk carries me too far ahead, out of the framework of the second decade of the twentieth century. Within it, I had yet another major experience to come; something to gain, and something to lose. In the April of 1920, full of hope and a passionate energy that would not let me rest, I began to write another epic poem, the work which the flat-earth theorist in the Laboratory so Calvinistically interrupted during office hours by reporting me to the Chief.

But I have told that story, as indeed I have told the whole story of an awakening from the fantasy of childhood to the still vaster actualities of life in the world of men and women, with responsibilities seen, recognised and usually accepted. I have learned that where they are not accepted, tragedy and retribution follow. That is a fundamental consequence, on which all religions have fastened, to hold human society together.

I had no sooner begun to write the epic poem than my wife gave birth to a daughter. I was still pen in hand, one afternoon in the room below, when I was summoned upstairs to greet the newcomer.

I took the infant in my arms.

"Put your pen down," said the voice from the bed, sadly amused at my absent-mindedness.

But I did not. I was concerned with this living creature in my arms. I looked at the miniature, and realised that she was breathing. I felt the slight rhythm of this movement, and suddenly I had the illusion that I was once again bending over my mother, trying to sustain the ebbing life with oxygen. I heard the hiss of the gas as my hand eased the lever on the metal cylinder.

"My hands are full," I said.

Still I remain suspended in wonder at the mysterious identity between death and birth, and I have not yet put down my pen.